Life on Purpose

Your true calling and how to create it

Philip Oude-Vrielink

First published 2013

ISBN 978-0-9875222-0-7

1.   Self-realisation.   2. Life.   3. Conduct of life.   4. Leadership.
5.   Vocation.   I. Oude-Vrielink, Philip   II. Title.

National Library of Australia Cataloguing-in-Publication entry:
Oude-Vrielink, Philip, author.
Life on purpose : your true calling and how to create it /
authored by Philip Oude-Vrielink ;
edited by Elizabeth Jewell Stephens.
ISBN 9780987522207 (paperback)
Self.
Life.
Conduct of life.
Leadership.
Vocation.
Stephens, Elizabeth Jewell, editor.
126

Cover design by Lucy Hardie
Cover photo by Philip Oude-Vrielink
Edited by Elizabeth Jewell Stephens

May you
manifest even more
of your magnificence

Table of contents

Acknowledgements

It is for you that I have written this book. Thank you for reading it. I have chosen to create something for you that delivers on my calling, which is to help you create yours. I am grateful knowing that you are receiving this. Thank you for participating in what this book details—the Life Calling Method™.

Thank you to my awesomely wonderful partner Sasha. Thanks for being endlessly supportive, patient and encouraging as I invested so much life into writing this book. Thanks for going out of your way to do what you knew was important to help get this work done, for sharing your enthusiasm, love and wisdom, reviewing the work and being awesome. You have my eternal gratitude.

My own ability to help lead, live and create what's important is informed by the work and efforts of many others. If I have not appropriately attributed or represented the work and creations of others, then the omission is mine and unintentional—and I appreciate being informed when this happens. My motto is: *Stand neither on the head nor in the shadow of others, but on their shoulders.*

Primary among these are two people, both friends and mentors. To Donald Epstein, creator of Network Spinal Analysis™ and Somato Respiratory Integration™: I have learned so much from you about our manifest nature and connecting with, accepting, celebrating and integrating the gifts of my experience. To Dennis Merzel (Genpo Roshi), creator of Big Mind Big Heart™: I have learned so much from you about our true nature and understanding, accepting and appreciating who I am, my life and humanity as it is. Thank you both for your ceaseless dedication to sharing and living your message. Thank you for being an example of what it means to share your message and gifts with the world and create a lasting legacy. You truly are an inspiration. I am grateful for your depth of ability to enable others to be clearer and more fully who they are. My ability to share with and support others to more deeply understand and appreciate their own lives owes much to your work and teaching and the depth to which I have been touched by what you bring to the world. On behalf of those I support and serve, thank you.

Another friend and mentor, Matt Church, creator of the Thought Leadership curriculum and a person brilliant at crafting message: thank you for helping me raise the standard of how I form and represent my message, and for suggesting that I write this book. Your idea around complete ideas, and expertise in how to capture, package and deliver message, is truly remarkable. What you teach has helped me clarify my thinking, especially in the sections on developing expertise and on being an authority.

I value, are informed by, and appreciate the work of adult development specialist Susan Cook-Greuter, psychology professor Mihaly Csíkszentmihályi, psychology professor Robert Kegan, and philosopher Ken Wilber. Thank you for what you bring to the world. My gratitude to you Robert and Susan to have been able to learn from you directly.

Elizabeth Jewell Stephens, thanks for bringing your wisdom, perspective and editing skills to this work. I deeply appreciate your hard work, practical insight, and drive to make every page beautiful. Your ability to be simultaneously supportive and respectfully challenging helped produce even greater clarity.

Thank you Suzannah for sharing your experience, awareness, and creativity through your review of the first draft. Thank you too for reaffirming the joy of mentoring, and sharing with me your extraordinary spirit, openness and sense of wonder.

To the people that I have had the great joy and honour of working with over the years: your participation, encouragement and response has shown me how useful this work can be and helped me continue to refine this 'Life on Purpose' or 'Life Calling' method. Thank you for being so open and courageous as you shared yourselves and brought yourself more fully into your own lives. The joy for me is witnessing you manifest more of your magnificence.

Special thanks to Adam, Anthony, Jeri, Justine, Kate, Katrina, Lucy, Maree, Martin, Matt, Matthew, Peter, Robyn, Steven, Suzannah, Tyrone, and Zaheed, as well as other participants in the Aware Leader Program™, for offering your stories of your own experience and how you are touching the lives of others. You all help to bring this book to life. Thank you too to Andrew, Anthony, Chris, Gareth, Ginette, Gus, Jane, John, Kirsty, Margot, Pat and Pete, for your trust, openness and enthusiasm. Thank you Frank, Iwona and Matt, participants so many years ago of the first-ever public version of what is now the Life on Purpose program, for being and remaining so incredibly encouraging.

To everyone that I have worked with: I am deeply touched and blessed to have worked with all of you. You're each a reminder that the wonderful thing about the work I do is that I get to work with such wonderful people.

About the author

At university, while studying biomedical and communications engineering, I, along with three others, formed the Chocolate Appreciation Society. It went on to become the student organisation with at one point almost a quarter of all students at the university as members. I hit my physical stride after high school and during my second year at university I trained with East Ringwood Football Club. I enjoyed being physically fit and for the first time seeing the possibility of excellence in a sporting field. What I did not enjoy with playing a contact sport is that I invariably caused and would continue to cause physical injury to others. Moreover, due to the time investment in training, I realised that I had to choose between football and my studies. Truth is, I didn't have the same drive for football as I did to be creative. I chose my studies. To maintain my physical fitness I then cycled and trained in martial arts that was offered at campus, appreciating the benefits of some degree of physical mastery.

Life at the time consisted of attending university and studying through the week, and weekends of partying, and recovering. As an example of my partying ways, I remember one Saturday party where I brought two-dozen cans of beer, in ice, in my own cooler. The party started mid afternoon, and by 3:00am I had the last of those 24 cans. As I opened that can, I had an epiphany—I realised that I could not continue to drink that much so regularly and decided to stop drinking, after that last can, of course. Besides, I'd already opened it. Now I drink alcohol so rarely I call myself "the world's cheapest drunk" and at most might have a half-glass with dinner.

During my final year at university I discovered that every one of the thirty students in my stream of engineering was also an artist of some sort: musician, painter, writer, sculptor, dancer, actor, or poet. I wrote poetry, or at least that's what I called it. Each of us was in engineering for its creative potential. We had all somehow kept that aspect of ourselves largely hidden from the others. As trained sceptics, we'd been taught to check assumptions, and this discovery certainly lifted the veil on many assumptions about engineers. I learned that a person is so much more than what they do.

After an assortment of summer holiday jobs of being a cherry picker, bottle-shop attendant, labourer, metalworker, and researching lightning protection for home phone users, my first professional role was with Honeywell Aerospace and Defence, designing and building a field computer for the Army. I enjoyed most the creative aspect of that role.

It was during that role that I spent some time overseas and met the woman I'd later marry. I moved overseas to be with her, though the marriage lasted less than a year. I'm grateful for the support of friends, as it was with their encouragement that I spent time with a therapist to find out how I had managed to mess my life up so thoroughly. It was during this time that I uncovered a ravenous interest in the human condition and human potential.

I decided to return to Melbourne and on the way I did what I had hoped to do at some stage of my life, and travelled through Europe on my motorbike. It was a basic Honda twin cylinder, with minimal electronics for easy field repair. After a year of enthusiastic travel through Europe and months trekking through Nepal, I returned to Australia and started work with Lotus Development, soon to become part of IBM. At the time I still had hair, and I remember that the recruitment agent said that my two foot long ponytail really "wouldn't cut it" in this type of arena. I donated the hair, though the first hairdresser I visited refused to cut it. I've had various roles since then, from systems design and project management, to business transformation and finally into leadership development.

Soon after my return, I started a graduate degree in psychology, though only completed part of it. I stopped to undertake yoga teacher training, and for several years part-time taught physical yoga and yoga meditation. Having a professional day job and working part time as a yoga instructor were simply different aspects of my life. I still practice yoga.

While my interests in all other explorations have waned over time, my interest in the topic of the human condition and life purpose has steadily grown. Indeed, it is due to my interest in understanding and sharing with others aspects of our human condition that I have studied a method called Big Mind and for many years have sought to and continue to share that method of personal enquiry and realisation with others throughout Australia and New Zealand.

I've been trained in some western scientific methods and more eastern approaches to understanding our nature. My friends say that the topic of the human condition and purpose is my obsession. I agree; it is my obsession. I can see why they'd say that, as I've made my life around it. And that's what this book is about.

I know that we have something that is the source of our fulfilment, which comes from acting on our deepest inner drive and sharing that with others. I know that we can discover and create our calling. My passion is helping people realise and create that.

I know that our authentic potential is always being revealed and that what matters is how we tap into and influence that. Each of us is able to identify that which gives us a profound sense of fulfilment and purpose in our lives. Every one of us is a leader, always influencing others, regardless of whether we're in organisations or not, and what matters is whether that influence aligns with what's important. This is all based on my experience of having worked with hundreds of people over the years.

For years, both formally and informally, I have been helping people lead and live more authentically and on purpose. I am most passionate about helping people experience true authenticity and fulfilling purpose in their lives. I realised many years ago that true authenticity requires the ability to identify and advocate on behalf of what's important, and that fulfilling purpose requires the ability to identify and create what's most important. I have developed my programs, practice and this book around these insights.

By reinterpreting their experiences in more effective ways, people often report how they have become more okay with who they are and what's important for them. As such they are more skilled or adept at bringing what is important into their work and lives. My work is kind of like a GPS for your life, helping you to orient, interpret and give new and more effective meaning to your own experience.

I have one criterion for assessing usefulness of something. When presented with information, an idea, or a method, I ask myself this question: "Does it produce more happiness, resilience or love in the world?" My hope is that as you read this book you find yourself answering 'Yes' to what you find and realise about yourself.

At the end of the day, I help people have a rich life of purpose, meaning and fulfilment.

Introduction

The purpose of this chapter is to set the context for this book, the Life Calling Method™ that this book details, and the broader topic of our life purpose or calling. This chapter will cover:

1. That our life is our purpose
2. Common doubts we might have about this topic
3. Existing approaches to 'life purpose'
4. What's different about this approach
5. Benefits of realising and living our calling
6. The model for realising our calling
7. The stages of creating our calling

Shaped by life

I've agonised over the question, 'what's my purpose?' For over 30 years, since around nine years of age, I'd agonised over my inability to answer that question. It is what I call my 'Great Wound'. Having no clear answer was just painful. It has only been in the last decade that this has changed.

For whatever reason, not being able to answer this question produced a lot of distress for me. I knew that I was good at certain things, yet felt bored with what I was doing and completely empty and unfulfilled.

I used to envy people who seemed to have a deep sense of purpose, and would enviously think, 'You lucky … person!' I would ask them how they came to know. Everyone answered the same way, "I just knew." I used to get even more discouraged by that. I was not satisfied with this answer, as revelation had not shown itself to me yet.

Over the years I've participated in every 'Find your purpose' program I heard of, and read every book on the topic that I could find. In good faith I'd invest my time, energy and money into them thinking, 'This might be the one that does it', only to go home with my question still unanswered, my yearning still not sated. I'd wonder if I'd even find this elusive 'thing'.

Ten years ago I used to write a daily journal. One day, as I was reviewing my journal, something caught my eye. I'd written a complaint about the work I was doing at the time. I'd written: "Though I'm very good at my job, what I'm doing just isn't important for me! It's just meaningless." Without realising it I'd circled *good at, job, and **important**.*

I realised that being good at something is one thing, delivering on what's wanted is something else, and doing what's important another thing entirely. I had identified and described three things. Three interrelated things. These three are central to everything you'll be covering throughout the rest of this book.

Curious, I quickly drew three concentric circles: Skill, Task, and Important. Seeing this relationship, I realised that my work did not include what was important for me. I understood immediately why I felt so empty and why the work that I was doing seemed so meaningless—it was devoid of what was important.

Something troubled me about what I'd drawn. Then I remembered what a friend of mine, Bill Williams, had helped me to understand many years earlier when I was experiencing significant relationship, let's just say, 'growth opportunities'. He helped me see that needs and the fulfilment of needs are two different though clearly related things. With his help I clearly saw that needs are a subjective experience, and that the fulfilment of needs is usually through something objective and concrete. For example, he'd helped me to appreciate that 'love' was a very intangible experience, and that people experience that through very tangible behaviours and forms.

Looking at the words, skill, task and important, I was troubled. I saw how 'important' did not fit with the other two. 'Skill' and 'task' seemed very tangible, quantitative, concrete and objective labels, something you could almost touch and see. 'Important' on the other hand seemed to be very intangible, qualitative, abstract and subjective, something that could not be seen directly—merely interpreted and experienced. I was comparing apples with oranges, something concrete with something experienced.

'Fulfilment', I realised, is a quality. It is not seen—though it is experienced.

Rather than convert 'important' into a concrete form, I needed to convert 'skill' and 'task' to their qualitative counterparts. I saw that the qualitative conversion of skill is 'gift', and task becomes what's important for others, or their 'need'. I now had my three factors: 'gift', 'need' and 'important'.

Realising that each of these was a quality that relates to something concrete, I excitedly decided to invent a process to qualitatively answer each one of those three. Stumped at first about how to do this, I was reminded that my own initial complaint revealed the insight that I was now exploring. Buried within our own complaints is something important for us, if only we know how to decode our own experience. I assumed that the combination of the three would produce the answer to my purpose. There was a large wall in the house I was renting at the time, and after a week of gathering information about my life it was awash with flip-chart paper, post-it notes and pencilled lines.

When I finished the process I'd created, I put my pen down and burst out laughing, like I had suddenly just got a joke that I hadn't been able to get for 30 years. It was a joke that for 30 years I didn't think was at all funny.

Then I cried. I was so touched by profound recognition that I just stood there for who knows how long. Written and circled near the top of that wall were the words, "My purpose is: Through insight to help people realise their purpose." I joked, "Well, if there is a God, I think I just peeked into its sense of humour. How perfect is that?" How perfect to have spent over 30 years trying to answer the very thing that I was here for. Then I added enthusiastically, "No wonder I get so excited when I meet someone who is trying to realise their own purpose in life!"

I was then able to make sense of the decisions I'd made during the preceding years about what I wanted to be doing. A few years earlier, I'd made a decision to 'Help people appreciate their humanity'. This is what led me to start studying psychology and to teach yoga. Not truly knowing why, I felt frustrated teaching yoga and stopped. I then decided I wanted to help people realise their true nature. This is what led me to bring Big Mind Big Heart to Australia. Going through that process for myself helped me to understand that what I really wanted to do was help people know who they are and why they are here. I want to help people know what will be their fulfilment.

Interestingly, each new version of my understanding of my purpose had included the earlier version. Moreover, the previous versions seemed to map out the pathway to achieving the next version. Helping people appreciate their humanity enables realising one's true nature. Realising one's true nature seemed to be the necessary enabler for realising one's purpose.

For a number of years I have been helping people to realise what they were here for. Each time my method improves and clarifies a little more. I felt exhilarated to be working with people in that way, and excited to be doing so. Despite all this, I noticed that I would feel frustrated whenever someone didn't act on their realisation. Some people would have profound realisations, and then simply allow that to be a pleasant memory. I was critical whenever others would do nothing with their realisation. Again, my complaint revealed something useful, that action is important for me. I realised that helping others achieve realisation alone didn't seem to be enough for me. There needed to be action. When I combine 'action' with 'realisation', I get 'actualisation'. I realised that what I really wanted was to help people to actualise their purpose. It was not only to realise it. In a sense, I wanted people to share the love, to not keep it to themselves.

My purpose is to help you realise and actualise your purpose.

To do that I've realised that we need to decode the shaping factors of our lives to reveal what is already important to us, to reveal what our lives are the answer to, and to uncover our most effective way of going about that.

What do you mean, I'm the answer?

What if what your life is the answer to, is what others are waiting to hear? What if your message is an answer to a problem of the human condition, of how to experience love in a particular way? What if you are already perfectly equipped to share your message with others? What if that's what your life has always been about?

This book is about living a life that matters, discovering your contribution, and answering what your life is the answer to. Our calling has to do with who we are, our essence. You have a calling, no matter how young, old, wealthy, healthy, successful, intelligent, or satisfied you are. It is unique. It is what you are here to contribute. It is realising what you care about most and seeking to create that.

Living your calling is a choice. Only you can make that choice. One of the intents of this book is to help you make a better-informed choice. The choice is completely yours to remain in your present circumstances or to do the personal work that will help you do what you came to do.

These may be familiar questions:

- Do I know my purpose?
- Am I on purpose?
- Am I making my contribution to the world?

Fulfilled people know what's important and live it. This is a journey towards the answer to one of life's biggest questions, a journey of deciphering your own life to uncover what your life is the answer to. This is what your life is calling you towards. Some call this your purpose. I call it our calling. By the end of this journey, you will hopefully know that your life has been shaped in a particular way. You'll know that the way your life has been shaped has sensitised you to something that is most important for you—your message. You'll know what you are most sensitised to because you'll recognise that that's the thing you already react to most strongly. You'll see that what you react to most strongly is all about the absence of what matters most for you. You'll use this evidence of your own life to reveal what is most important, your message, and the contribution that you are here to make. You'll see how you are primed to recognise the absence of what's most important for you when it shows up in others. The absence in others of what's most important for you provokes your highest empathic response, your Peak Empathic Response.

People consistently report that their message—which includes qualities such as trust, worthiness, flow, acceptance, dignity, inclusion, and empowerment—is an aspect of what might otherwise be called 'love' in a universal sense. They say that the absence of their message reduces the experience of love, and that the presence of their message enhances it. When they realised their message, they realised that it was an aspect of love—their personal version. You'll realise too that your message is an aspect of love, a differentiated form of love. You'll do this through seeing that throughout your life you have been sensitised to the absence of that differentiated love. In other words, our calling is to help people experience love according to our differentiated or personal form.

You have been sensitised to something, the absence of love in a particular way. You could say that this is the registration of the problem that you are the answer to. You probably just didn't know it consciously. It is what you have been most sensitised to, and as such it provokes your Peak Empathic Response. Not only does it happen to be something you're most passionate about creating the solution to, you feel compelled to do something about it. You can't not do it.

What you are here for is what life has shaped you to be.

Then you'll uncover your style or method for creating your message. This is the way we create our calling that is both abundant and most effortless. It's your gift, your natural talents. We'll then connect the two and find that your calling is to use your gift in service of your message on behalf of others. Your calling is to use your gift to help people experience a differentiated form of universal love.

Ultimately, it's all about action. To derive the greatest benefit from this book, it's important to get into action, to do the work. Don't just leave it conceptual. Only doing the work leads to lasting change. I encourage you to do the work.

My hope is for you to bring more of who you already are into your life. You are not broken. You never were. Sure, we can all show up in life more effectively, we can always be more functional, but that does not mean we are broken. You are already magnificent. My hope is for you to manifest even more of your magnificence.

My wish for you is that you experience incredible joy, clarity, and more of the fulfilment that comes from realising and creating the contribution that you are here to make, from sharing with others what your life is the answer to. I have realised that my calling is to illuminate fulfilment through actualised calling. My life has not been the same since I committed to acting on that. This book is one way in which I am delivering on and creating what my life is the answer to. I feel a great joy and fulfilment at the thought of you reading this book, discovering what your life is calling you towards, and using your gift to help people experience love in the differentiated form that you are here for. Nothing for me could be more exciting. It is my hope that you too experience that excitement.

If at any point you find yourself scoffing or in opposition to anything I suggest, please persist and discover what your own life reveals to you. Those who have persisted have consistently been delighted with what they found.

As Arthur Schopenhauer points out, new ideas or newly discovered truths have to pass through three stages:

1. First it is ridiculed
2. Then, it is violently opposed
3. Finally, it is accepted as self-evident

Those who persist and do the work consistently see the principles and ideas described in this book as self-evident. Those who persist experience what's most important to them as self-evident.

My hope is that you persist, and hope that you find what you uncover about what you are here for as self-evident.

A life worthy of you

Vicktor Frankl in *'Man's Search for Meaning'* says that many people "lack the awareness of a meaning worth living for". He says that the problems caused by a lack of meaning are not only common, but also rapidly spreading throughout modern society. Frankl says that the main problems of this lack of meaning are boredom and a sense of purposelessness, meaninglessness, and emptiness.

There seems to be a growing tide of dissatisfaction and meaninglessness in people's lives. We have success like never before, yet a growing sense of emptiness. People don't know what guides them. People don't know how to bring fulfilment to a successful life.

Frankl observes that people have "enough to live by, nothing to live for; they have the means but no meaning." People today seem more than ever to be experiencing their lives as empty, meaningless, and purposeless. One can hardly read a report on the state of workplace engagement without getting a sense of how right Frankl was. Disengagement due to people's disconnect from a sense of meaningfulness in what they do seems everywhere—maybe not for all, but certainly for many. You could almost say that a sense of meaninglessness is reaching epidemic proportions.

So what is to be done? Find and live the theme of your life. Find what it is about you, which, when acted on, will give you a sense of purpose and meaning in your life. As Frankl says, once an individual's search for meaning is successful, it "renders him happy".

Really though, when is the right time to know what we're here for? When is it the right time to reveal what will help us to:

- Feel alive, energised, juiced, good
- Feel connected
- Make our contribution
- Feel happy, fulfilled, content, satisfied
- Have a clear sense of inner guidance

The time for this is always now. Life is different when you understand what guides you.

If you aren't living your purpose, you are probably living someone else's purpose. You are a force, and if you don't ignite that force into action, you're subject to the forces of your immediate environment and moved towards wherever others want you to go. Without utilising the wind and generating force against the water, a boat will travel wherever the winds and tides take it. Who's powering your boat?

To ignite that force requires action. As Thich Nhat Hanh says, the only thing we truly own are our actions. Our responsibility is for what we do. That said, it can be confusing and difficult to act without clarity, the clarity that comes from stepping into what life is calling you to be.

People in all occupations, from highly successful business leaders to artists, often feel a sense of dissatisfaction, frustration and emptiness with what they're doing. Skilled professionals often report that just being good at something isn't enough. Many wonder about why engagement with others seems so hard, why trust so elusive, and their ability to influence so limited. Many more often feel a lack of fit with their organisations or of a lack of fulfilment in general. Others have a sense of wanting to make a contribution, yet are confused about what that may be. Though purpose is known to be centrally important for leadership, relating, and life, existing approaches to the topic of purpose often seem somewhat superficial. I understand this all too well, as I was feeling that emptiness for several decades.

What's really going on though is that there's a lack of clarity about how to identify a sense of purpose and how to create it. While the need for a sense of purpose is agreed, how to identify and create what we're here for is not.

Many who approach the topic of their life calling seem to have immunised themselves against the topic. Many people have questions, statements and doubts about the question of their life calling. Some of these are as follows:

'I'm not sure that I have a purpose'

Everyone willing to understand themselves can identify something that they consider to be most important for them. This is your purpose, not for you, but on behalf of others. The question 'What am I here for?' isn't the best question, as it's very concrete. Your purpose or calling is at first qualitative, not concrete; intangible not tangible. You are then free to choose what concrete form or forms the creation of that quality can take.

'A purpose is only for the lucky few'

This is a bit like saying, 'Because someone else always seems to win the lottery, I'll never be rich'. Everyone can identify a something through which they may derive fulfilment and a sense of passionate purpose. It's whatever it is that happens to be most important for you.

'Purpose is an act of revelation and grace'

While revelation can and does occur for some, we can always learn to decipher the clues of our own lives to reveal what is most important for us already.

'I am an accident'

Everything about the way you have experienced your life thus far has shaped you into who you are right now. Even if you want to believe that your life has been an accident, this does not change the fact that it is your own life that has shaped what is most important for you already. It does not change the fact that there is something you can identify as being already most important for you.

'I am too broken'

We all have areas of our lives that we'd like to improve on. I am yet to meet anyone who does not recognise in themselves areas they'd like to improve. What's different is the meaning we might give to that awareness. Having and acknowledging that you have areas for improvement does not mean that you are broken. It simply means that you are human, just like all the rest of us—a human in process of becoming even more perfect. Recognising that you have room for improvement does not deny the room for improvement, nor does it judge that this is the case. Is it okay to acknowledge and accept that you are human?

In fact, it might well be that your message for the world lies hidden in the areas that currently are the basis for your imagining you might be broken.

Moreover, I regard any perception of humans being 'broken' as dishonouring of our human condition. It's an unhelpful evaluation of something every alive human has—opportunity for growth.

Then there are people who accept that there is or may be a life calling, yet manage to buffer themselves from acting on it. Some of the common questions and statements are outlined in the following:

'What if I get it wrong?'

You cannot get it wrong. There are only deeper layers of clarity that become known through doing it, through acting 'as if' what you currently know to be your purpose actually is your purpose. Your understanding and definition of what your life is the answer to will evolve as you act on what you know as if it were true. Purpose can and often does change as new clarity comes to hand. That new information and clarity results from our actions.

'What if I'm not good enough?'

Your life itself has shaped what your life is the answer to. It is your very life that has shaped you for this. You are already good enough to do something and create a concrete form with a certain number of people, of your own choosing. For example, that could be as simple as smiling to the person who serves you at the store.

We each choose the span and scope of our concrete form, and each of us is already ready for whatever we choose to be the next step in front of us.

You are perfectly ready for your next step, even if it does not seem like it, and even if you don't get it perfect the first time.

'What if I don't like what I find?'

Many have shared with me that they had this concern at first. Some have revealed that there was a part of them afraid of what they might find and felt a tendency to shy away from exploring further. So if this is happening for you, know that this is very common, understandable, and that you are not alone.

This seems to come from a concern that our purpose or calling is somehow separate from our life. It isn't. One of my hopes is to help you realise that your calling not only is your life, that you have already been living it, though not necessarily consciously.

'Purpose is not practical or relevant in the commercial world'

People in all occupations, from change agents to CEOs, report that nothing could be further from the truth. Purpose can define the method you use to create your successes, so that it is through how you achieve your successes that you experience fulfilment. It can be your 'signature style' for creating success. You only need to know how. You can have both success and fulfilment, both a life of riches and a rich life. As some of these senior leaders have shared, when done in an appropriate way and in the right circumstance, purpose supports the ability to achieve even greater productivity and success.

We also happen to be naturally passionate about our purpose. For example, one senior leader realised that his purpose was to do with empowerment. For him, his focus is on achieving results and empowering his staff. Empowering his staff is for him the experience of fulfilment. Moreover, how much more productive do you think his staff are as a result of his creating an empowering workplace and a work design that was redesigned to empower? Not only does productivity research continually point to the importance of empowerment, he was intrinsically motivated to empower others.

Tyrone's experience

Tyrone is the youngest of three children born to Chinese immigrant parents. With his American spouse he has two young children, a boy and a girl. When he lived in Detroit for two years he says it was often curious for people to experience someone of Chinese appearance with an Australian accent. He loves the movie 'Sound of Music' and once watched it eight times in a day with his grandmother. He is currently studying a Masters in Applied Finance.

"Purpose", he says, "is applicable to all of my life, work and personal." He says that he always seemed to have a general sense of direction, though it was at best "very hazy". Admitting that he initially thought that 'purpose' was a specific thing he had to find, he now realises that his purpose, to "help people feel valued and have self-worth, can be brought to every interaction with others, and there are many different ways this can be done."

Tyrone says that the notion of purpose, "is not fluffy or esoteric and it makes sense that you build up your own story. It makes sense that your purpose is based on your life, what's happened in the past, what's important to you. You just need to gather the evidence and translate it properly."

His own translation also changed his experience. "How you see the world is pretty much influenced by a significant event or events in your life. In my instance, this event was seen in a negative light, in that I had wished that it had never happened. Now I see the gift in that event and how it has actually turned out to be a positive driving force for me."

Asked how his experiences are now perceived as a gift, he explains that, "The event is something that has shaped me and has made me sensitive to certain things in life. The event, which I thought affected my sense of self-worth, has made me become more sensitive to that, especially in others. That has enabled me to turn that experience around, and help elevate others' sense of self-worth."

Echoing the notion that in giving we receive, Tyrone realises that, "As I focus on helping elevate others' sense of self-worth, I feel a great sense of satisfaction and my own sense of self-worth is elevated." Though he admits that his behaviour hasn't changed much at all, he says that, "It's more a case of I am consciously aware of what I am trying to do. I have a reason now behind my actions, and reason even for existing."

He appreciates the scepticism many people experience about 'purpose', though with the benefit of hindsight sees the logic to it. With refreshing honesty, he admits, "If anyone had come to me and said you're going to clarify your life's purpose, I would have been very sceptical or even cynical. I'd have imagined that the purpose I would have come up with would be completely unrelated to my life. I didn't think that it would be relatable, nor did I think there would be any logic to it. Purpose is more a matter of uncovering what you innately know is there, and really about connecting the dots to both your past and the way that you operate."

Tyrone, concerned at first that purpose would somehow be different from his life as it is, now realises, "There's a preconception that purpose is something completely different from your own life, somehow separate from life. It's not. That infers that there is something wrong with your current life, you know, like your purpose is to be a missionary and you are working in an office. It is not that at all. There is no massive adjustment or change needed in your life. The purpose in your life is your life."

As a white-collar professional working in the finance industry, Tyrone says that purpose and message are completely relevant to working in an office. "I help others feel that their input is valued, that their contribution is worthwhile. It's all about people and our success or failure is driven by how we interact with each other. Tying this back to my purpose, everyone has input to give, and in receiving that, not only do we end up with a better outcome, people are more actively engaged and feel better about it." Tyrone sees a participatory form of leadership as one way of creating his purpose, saying, "A professional workplace is filled with people. If you don't think that your life is connected to other people, I think that you are somewhat deluded. In a small amount of space there's a lot of people. So how you work with people, including customers, makes a world of difference. Purpose is as relevant to your work as you choose it to be. Tell me that a moment of interaction is not an opportunity to affect them positively and make a positive difference."

Others need not even know. "My job has not changed", Tyrone informs, "but my attitude to it has and with it my enjoyment. It's not about announcing it to the world; it can just be the way you do things. Very often you are the only person who knows what's really going on, but the effect on others is no less positive, as long as you are living to that purpose."

Summarising what 'purpose' is all about, he confidently states, "Purpose is just about you interpreting your life differently and looking for the opportunity to make a difference, whether you're at home, working in an office or a building site."

Let's have some words

Before we continue, it's important to share with you what is meant with a few terms; in particular, 'success' and 'unconscious revealers'.

Success

'Success' is simply the ability to achieve what you have set out to achieve. This is not intended to mean only the typical meaning of success that is pervasive in our culture of being an entrepreneur, reaching a senior position in an organisation, having amassed great wealth, or become a high earning professional, unless of course you are someone who sets out to actually achieve these things.

In this book, 'success' is literally having achieved what we set out to do. It therefore includes someone who has set out and achieved such things as travelled the world, completed a degree, become an artist, learned to parachute, become a teacher, trekked through the Himalaya, built a house, created a welcoming environment to which to invite guests, raised children, or started a business.

Revealers

Throughout this book you'll be collecting information about how you and others experience and perceive your life. This information reveals things about you that is very useful. The reason that this information is important is that it helps to reveal to you what is actually important and most important in your life, and your gifts.

There are two types of information—what you are already aware of, and what you are not aware of.

You are already aware and conscious of certain things—what you want, what you know about things, your aspirations, what you might be skilled at doing, what you are interested in, what gets your attention. You might want a promotion, or have an interest in the environment or politics, care for and love your family, be good with your hands or with analysis, and pay attention whenever there's news of child neglect. All of this you might know consciously, and this 'conscious' information reveals certain things about you. These are your 'conscious revealers'.

To reveal information about you based on what you are aware of and know consciously is to use your conscious revealers. Every other method that I have seen and participated in asks you to take the conscious route, to use what you are aware of about what you know and want.

There are plenty of things in your life that you are not necessarily aware of though. There is plenty about you that right now is outside of your awareness; there is plenty that you are not conscious of right now. Do you always understand your motives when you get frustrated or angry? Have you ever been worked up about something without clarity about why? Have you ever felt deeply and cared passionately about something without knowing why? Do you really know why you feel strongly about and even react to things at all? Not necessarily all the time, but at least some of the time?

So you can say that there are things that are currently outside of your awareness. You could describe what is currently outside of your awareness, what you are not conscious of, as being what you are currently unconscious to. Everyone, including me, including you, feels strongly about or reacts to certain events in their lives. Your reactions may be fleeting, or may be enduring. You might verbalise them, or they may remain known only to you. Either way, a reaction to something has occurred. Your reactions at the time they happen are outside of your awareness; they are not something that you are conscious of at the time.

For example, say you get upset with someone during a conversation because you perceive that they're 'not listening'. That judgement was automatic and unconscious, as you cannot know for sure that they weren't listening. It is possible that they were listening completely according to their version of what listening completely means. For you, this is an unconscious revealer. Your unconscious judgement of their 'not listening' reveals that what's actually important for you is 'attention'. When you do that for a large number of events and record them, your map of what's important gets revealed. It's all revealed through the unconscious reactions you have to your own life circumstances.

The approach to your purpose and calling that you'll be reading about in this book is mostly reliant on your reactions and the perceptions you have when you react—your unconscious revealers—to make sense of how you experience and react to your life. Doing so will reveal a wealth of information that is not otherwise accessible to you. I am not aware of any other approaches to this topic that rely on and utilise your unconscious revealers so specifically.

True yet partial

Over the past 30 years I have probably read the book and participated in the program that purports to answer one's life calling. I admire the authors and trainers who created and developed what they shared. It's just that none of them did it for me. Though I had great and useful insights, I always felt like I'd missed the mark, and that something was still missing. I was never satisfied with the degree of depth I achieved.

Many people that I interact with seem to have 'tried it all' as well. They are rightfully sceptical that something might touch them at a deeper level. They're suspicious that in following a process they might reveal something they can look at and say: 'That's me! That's what I'm about! It always has been!'

Some of the common statements and responses follow.

'Not possible—it can't be true that purpose or calling can be realised'

It's possible for us to realise something that we regard as most important to us. It's something that evokes our Peak Empathic Response when we see that missing in others, and we can be very passionate about wanting to do something about it. It's something that when we act to create on behalf of others, we experience happiness and fulfilment. Only you doing the work can validate or refute whether that's the case.

'Another program promising purpose'

What's different about the approach that you'll be using in this book is that you'll specifically rely on and utilise unconscious revealers as a primary source of information.

You'll use your reactions and the perceptions you have when you react. You'll use your own and others unconscious revealers. You'll do this to make sense of how you experience and react to your life. This reveals a wealth of information for you.

Most methods ask us to take the conscious route, to use what we are aware that we know and want. To reveal information based on what we are aware of and know consciously is to use our conscious revealers. To make sense of our conscious revealers—is to make sense of what we are aware of and consciously know and want. It can miss other important sources of information.

'Purpose is known only to an unknowable external intelligence'

Maybe. While you may not know exactly the intention behind the events you've had in your life, you can certainly make sense of how you experienced those events. Whether there's an intent behind the events, and what meaning we give to how we experienced those events, are two different things.

I don't know whether there is an external intent to the events in our lives. I do know that we can interpret the meaning we give to them.

'Our purpose cannot be revealed through focus on ourselves'

Maybe not, though your purpose can certainly be revealed through focus on how you react to and experience life and others, and how others experience and react to you. I never uncovered my calling through a focus on the conscious aspects of myself. We uncover something magnificent through a focus on the unconscious or subjective aspects of ourselves.

'If every other method I've tried hasn't really worked, how will this?'

This is a terrific question that still holds the door open to validity. Though elements of this approach may seem familiar for you, this is a new and unique approach that consistently helps people gain clarity about their own lives. It is different from existing approaches in many ways. Existing approaches to the quest of answering purpose can be described as follows:

1. You're born with purpose.

This approach basically says that you either know it or you don't. Searching for it won't help. It may be true that you're born with something that's most important for you. I certainly know people for whom this is true, they just always had a sense of what they were here for. What I do know though is that, regardless of whether or not you're born with a sense of purpose, you can decipher the way you experience and react to life to reveal what is most important to you. Whether you were born with that or not does not seem to make any real difference. Participants in this approach often report that their lives suddenly make sense, and that they appreciate it in a way that they never had before.

2. Purpose arrives by epiphany

This approach says that your purpose or calling in life will arrive on you unexpectedly—so just wait for it to arrive. I do know people for whom their calling was experienced this way. They just woke up one day or responded to a circumstance before them, and found what gives them a great sense of fulfilment. However, relying on this approach is a bit like making your business strategy to be winning the lottery. However, in what you'll be doing here most participants experience the epiphany of 'so that's what my life is all about!'

3. Life review

This technique says to list the significant events in your life, look for patterns in and through them, and that's your purpose. This can certainly work if you happen to be able to make sense of those significant events in your life. However, if you're not skilled at deciphering your significant life events, you may not arrive with much. What you'll be doing here will help you to decipher those significant events in a particular way that will help you reveal to yourself what already matters. The method you'll be learning goes much deeper than other methods I've ever come across.

4. Obituary

This technique asks you to define what you'd want others to say about you, or what you'd want your grandkids to know about you, upon your passing. While this can be great at revealing the values that you *want* to be important, it doesn't necessarily include the values that *are already* important. While there is merit in appreciating where you want to go, there's also merit in appreciating what already is. What you'll be doing here is recognising what already is.

5. You are strongest in your gift, and you're meant to use it

This technique asks you to write down your talents and look for patterns or common themes. I agree that this technique is important, and I agree that things work best when we use our gift. However, we humans have this interesting habit of tending to discount our gifts. Your gift, after all, is something in you that is abundant and effortless, and we live in a culture that tends to value things that are scarce and effortful.

The other limitation of this technique is that it is based on what you know consciously. It uses your conscious revealers. There is an additional wealth of information to be garnered through your unconscious revealers. What you'll be doing here will include both the conscious and unconscious revealers.

Moreover, your gift, by itself, is not innately motivating. Using your gift means that what you're doing can seem more effortless than other ways of doing it. It does not automatically mean that what you're doing is important.

6. Identify what you are passionate about and do it

This technique asks you to pay attention to whenever you feel passionate about something, record those events, look for patterns and make sense of it. I agree that doing what you're passionate about is important, essential even. However, while you may know you're passionate, you might not always know what you're passionate about, let alone why. What I have realised is that what is essential to you, and matters most for you, is what you'll tend to be naturally passionate about on behalf of giving to others.

What you'll be doing here relies on that being the case, and has been the experience of participants.

7. Purpose = passions + values + talents

This technique asks you to identify your passions, your values and your talents, and says that your purpose is the intersection of those three. I absolutely agree that purpose involves what you're naturally passionate about, what's important for you, and what your gift is. The challenge is in identifying what they really are. The other concern I have with this approach is that it appears to assume that your passions and values are separate. What you are most passionate about is what's most important for you, and is your highest value. What you'll be doing here will be identifying what your values already are, what's most important for you and what you're likely to be most passionate about, and what your gift is, though you'll be using your concrete experience to identify what these are in a qualitative sense.

8. Do things that meet a need

This technique says simply to identify something that needs to be done, and do it. I agree that serving others is important. Research into 'happiness' says doing so is the factor most highly associated with increased happiness. That we are here to serve others in some way is a primary assumption of what we'll be doing here. When we uncover what matters most—our message—we realise that's what evokes our Peak Empathic Response. It's something that we feel drawn to do something about—not for us alone but on behalf of others. Our message is an answer to a problem of the human condition. Our message serves a need. It happens that we'll serve others in a way that we're likely to be most passionate about.

9. Adaptive path

This technique says that you can just make a decision and notice what your experience has to say about doing so. I completely agree that this technique can work, assuming you have the time that this adaptive process may take. This is especially the case if your starting point is way off the mark. Before I came up with the current approach, this was the technique I'd been using for many years. After some ten years, I'd gotten to 'Help people appreciate their humanity', and paying attention to acting on this helped me to adapt my understanding of what I was here for. What you'll be doing here will give you a jump-start on your starting point, to help you get as close as possible to what the essence of you is really about. From a better starting point, listening to the feedback of your own life and adapting can be thought of as minor course corrections, rather than massive adjustments.

10. Science of success

This approach says you just need to decide what you want it to be, choose your values, set your goals, hold yourself accountable, and keep going. In other words, it's all about how to create what you intend to. I agree that knowing how to create success in your life is important. It's just very different from fulfilment. These approaches seem to be teaching how to be successful, including in matters of purpose. Unless you're someone for whom achieving what you want is most important for you, I very much doubt that a focus on what you want your life to look like will, by itself, reveal your life's purpose. I doubt the science of success is the best approach for the art of fulfilment. The ability to succeed is great for delivering, not discovering, purpose.

The science of success is best applied to the concrete forms you choose your life calling to take. Your purpose requires that you take action, as only through living it in some way can you experience fulfilment. Fulfilment is the consequence of acting on your purpose. The more adept you are with successfully creating what you want, the more skilled you'll be when it comes to creating the concrete form or forms you choose your life calling to take.

What's different about this approach?

In the approach you'll be taking here, you'll be including elements of all the above techniques, as all of them are part of the overall story. They are all true yet partial. What's different is that while the above techniques typically rely on what you can be aware of and consciously reveal (your conscious revealers) and figure out, what you'll be doing here is heavily utilising what is revealed by that which is outside your awareness (your unconscious revealers) to uncover the truth as it is.

This approach:

- Is not about interpreting the meaning of some sacred texts or trying to figure out some preordained reason for your life.

- Is about deciphering the way your life has been shaped and what your life is already the answer to.

- Will seek to help you appreciate that you are here to create a differentiated form of love, love, not in the romantic sense, but in the universal sense. In fact, once you have formed your message, your self-evident truth, your test question will be, 'Can you have love without that?' With conviction participants say, 'No! Not according to me, anyway!' They realise that their message is to create love in some way. Examples of this are: empowerment, connection, trust, inclusion, and worth.

- Is about first answering what your purpose is in an abstract sense, before you choose to create it in concrete form.

- Says you get to choose and create the form your contribution takes, which assumes an ability to create. Why it is important for you to choose is that you know your personal circumstance better than anyone, you know the reach that you are capable of, and you are in the best position to choose the most appropriate concrete form that your contribution may take.

What I have discovered is a new way that utilises your unconscious revealers, using the unconscious aspects of our own experience to reveal what your purpose or calling already is. Using your unconscious revealers tends to be a more direct path than using conscious revealers, and can be a very profound experience.

You'll be using:

- Your reactions to life to reveal all the things that are already important. This can then reveal what that's all about for you.

- Your Great Wound to reveal your Peak Empathic Response. This is related to what's essentially important for you, that which you care most about. It reveals the form of love you're here to create.

- The experience of your perceived differences from others to reveal your gift.

So yes, what you are here for is to create a form of love in the world, in some way, with a number of people that's for you to decide on. Finding your calling is a conscious, deliberate effort that gives your life a larger meaning and source of fulfilment. Your calling is unique, it's your signature form of love; and it asks you to utilise your gifts in service of what's most important for you on behalf of others.

Your sense of purpose changes, and you are rarely consciously born with it. You generate a sense of purpose through choosing to create what's important—what's most important. Because this is a 'sense of things', it comes from within, and only you know if you have a sense of purpose.

Your sense of purpose is your life, though very often you don't realise that and how to decode what it means. You already know, though probably unconsciously, what you are to bring into the world more consciously, and you'll be making that conscious to yourself. Moreover, you'll recognise what's most important for you when you hear yourself articulate it. You already know a tremendous amount about it; I call it your area of genius.

Now I'm perturbed

Recollect if you've ever seen popcorn being made. The heat pressure on the corn kernels is what causes the kernel to transform and 'pop', becoming fluffy and tasty. Once popped, there's no going back for the kernel. It's an irreversible transformation. Similarly, when coal is put under immense pressure for many millions of years, it permanently transforms into the precious gem we know as a diamond. To transform, the popped corn required the heat, and the diamond required the sustained heat and pressure.

'Perturbation' is a term coined by Ilya Prigogine, winner in 1977 of the Nobel Prize in Chemistry. He was a Belgian physical chemist noted for his work on complex systems and irreversibility. He studied how organisms behave and transform when put under pressure. Perturbation deals with how organisms, such as humans, change and transform.

According to Prigogine, when enough pressure is applied a tipping-point is reached where one of two things happen:

1. **Uncontained.** Without something to assist the organism to withstand the pressure being experienced and support its transformation, the organism is said to be uncontained. The organism will move to a chaotic state or disintegrate. This is known as entropy.

2. **Contained.** With something to assist the organism to withstand the pressure being experienced and support its transformation, the organism is 'contained'. The organism can then be held in place while it reorganises itself into something more complex and capable of withstanding the pressure being experienced. This is an irreversible process. In becoming more complex, the organism will take on the properties of the pressure being experienced. In other words, the pressure being experienced is used as fuel for transformation. This is known as enthalpy.

To summarise this book and what you'll read about the approach to your calling and life purpose, it is the process of perturbation. Your life has experienced many shaping pressures, large, small, and in some cases, extreme. You're still here or otherwise hopefully not in a chaotic state, which means that in many respects, those experiences were contained. They were fuel for your transformation. You took on some of the properties of the pressure being experienced. It shaped your life. This is represented in the image below.

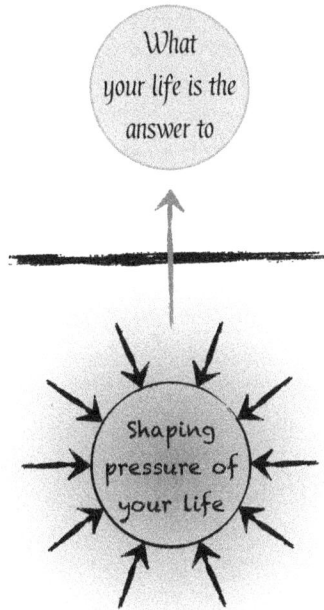

From pressure to transformation

Perturbation describes the process of changing, of what happens when the pressures we experience result in our transforming. When we have transformed, we have grown in some way. There seems to be a wealth of information and debate about which factors are involved in our own growth and the factors that shape the transforming that occurs. Often this is reduced to the 'nature vs. nurture' debate. This debate looks at the extent to which our current state is due to our innate nature, versus the way we were nurtured.

Different people will experience the same environment or nurturing situation differently. What we call 'pressures of life' are the way we are experiencing our environment. What is 'pressure' to one person is barely noticed by someone else. A situation that is anxiety producing for one person is an exciting opportunity for another. The way we were nurtured has to do with what happened in our environment and the way we experienced those external conditions. It's our nature that determines the way our environment is experienced.

From our own perspective then, our innate nature is the essence of who we are, and what we call nurture is the way we experienced our environment. Therefore, what determines the way we humans transform and evolve is a combination of our nature, nurture and experience. Who we are being at any time is a combination of our essence, our environment, and our experience.

To our essence, the environment is a constraint that determines which aspects of our nature are influenced to respond. Our essence determines the way we tend to experience those external situations and what habits we form in response. It's our experience that shapes the way we perceive, give meaning to and make sense of our environment, and the way we behave and act accordingly. The following model represents this dynamic that determines how we develop and show up in life.

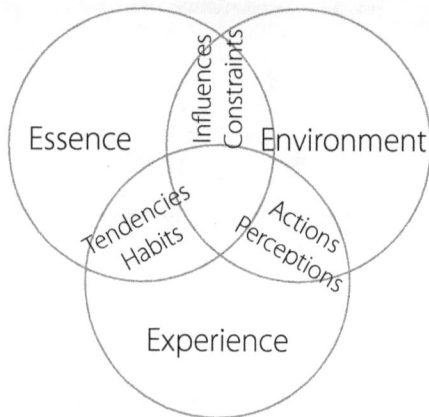

Who we are is a result of our essence, environment and experience

Perturbation describes how things transform in response to external pressure. What we call these external 'pressures of life' are the way we experience our environment and are what had us transform, evolve and grow. It's the way we experience our situations in life that determines whether we are experiencing the pressure to grow. It's our essence that determines the way we tend to experience and are influenced by that environment.

When we have experienced extreme pressures, we've been influenced in extreme ways and tended to experience those situations in particular ways. Those pressures shaped our life and led to what our life is about—which is the meaning we gave to significant events in our life. Those significant experiences were experienced in a particular way, with a particular meaning, or as a particular message. What our life is the answer to, our message, is determined by the way we experienced that extreme pressure.

That our life has been and will continue to be experiencing shaping pressures that support us to transform in some way, is one thing. Another is opening up and into that transformed version. The ongoing shaping pressures of life don't have to be extreme. They can be quite small. They're just situations in our environment that are experienced as pressure. In containing and surmounting them, we grow in some way.

However, 'pressure' can be the source of development and happiness.

Have you ever had the experience of being so involved in something that you lose track of time? Have you ever been so involved in what you're doing that you're just doing and there's no sense of self-consciousness? If you have, then you've experienced an optimal state of experience called 'flow'.

While many are familiar with the term 'being in the flow' and we have a sense of when we are in the flow, the conditions for experiencing flow are not so well understood. Mihaly Csíkszentmihályi, author of the book *'Flow'*, describes optimal experience as a state of flow, and that people are happiest when experiencing it. You're likely to be in a state of flow when you are fully immersed in an enjoyable activity and have a feeling of energised focus, full involvement and success.

According to Csíkszentmihályi, flow conditions exist when an activity has the right balance of challenge and skill. A 'challenge' is still 'pressure'. As in learning to play tennis, your skill is initially low. In playing with this level of skill, you'll be facing a challenge. If the challenge is too high, you're likely to experience some pressure and anxiety. If the challenge is too easy, then you're likely to experience some boredom. Provided the pressure and challenge are neither too high nor low for your level of skill, flow conditions exist. As your tennis skills improve, what was the appropriate level of challenge and pressure becomes boring, so a greater challenge and pressure is necessary. If you happen to meet a greater challenge and pressure, such as a more skilled opponent, then you'll experience anxiety and, if you want to continue to play tennis, you might decide to increase your own skill in response. Either way, you arrive at a more skilled level capable of meeting the greater challenge, and have a greater ability of responding successfully to that level of pressure. The new situation is more complex because it 'involves greater challenges, and demands greater skills'. What we call 'pressure' is simply a challenge that we have not yet transformed through.

In flow, you are neither anxious nor bored, but just right. There is neither too much pressure, nor too little. Whenever you consider any situation you're in as too challenging, you'll experience anxiety, as the experience of pressure is uncontained. If that anxiety can be contained, you have the conditions for transforming. In experiencing pressures of life you can be said to be experiencing pressure, anxiety and stress when there is uncertainty about your ability to successfully navigate and transform through the situation.

This is represented in the following diagram from the book *'Flow'* (reproduced with permission from Mihaly Csíkszentmihályi).

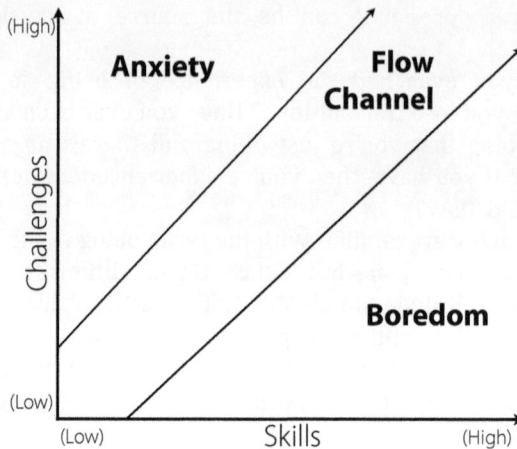

Why the complexity of consciousness increases as a result of flow experiences

According to Csíkszentmihályi, the three steps to gaining strength from 'stressful' situations and pressured environments, and then transforming from them are:

1. Confidence in our own ability to prevail
2. Focus on and being involved with what's happening in our environment, and
3. Being open and alert to possible responses

Any situation in life is a possibility for our growth, if we make it that way. As Csíkszentmihályi says, "These transformations require that a person be prepared to perceive unexpected opportunities" and respond to them. To respond is to act.

The same applies to what our life is calling us towards. If our choice for action is suitably challenging (neither too anxious nor boring), "a person may experience flow continuously in his or her calling".

Is it worth it?

Besides the obvious benefits of a sense of meaning and purpose in life, the benefits of sharing with the world the essence of who you are can be summarised as follows:

1. Clarity and priority

Your life purpose is a foundation on which to make decisions. It's a GPS for your life. Things get really clear when you know what's most important. Your priorities are what's important for you. Knowing what's most important helps you to stay closer to it.

2. Investment

With a clear sense of purpose, you're able to invest your time, energy and resources appropriately towards seeing the concrete fulfilment of your purpose.

3. Focus

Purpose provides the focus of knowing who you are, where you're going and where you want to be.

4. Persistence

Success is invariably due to persistence and the determination to persist. Obstacles become just another part of the purposeful life you're living. They are seen through the lens of the contribution that you are here to make. You are not stopped by them—you flow around them.

5. Motivation

Your purpose, what you care about most, is a source of great motivation. What could be more motivating than knowing you are working towards something that matters most to you. Without having a sense of purpose, motivation can be difficult.

6. Well-being

Recent research suggests that those who live life with a sense of purpose experience protection against poor health and better physical functioning. This is even more so than people who focus on achieving feelings of happiness. In one study, the researchers concluded that living with a sense of purpose should be added to the list of healthy living strategies such as exercise and healthy eating.

7. Appreciation

When living life on purpose, not only does life have meaning, there's an appreciation for the way your life has been shaped and the experiences you've had that shaped it. It is those experiences that have sensitised you to and clarified what your purpose actually is.

8. Orientation

Knowing what you are here for helps to make clear the adjustments needed in your life to create the fulfilment of your purpose.

9. Growth

To create the contribution you're here to make will require you to become the person capable of creating it, and your character will mould to fit it.

10. Happiness

Purpose is about giving, not getting. Happiness research consistently reveals that contributing to the well-being of others is associated with happiness. That is, happiness is the result of giving to others.

11. Fulfilment

Fulfilment is the result of using your gift in service of what's most important on behalf of others.

12. Authenticity and leadership

With clear life purpose it's possible to be truly authentic around the essence of who you are as you share that with the world. In addition, research shows that authenticity is the factor most highly correlated with leadership effectiveness.

Health, happiness and leadership

Recent research and authors suggest that a sense of meaning and purpose contributes to health, happiness and leadership.

1. Health

Recent research finds that positive psychological well-being (of which purposeful engagement with life is a part) and purpose in life correlates with a reduced risk of mortality from all causes.

The authors of such research conclude that:

- "Positive psychological well-being has biological correlates that may be health protective, with distinctive patterns for men and women."[2]

- "Greater purpose in life is associated with a reduced risk of all-cause mortality among community-dwelling older persons."[1]

- "Positive psychological well-being has a favourable effect on survival in both healthy and diseased populations."[31]

- "Subjects who did not find a sense of 'ikigai' (a life worth living) were associated with an increased risk of all-cause mortality. The increase in mortality risk was attributable to cardiovascular disease and external causes, but not cancer."[30]

2. Happiness

"The only ones among you who will be really happy are those who have sought and found how to serve." ~ Albert Schweitzer

Csíkszentmihályi says that we experience happiness when we experience flow. In addition, when we look at recent published works on the topic of happiness, a common theme is that happiness increases as we focus on contributing to the well-being of others. To cite but a few authors who have written based on recent research:

- Richard Layard, in *'Happiness'*, says that selfishness does not lead to happiness. People feel happy when they are contributing to the well-being of others, and experience gratitude. He says that the most profound motivation in the world is love, and that if you increase the amount of love in the world, you increase the amount of happiness.
- Sonja Lyubomirsky, in *'The how of happiness'*, says that the ultimate happiness secret is to be kind, to do good for others.
- Martin E.P. Seligman, in *'Authentic happiness'*, says that helping other people is the single most important element in long-term happiness.
- Research conducted by MetLife Mature Market Institute revealed that people with a sense of purpose in their lives are more likely to report being happy and describe themselves as living in a positive state of being.[12]

Combining or stacking these two factors, we can increase our happiness through contributing to the well-being of others in a way that produces flow for us.

3. Leadership

When you have such things as clarity, priority, focus, persistence and motivation, then you have what most schools of thought on the matter say are the essential ingredients of effective leadership. With clear life purpose it's possible to be truly authentic around the essence of who you are and share who you are with others. Research, such as that from The Leadership Circle™, shows that authenticity is the top factor correlated with leadership effectiveness.

For example, Bill George and Peter Simms, in their book *'True North'*, say that authentic leadership is all about how well connected we are to our 'internal compass', our true north. It establishes our authenticity and inspires others to follow our lead. Their point is that it guides us to who and to what we are, as it is based on our values and deepest convictions. They also give examples of how leaders have made their greatest contributions when they were enthusiastic about their work.

Authenticity isn't just about knowing what's important; it's skilfully bringing what's important into your environment. This book will help you realise your deepest conviction, your natural authenticity, and your self-evident truth—your true north.

Zaheed's experience

Zaheed was born in Johannesburg, South Africa, and moved to Australia when he was two years old. Out of four children, he's one of identical twins. He's a married father of three who works as an in-house corporate lawyer. He's been involved in multibillion dollar mergers and acquisitions, and has been acting Company Secretary for a large ASX listed public company. He trains in karate and has an active interest in sports cars. He says that he turns into opportunities for having fun whenever someone confuses him with his twin brother, something which understandably, happens frequently.

Zaheed's experience is a clear example of the personal benefits of doing the work to realise, act on and live life on purpose. "The biggest difference", reports Zaheed, "is renewed confidence, confidence in just doing what's important and knowing that, rather than searching for answers, they are already within you. I have access to and confidence in my own wisdom."

Things have become much simpler for him. "When you discover your own insight, you don't have to be told over and over again. You just know. Actions flow effortlessly then, as it is self-chosen, not imposed on you. Imposed methods are never going to work. Diagnostics can give you useful feedback, though they don't inform you anywhere near as well as your own wisdom. When insight is personal, there is nothing to remember. By knowing what's important, actions flow more easily and immediately. Now I just act. With a values diagnostic you can't be sure if it's real or not. With my own clarity, I have no doubt that it is. Not only am I clearer on what's important, I find myself spontaneously acting on it."

He appreciates his past experiences more. "When you look at everything that was perceived to be 'bad', 'negative' or 'reactive' about yourself, the labels themselves sound bad. When you realise that these labels are actually pointing to something you value, like health and love for example, you don't see them as bad any longer and you appreciate them. It was a profound moment for me, like a slap across the face, when I realised that the great pain you have gives you the ability to relate to others. All this time I was unconsciously suffering in pain, to then realise it's a gift to be shared. I was shocked by the beauty of it all. I am much more in tune with people who have challenges in life. Pain means that I can relate. I accept people for who they are. I accept me for me."

Purpose is natural according to Zaheed. "When I act consistent with my message I feel like I am more me. I realise too that I had always been living my purpose, though unconsciously. We are already living our purpose. Now we can do it more consciously."

Motivation is higher and action more immediate for him. "Not only do I know why I feel so motivated for certain behaviours and acting in a certain way, I experience those qualities at the same time. It bothers me when people are beating themselves up. Now I'll spontaneously respond and invite an interaction with others, and leave them free to choose their response. I am there for people more than I was before."

Zaheed reports that for him, a sense of purpose is integral to his work as a lawyer and central to authenticity. "I used to think that my job was to be a consultant and give advice. Now I realise that much of what I do is in the moment-to-moment interactions of acceptance. That is what I get paid for and at the same time I am living my purpose. It does not matter what job I am doing, I can always live my purpose. My message defines how I go about my work. For example, on a recent merger and acquisition deal, lawyers from the external law-firm provided feedback that I was received as calmly assertive, strategically commercial, respectfully effective, and strong. It's rewarding to be told that the qualities that are important for me are how others perceive me. To know that it can happen, though not always and not with everyone, gives me more motivation and enthusiasm to keep going."

He also feels more energised and fulfilled. "When I am acting on what's important, I'm juiced up about life. In fact, I get juiced up just talking about what's important. The more I act on what's important, the more pumped I feel. I go to bed tired but pumped. It's fulfilling to act on what's important. I focus on the tangible, concrete things that reflect what matters, like being a great husband, father, son, friend, and I feel awesome. When I know I've done the things that matter, I feel great, content and satisfied."

His advice to people exploring purpose is to "Know what matters and live it. Know what's important and do the work. That's not to say you won't have ups and downs, but you will be more fulfilled by pursuing it. Everyone experiences pain and hurt and suffering, but you can still be content."

Purpose on purpose

So what brings someone to a book like this? It could be any number of things:

- Perhaps you're just wondering: 'Is this all there is?'
- In good faith you've done as others have advised, you've tried to identify your values, passions, and talents, you've tried just going for it, and it all somehow seems like it is missing the mark. No matter how much energy, time and money you invest, it seems like you just don't know how to find what your purpose is. With good intention you have tried many other 'purpose' programs, yet still seem to be searching for that sense of deep recognition you know is there.

- You know or have a sense that you're here for a reason, but you don't know what. You might even have a missed sense of opportunity and feel an underlying anxiety about the passing of time. Perhaps too you might wonder how others have been able to find their 'thing'. What reassures you is maybe that either life is random and you're not actually here for a reason, or you are already doing what you were born to and you just don't know it.

- Supporting your family or some other aspect in your personal life is important to you, and rightfully you stay true to what's important for you. You perhaps keep at your unfulfilling job simply because it provides you with at least a reliable and possibly even the best way you know how to deliver on what's important for you. It may even feel like, and is, a noble sacrifice that you are making. You don't like your job, might even regard it as a chore, but you keep at it because it supports your ability to do something else that's important. You might even have given up on the hope of experiencing fulfilment at work, and instead find fulfilment in what your work can provide. Perhaps you've given up on the possibility of living life at work with meaning.

- In the beginning you loved your job, were excited about its potential and what you can and did achieve. Material success might not even have been your prime motive; you did it just because you loved the job. That was in the beginning, but for some reason that same job now no longer satisfies, has you feeling empty, and you're ready to jump ship.

- You're in a workplace or environment where you are experiencing alignment, and you have strong sense of fit and belonging. However, while you're passionate about your work and the environment in which you're doing it, what you're doing seems so tiring, perhaps even exhausting.

- You might even have done a lot of personal enquiry and have a deep sense of purpose and what you are here to do. However, for some reason you still feel down, and happiness seems somehow elusive to you.

- You've been blessed with a natural talent, like art, and are really good at something, perhaps even receive accolades and admiration from others for the quality of your work. However, you don't seem to be passionate about what you're doing, perhaps don't even know why you're doing it.

- You're doing a lot with your life, perhaps even feel stretched and possibly very busy much of the time. You may be staying true to and fulfilling those noble commitments that you have already made, like raising a family, completing that big project, or finishing that great undertaking that'll be a long time to fruition. However you have the sense that there is more to you, there's a sense of there still being some untapped resources that could be brought forth, you intuit that you can still contribute a lot more, and still you seem unable to scratch that itch.

- You've had a good or great career, and you've developed appreciative reputation around your expertise in your field. However, you have a dawning sense that what you're good at no longer seems to satisfy like it once used to.

- You have done the years of hard work and achieved success in life, perhaps even achieved a life of riches, and want for nothing of a material form. However, you've come to the realisation that it all seems a little empty and you realise you'd also like a rich life.

None of this is your fault. How could it be? You do what you do in good faith, for good reason, with great integrity. There's even a certain nobility in what you do. Inexplicably, things change. Your life, for some reason seems to want more from you. Life seems to be trying to reorganise your life. For some reason there's this new pressure that you are experiencing. You might not even realise that this pressure is somehow trying to bring about some form of reorganisation in the way you are living your life to get you to share with the world more of the essence of who you are. You might be at a loss how to identify this intangible, ineffable, elusive essence, this deep aspect of you that is trying to come through into the world just that little bit more.

What's going on though, and perfectly understandably too, is that we don't know how to identify what we're really here for in a deep way, a way that makes sense of our life in a way that reveals what we're here to contribute. What's happening too is that, while success seemed to be so satisfying at first, we don't really understand why it no longer does.

The shift from success to fulfilment

This all makes perfect sense though. After a while, we start to realise that continued success and progress, for some reason, no longer seems to satisfy as it once did. For many it's almost an inexplicable 'What the...?' experience.

If this decline is allowed to prolong, it can result in a growing feeling of meaninglessness and emptiness. If allowed to continue for a long time, it can lead to decline, feeling restless, frustrated and wasted;

and being perceived as demotivated, a misfit, and possibly even incompetent. Hopefully, if a sense of purpose is found, it can lead to rejuvenation and fulfilment, especially when acted upon. This journey is represented in the following diagram.

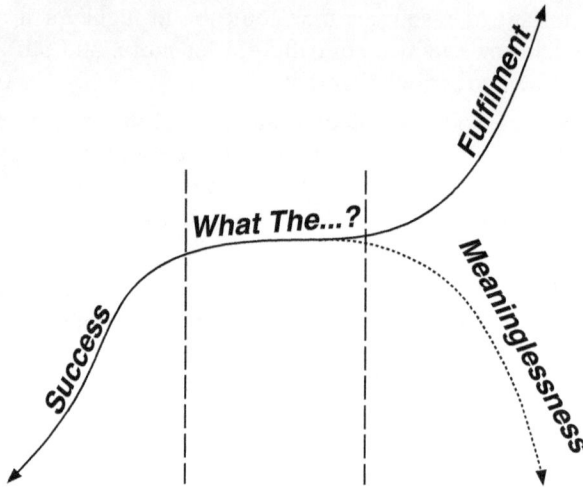

Sometimes success no longer satisfies

Many people ask 'What am I here for?' or 'What is my purpose?' and yet still stumble with its answer. It can feel a little like stumbling around in the dark, the dark that comes with a lack of deep insight. What I have realised is that the question, 'What am I here for?', especially when asked in a concrete way as if it was, 'What am I here to do?', is not actually the best question.

Achieving purpose and fulfilment is an abstract and intangible experience. You know it when you experience it. You can't see it. You can't touch it. It is not a concrete 'thing'. Yet the question is usually asked in a concrete way. This is represented in the following diagram.

Qualitative

Existing approaches
focus here

What is my purpose?
What am I here for?
What am I here to do?

Concrete

Many approaches to 'purpose' focus attention in a concrete way

The better question is a qualitative one. Literally: 'What quality am I here to create?' To answer this question is for you to awaken to the essence of who you are. In a way, this may be your purpose. The qualitative question comes first. Your first purpose is to awaken to the essence of who you are and what you're here for. The answer to this question leaves you free to choose the how, the concrete form it may take.

The quality that each of us is here to create is an inner experience. You have an inner and intangible purpose. That aspect of you is changeless, though your clarity of understanding about that may well change. What ever concrete form you choose for your inner purpose could be called your outer and concrete purpose. Your outer purpose can and may very well change a lot and often. What you are here for is your inner purpose that shows up as an outer purpose.

This is what I understand to be what Eckhart Tolle describes as the difference between your inner purpose and outer purpose. In his book 'A New Earth', Tolle says that we have an inner purpose and an outer purpose. Our inner purpose is primary and concerns Being; and our outer purpose is secondary and concerns doing. According to Tolle, our inner purpose is to awaken; something common to all of humanity. Tolle is clear that our outer purpose can change over time, and that it varies greatly from person to person. I agree with Tolle that finding and living in alignment with our inner purpose is the foundation for fulfilling our outer purpose. Aligning with our inner purpose and fulfilling our outer purpose is the basis for true success.

The intent of this book is to help you realise what your specific inner purpose is. Your outer purpose, or rather the specific and concrete forms that it may take, is for you to choose. More than likely, as Tolle says, your outer purpose will change over time.

This is represented in the following diagram.

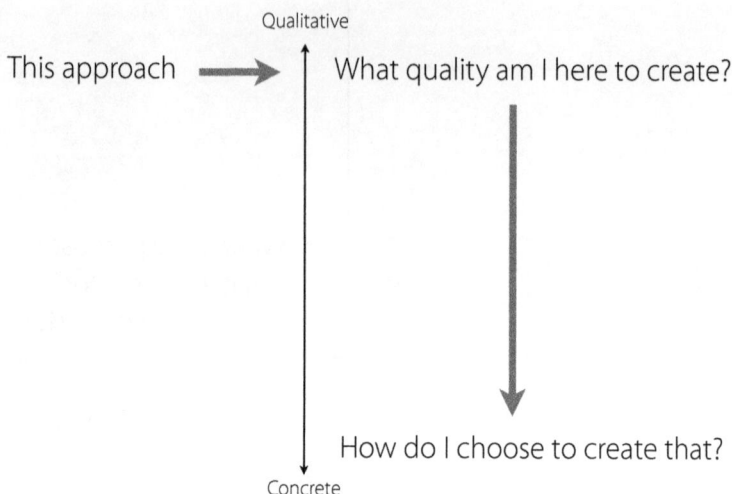

Qualitative

This approach ⟶ What quality am I here to create?

How do I choose to create that?

Concrete

The focus of this life calling method is at first qualitative

It is not just that it's important to identify what quality you are here to create before you can choose the concrete forms it might take. There are many dimensions to the nature of what your life is calling you to, and unpacking those can help you to understand how things inexplicably change.

The common employment arrangement is that your employer has a task that needs to be done and it is your talent that completes the task. That's your common commercial exchange. However, when that exchange is separate from and does not include what's important for you, it's eventually going to feel empty and meaningless.

Talent   (Important)

$ Exchange

Task

The usual workplace commercial exchange of talent for task

Now as I said earlier, what you are called to create, and the source of your fulfilment, is the intersection of what's most **important** for you, your **gift**, and delivered in service for others because that's important for others and meets a **need** that they have. Later we'll find and define how what's most important is your **message**. The model then becomes as shown below.

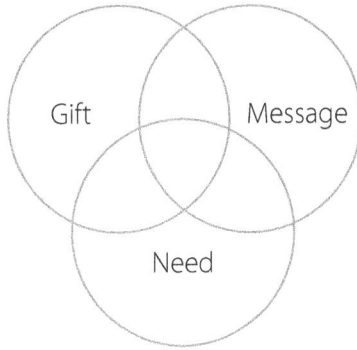

Our calling is the intersection of gift, message and need

The intersection of your gift serving a need that's important for others is your contribution, you're providing value and serving others, and when acted on increases satisfaction. Where what's most important for you—your message—meets the need that's important for others, you have alignment and a feeling of belonging. When your gift intersects with what's most important for you, you have a sense of purpose and feel a sense of meaning.

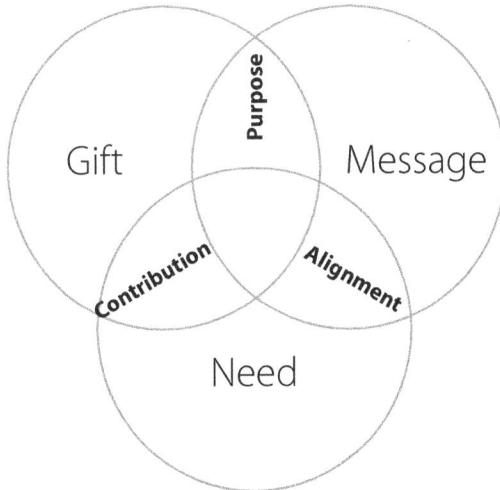

Leading to a sense of purpose, contribution and alignment

Without utilising your gift, whatever you are doing will be far more tiring than it could otherwise be. When what you are doing does not include what's most important for you, it'll feel empty. If what you're doing is about you and not about serving others, it'll probably be depressing.

Without a sense of purpose, you're likely to feel somewhat restless, and others might see you as unmotivated. If alignment is substantially missing, you're likely to feel rather frustrated, and others might see you as a misfit. Where there's an inability to make a contribution, you'll probably feel a little like you're going to waste, and others might perceive you as perhaps incompetent.

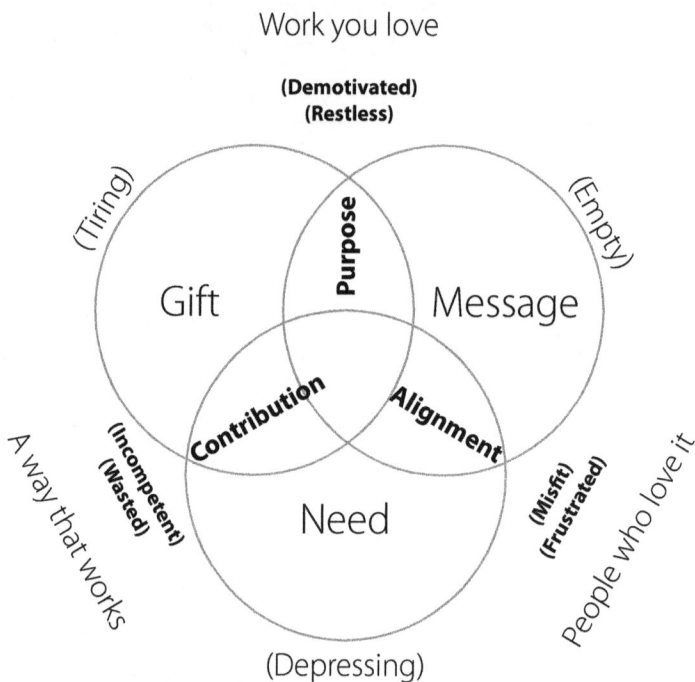

The life-calling fulfilment model

When you're on purpose, you're doing work you love. When what's important for you meets a need that's important for others, you're interacting with people who love it. When you're making your true contribution, it's in a way that just works. In other words, when you're using your gift serving others in a way that you're most passionate about —its work you love, with people who love it, in a way that works.

While purpose gives many benefits, it does not necessarily make your life any easier. Pursuing your purpose can lead to all kinds of additional shaping pressures that require your growth to achieve.

What's creating on purpose?

What you are here for is your message, a message that is the answer to a problem of the human condition. You'll find later that your message is how to experience a form of universal love. One of our world's greatest teachers said this to be so. It's a very qualitative message. It's not for you. It's to be shared with others.

Another of our world's greatest teachers said that suffering is due to the avoidance of pain; that this avoidance is due to the meaning and stories we habitually give to our circumstance. In other words, we turn circumstance into things through the stories we tell ourselves and others and believe them to be true. We usually do this habitually and unconsciously.

So what we are going to do is use our unconscious revealers to give new meaning to our experience. We are going to use them to reveal what our own life is revealing is already important for us. This works because we more than likely already unconsciously know what's important to us, and we can use our unconscious revealers to become conscious of what's important for us. Once we consciously know what's important, we can start to consciously create that. Where the creation of the quality that we are here to create becomes so habituated that doing so becomes an unconscious action, then we're unconsciously creating. When we act on what we realise, we actualise. We'll be moving from realisation to actualisation. This is illustrated in the model below.

Anyone who does the work may experience a high level of fulfilment in their life by creating, in a way that works for them, what they are here to create and live the theme of their lives.

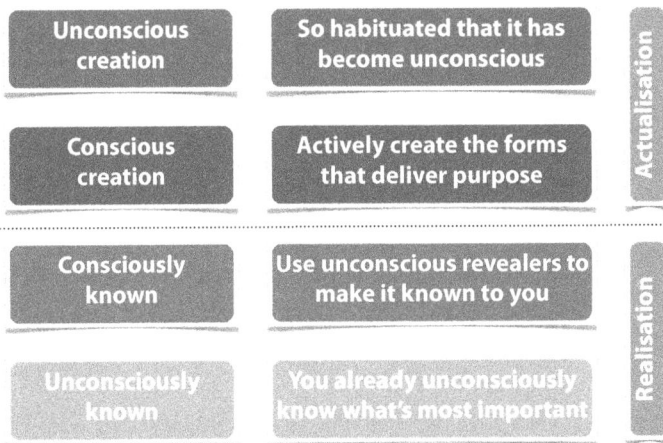

Unconscious creation	So habituated that it has become unconscious	Actualisation
Conscious creation	Actively create the forms that deliver purpose	
Consciously known	Use unconscious revealers to make it known to you	Realisation
Unconsciously known	You already unconsciously know what's most important	

From unconsciously known to unconscious creation

37

The following model, the Stages of Actualisation, illustrates the different stages that people can go through. These 'Identify to Actualise' stages are the key focus of this book and the journey of living the life you are called to. I'll expand further on this model as we go along, and give specific strategies that you can use to move through these different levels.

A word of caution though. While there are a few who do succeed in jumping past stages, for the majority of people, it is very tough going to try to by-pass a stage. The suggestion is to go stage by stage, even if it is only briefly. Indeed, the stages are inclusive and each subsequent stage includes, requires and is supported by the best of the previous ones.

Stage	Focus	Be
Being	Be	Grateful
Actualise	Result	Activated
Transform	Method	Convinced
Learn	Discover	Curious
Permit	Allow	Accepting
Identify	Explore	Honest
Denied	Accept	Open

Stages of Actualisation model

Though this will be elaborated in more detail later, this model is essentially saying:

1. The first thing to do is to accept and be open to the possibility that you are called to share your essence and serve others in some way.

2. The next thing to do is explore and be honest with yourself to identify what will enable you to create a life of meaning and not just means. You identify your calling, the message you are here to share, a message that others are waiting to experience and perhaps hear.

3. Then allow yourself to have a message and give yourself permission to act.

4. To learn is to discover what you know about your message by being curious throughout your discovery. You learn about what others know, about what you know about what others know, what you uniquely know about your message, and how to create it.

5. In the transform stage it's important to be convinced of the self-evident nature of your message, since it is used as the criterion that defines how you undertake your current activity, work or area of exchange. Your message becomes the indirect or implicit result you want to create. Your message becomes your method and criterion for how you do things.

6. To actualise is to make your message—your calling—the direct or explicit result that you are seeking to create. Ideally you are activated through the pursuit of creating that.

The remaining chapters of this book will elaborate on each of these stages. The 'being' stage, not explicitly covered, is lived—it is self-evident to those who are living their message.

What's important?

We're at the 'identify' stage of the Stages of Actualisation. This stage is about identifying what you are called to by honestly exploring your own life. Three chapters cover this stage of the Life Calling Method™:

1. What's important—identifying what's important for you
2. What's my message?—realising your message
3. What's my gift?—discovering your giftedness

Stage	Focus	Be
Being	Be	Grateful
Actualise	Result	Activated
Transform	Method	Convinced
Learn	Discover	Curious
Permit	Allow	Accepting
Identify	**Explore**	**Honest**
Denied	Accept	Open

Identify stage of the Stages of Actualisation

What's so important?

There's a shift from experts being the authority on things and people, to experts being the authority on things and process. Truth is, *you* are not an object, and *you* most certainly are not a thing. Just because we can know things about you, does not make you a thing. Someone else might have some expertise regarding things about you, but they can't be the expert on *you*. Truth is, *you* are the authority on *you*. No one else is. The best anyone else might have is an opinion about *you*, or a method you can follow to deepen your awareness. For example, a doctor might know about and might assume to know certain things about your broken bone, but they cannot reasonably assume to know about *you*. It's up to us to endorse and sanction the opinions of others, or not. Doing so often can be very helpful, though not always.

I don't appreciate when people presume to tell me about me. I know I do this myself sometimes when I'm reacting to something I think someone has done. I've even had people tell me what my intent was, what I was thinking, why I did certain things, and what I'm meaning. None of it was true. I have done this to others, and no matter how convinced I was at the time, none of it was ever true.

For it to be true, we'd need to have telepathy. Last I checked, telepathy is not a well-established attribute of our human species. Whenever I hear this from others, all I usually hear is the other person telling me about themselves. They are not telling you about you, but are simply revealing themselves.

Others can only tell us about their experience of us. When they do that they are telling us about their interpretations about their experience of us.

So one form of expertise is that an expert is an authority on things and us. I don't regard this as honouring of our human condition as it could be. What's more honouring is when expertise is about things and processes that we can follow that help us to know ourselves in greater depth. As long as others are the authority on us, we aren't. A better expertise is when it's about things and what supports us to become even more of an authority about ourselves. I want others to help me empower me through being more of my own authority.

It's the same thing with personal values. In some arenas, other people assume to be the authority on what our values should be or are. They may or may not be correct and accurately represent what is actually important for you. For many people this approach can be very profound. In general, this approach involves someone external from you, usually an authority on values or some diagnostic tool, defining or identifying your values. Since someone external from you identifies them, your values are externally identified. The difficulty that I've always had with this approach is that I've had to invest time and energy remembering what they were, and then trying to identify which of them apply in a given situation and how. The other concern that I've had is that these values always somehow seemed outside and external to me.

The alternative is for someone external from you, usually an authority on a process you can use, to help you realise what's important for you already. Through a process, you reveal what is already internal to you. In other words, you internally reveal what's important for you.

This is represented in the following model that shows the shift and charts the evolution from externally identified values to revealing internally what's important. This is especially relevant to life in organisations. The following model shows their hierarchy with increasing degrees of leverage and impact.

For a long time, the notion of values was absent from the organisational landscape, and the conversation was around 'what values?' and the inevitable values conflicts. Organisations responded to this chaos by defining what the 'organisational values' were for everyone, and the conversation was around 'our values' and what they meant, usually as defined behaviours. Compared to having no values, this made a big difference. The defined values approach tends to assume that when people had their values defined, they'd all act accordingly. Problem is, things don't always turn out as assumed.

Values type	Stage	What	Topic
	Message	I'm about	Calling
Internal	Central	They're about	Purpose
	Revealed	They are	Authenticity
	Diagnosed	I believe	My values
External	Selected	I want	My values
	Defined	I'm told	Our values
Absent	Absent	No values	What values

From externally identified to internally revealed values

In response to the realisation that individuals do have values separate from those defined by the organisation, people were encouraged to choose from a list of possible values and select what they thought their values to be. The conversation was around 'my values'. This was another improvement. It was assumed that once we've selected our values, we'd live them.

Then people realised that what they think their values are can change quickly depending on circumstance. Diagnostic tools were developed where people would fill in questionnaires and, based on what they believed to be the way they live their lives, their values would be diagnosed accordingly. Another big improvement, as this tended to identify the more enduring values of people. It also gave people the language and words for what their values were. The conversation at this stage was still around 'my values'. It was assumed that when people had their list of diagnosed values they'd be more likely to act according to them. This approach still had the issue that people had to remember and remind themselves of their values and how to apply them.

For people who are comfortable with the externally diagnosed approach and do not wish to understand themselves through their own personal exploration, this is a terrific approach, and I know of people doing great work with people and organisations using it.

The tipping point is when we have an interest in knowing what's important when it's important. When we realise what's important is itself important to us, we're certainly ready for the internally revealed approach. The revealed stages involve using our own life to reveal what's important. We're looking at our own experience of life to reveal what is already important for us. Our own life becomes the diagnostic tool. We use our transitory experiences, our experiences that come and go, as the basis of what gets revealed. We just need to know how to decipher the clues that our own life produces. The interest at this stage is about being true to oneself, true to what's important, in our own authenticity.

Examples of what is revealed as important are such qualities as:

Respect	Harmony
Trust	Clarity
Patience	Dignity

Knowing the different elements that are important for us does not provide the overarching context or meaning that draws them all together. Revealing all the different elements of what's important usually leads to the desire to know what they're all about, to know what the central theme actually is. Once we have information about the different aspects that are important for us, we can go through a process of identifying what all of those different elements are all about, and find what is centrally important. We identify the one central theme that explains and includes everything else that's important for us. We find that everything that's important is a variant of what is centrally important. This is all about 'What is centrally important for me?' and the interest tends to move from 'What's important?' towards 'What's important in life?' and the question of 'purpose' itself often becomes important.

The same process can be used with groups of people and organisations to identify the alignment that already exists and to dynamically reveal what the group and organisational values already are.

Examples of what is revealed as centrally important include:

Harmony	Freedom
Connection	Trust
Empowerment	Respect

Identifying the different aspects of what's important as well as the central theme is a bit like baking a cake. There are many ingredients to a chocolate cake. The different elements of what's important are like all the ingredients, and what's centrally important is like describing the cake that the ingredients create. Just like there are many ingredients in common with many different cakes, many people have similar ingredients of what's important, and identify a different cake.

When we identify what is centrally important, which is what everything that's important is actually about, we tend to start to wonder about what our life is about, what our contribution and message might be for the world. We start to wonder, 'What am I about?', and consider what our life is calling us to.

Still based on your experience of our own life, a similar though different aspect of your life experience will be used to reveal what is most important for you. Where the revealed stage makes use of your in-the-moment experience to reveal what's important, what's most important is revealed through particular significant events or themes that you have experienced in or through your life.

What's important is what matters to you, is what moves you, is what you get upset about and react to when it's compromised. What's important is a foundation for your life that you can never lose.

This section explores how to identify the revealed and central stages of what's important for you.

Curiouser and curiouser

"Your living is determined not so much by what life brings to you as by the attitude you bring to life; not so much by what happens to you as by the way your mind looks at what happens." ~ Khalil Gibran

Have you ever been in an argument with someone, only to realise later that what you were arguing about was actually about something else? Imagine an argument about the bedroom window that goes something like this:

"I want the window open."

"I want the window closed."

"No, I want the window open."

"Well, I want the window closed."

First, most people ask for a solution and the concrete means for what they think will give them what they actually want. For example, the window open might be about fresh air. The window closed might be about being warm. At the window open or closed level of discussion, it seems like it's a win-lose situation, as it's not possible to have both. If the couple could realise that they were actually discussing fresh air and warmth, then they could start to work together on how to create both fresh air and warmth. One option might be to open a window in an adjacent room, and the person who wants fresh air sleeps closest to the door.

Assume that this conversation goes backwards and forwards like this several more times. It could result in mutual frustration and an argument something like this:

"You're being disrespectful!"

"You're being inconsiderate!"

"No, I'm not!"

"Yes, you are!"

The conversation has moved on from being about the window to being about the manner in which the conversation was held. In their frustration, both perceived that the other person was compromising something important. For the person who saw that the other person was disrespectful, it was actually about respect. What is important for that person is 'respect'. They perceived that they weren't experiencing respect, that respect was being compromised, and made it about the other person being disrespectful. For the person who saw that the other person was not being considerate, it was actually about consideration. What is important for that person is 'consideration'. They perceived that consideration was being compromised, and made it about the other person being inconsiderate.

If neither person realises that their argument was actually about respect and consideration, they might continue to act in ways where the other continues to perceive that what is important is being compromised, that the other was disrespectful and inconsiderate. If instead they both paused and asked, 'How can we do this in a way that is both respectful and considerate?', then they could start to work together on how to do things differently in a way where both experience what is important, not the compromise of what is important.

All of us get upset with others one time or another. As humans, that's what we tend to do, though—we experience that what's important for us is being compromised, and make it about what the other person is being or not being, doing or not doing. For example, say you get upset with someone during a conversation because they have said something that you perceive as 'being disrespectful'. You might even have an explanation or reason why you're upset: 'I'm annoyed with that person because they're disrespectful'. That judgement was automatic and unconscious. Even though it can seem real and true, we cannot know for sure that they were disrespectful according to their criteria. 'Disrespectful' is an assessment we've made about the other person, a judgement about them or their behaviour. It is possible that they were completely respectful according to their version of what respectful means. We have a different criterion. For us, this is an unconscious revealer. Our unconscious judgement of their 'being disrespectful' reveals that 'respect' is actually important for us. If it wasn't important, we wouldn't react to its perceived absence.

Here's an example. The situation is that Jane became aware that Mary was upset with something Jane had done. Jane had invited Mary to discuss and resolve whatever it was, and Mary declined Jane's invitation. Jane interpreted Mary as being spiteful and disrespectful, perceived that Mary was disconnected from her, and judged Mary as not being a true friend. What this was actually about for Jane was respect and connection.

So what's going on? It all depends on the perspective we take. There are three perspectives that are involved:

1. What happened; the circumstance (our 3rd person perspective)

2. Your relationship with that circumstance (our 2nd person perspective)

3. What it is actually about for you personally (our 1st person perspective)

It's crucial to know how to recognise and identify what is personally important. Let's look at what those three perspectives are:

1. **Event.** There is something that happens in our environment, some observable facts. It's what an alien would report happened if they were to witness and observe the event. In the above scenario, it is: 'We were in a conversation. I invited her to discuss, and she declined'. It's just the facts. There's no assessment, interpretation, or judgement. It's our 3rd person perspective of what happened.

2. **Story.** We have a relationship with what happened. It triggered a reaction in us of some sort. What comes with that reaction is usually an assessment, interpretation, attributed meaning, or judgement of the situation or person. Often, we are not even aware of the assessment and interpretation we may have made, it can happen so quickly. In the above scenario, it is the interpretation of Mary as being spiteful and disrespectful, that Mary was disconnected from her and the judgement that Mary was not a true friend. This is our 2nd person perspective.

3. **About.** That interpretation, your relationship with the situation, reveals what's important for you. In the actual interpretation and judgement you look for the qualitative word or words. What's important is revealed through the qualitative word or words in the 'story' you had in relationship with the situation. Rewording those qualities in 1st person reveals something important that was perceived as

being compromised. In the above scenario, what's important is respect (revealed from 'disrespectful'), and connection (revealed from 'disconnected'). This is the 1st person perspective.

My perception of you is a reflection of me; my reaction to you is awareness for me. That said, the reflection is not always literal.

Imagine if Jane presented to Mary her interpretations of her: 'Mary, you're disrespectful and disconnected from me'. Mary's response is likely to be one of defensiveness and denial: 'I'm not disrespectful...' and we could imagine the probable argument and additional pain that this would generate. Just because Jane's interpretation appears true to Jane, it is not objectively true. If presented as true, someone else could understandably argue that it was not true. It is therefore arguably true. Jane's interpretation of Mary as being disrespectful and disconnected from her is clearly an arguable perspective—it's an arguable truth. How often do we present our arguably true interpretations of others to them as if those interpretations were self-evidently or unarguably true? If we share arguable truth, then we usually end up in the inevitable—an argument. It's an inevitability that we have helped to create.

By contrast, what is important personally is unarguably true. Imagine if Jane shared with Mary: 'What's important for me is connection and respect. When you declined the invitation to discuss what you were upset about, I experienced that as disrespect and disconnection. Would you please help me to understand what was going on for you?' Mary might then share that she declined because connection and respect were so important for her that she chose to temporarily withhold any discussion for fear of having it come out inappropriately, in a way that was disrespectful towards Jane and broke connection. How differently does that scenario play out if they were to both discover that what was important for each of them was the same thing? Once what is important is known, one can share what is unarguably true in a way that maintains, uplifts and upholds the other.

The extension of this is the skill of advocating what's important, having important conversations, and of moving from conflict to connection to co-creation. This is authentic relating and leading.

The whole point of this book is not so much to improve the quality of our relationships, which a practical application of it can do, but to help us discover our mission. The intent of this book is to help us step into what life is calling us to be. It will indicate the basics for authentic relating and leading, though will not be a complete coverage of it.

Please remember though that because something is important for us does not suggest that we are perfect at that value. Most of us, from time to time, compromise what's important for us. This is different from the fact that it is important for us. For me, I feel guilt when I act contrary to what's important for me, and I feel anger when I have dropped my own standard and have not acted appropriately on behalf of what's important.

The point is that we can use our relationship with something 'out there' to indicate something important to us 'in here'. This is represented in the following diagram.

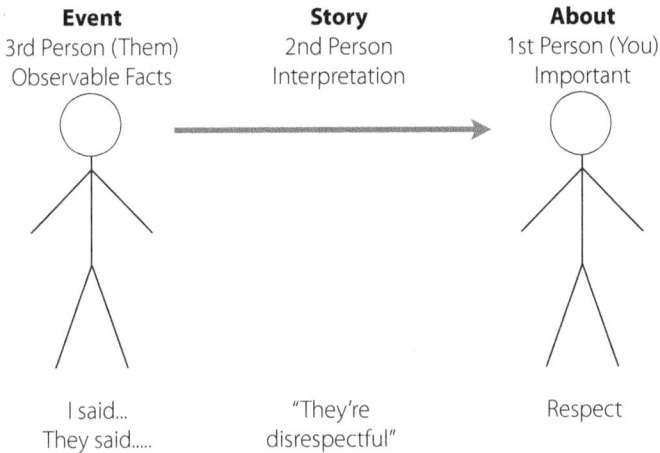

Event	Story	About
3rd Person (Them)	2nd Person	1st Person (You)
Observable Facts	Interpretation	Important
I said... They said.....	"They're disrespectful"	Respect

How our interpretations can reveal what's important

Something to note is that identifying what's important for us personally means finding the word that does not infer dependence on another person. It needs to be independent. If the word infers an 'other' or someone else is doing or has done something, then it is still in relationship —with someone else. For example, say I interpreted that someone else was being 'disrespectful', it could be easy to assume that what's important was 'being respected'. However, 'being respected' still infers a relationship or dynamic with someone else and that someone else has done something. The inner experience that really matters, is 'respect'.

Words that end in 'ed' such as, respected, trusted, valued and connected, generally infer a dynamic with someone else in that someone else *has* done something. In a similar way, words that end in 'ing' such as, respecting, trusting, valuing and connecting, generally infer a dynamic where someone else *is* doing something. Describing qualities in terms of what others *have done* or *are doing*, are not statements of qualities, values or of what's important. They are perceived methods. They are statements of the actions that need to be taken that describe how we can experience what's important. In other words, they are methods for experiencing what's important. For example, others being 'trusting' or 'trusted' are perceived methods for us to experience trust.

If you are one for the particulars of the English language, what is important for you personally is always a virtuous noun.

The other aspect to be appreciated is that becoming proficient in this activity, like all other new skills, takes practice. Becoming adept at identifying what's actually important takes time. Be patient and disciplined. The benefits of doing so include the following:

1. Growth through knowing and being able to act on what's important.

2. Understanding what's important for you is a great way to understand yourself and identify what orients you in your life.

3. You can pre-empt the compromise of what's important and share with your environment not only what's important but also the behaviours that you'll perceive as compromising it.

4. The ability to take responsibility for your own experience and for what's actually true.

5. Identifying what is important in 1st person is a consciousness-raising practice. You'll become more self-aware.

6. Bringing what is actually important into your personal and professional relationships builds effective relationships—authentic relationships.

7. You can share what is unarguably true with others and not be subject to your assumptions and interpretations of others, thereby reducing the opportunity for conflict and increasing the opportunity for trust and connection.

Ultimately it can help you be more loving with others.

Some examples are included in the following table.

Event (Observable facts)	Story (Interpretation)	About (Important)
Student arrived into class after the second bell that indicated class commencement.	He's being disrespectful of me and irresponsibly setting a bad example for the other students'.	Respect Responsibility
Mother talks about what she is missing in her life. Happens whenever we talk.	'She's being an ungrateful complainer and I don't like how I'm uncomfortable whenever she talks that way'.	Gratitude Comfort
He arrived ten minutes after the meeting started. He told the story of how he became late. The attention of the group was on his story for five minutes.	'He's being disruptive and isn't honouring everyone else's time'. (Opposite of disruptive = harmonious)	Harmony Honour

Example interpretations

Martin's experience

In his birth family Martin has three younger siblings, and in his adopted family, two older sisters. Martin is a married father of two teenage children, and with his family lived in Ireland for three years. He loves being by the water and fishing; and is especially proud of the time both he and his son each caught a large fish called a Spanish Mackerel. His enthusiasm for wine sees him planning holidays around different wine growing districts throughout the world. He is a deeply caring and reflective individual.

Martin is articulate about how insight, action and change interrelate. "Growth", he says, "comes from changing behaviour, which takes time. You can have astounding insight in an instant. Allowing that to permeate your being and show up as changes, takes time. Application of insight takes time, which is practice."

The practice of understanding how our triggers, stories and values relate was significant for Martin for simply accepting his own humanity. "I understand myself more", says Martin, "I fight myself less. I accept that I am a work in progress. I'm not expecting myself to be perfect. I understand why I act certain ways. This frees me up to act differently."

It has also helped him to be more accepting of others. "I used to think that everyone thought the same as me", he admits, "and what underpinned my frustration with others was this assumption. If everyone else thinks the same as me, why don't they act the same as me? I'd be confused about how others would respond. It's then very easy to make a judgement about them. Realising that not everyone thinks the same, has the same values, or the same gifts as I do, has taken the pressure off. Now I simply accept how others are. As I accepted myself more, I accepted others more."

"Values are not static", shares Martin, "we know what's important through the way we react to circumstances in our lives. I've learned to look at the circumstance instead of my reaction to it. This is soothing as it allows me to understand how I create my experience."

Relationships are important for Martin, and he says that his acceptance and understanding of his own experience opens communication. "I'm more open with my wife about what matters and why it matters. Rather than just reacting and it seeming like there's no alternatives, it allows her the freedom to choose. It gives you a platform to discuss and move through obstacles. I am clearer on what I can do to experience greater connection in my relationships."

"I only have a certain amount of time", says Martin talking about time pressures that most people share. "The question I have is where I put my time and effort. Knowing what's important helps me make choices more easily. I just choose for what's important. That's enough."

Martin is passionate about the importance of being clear about what matters. "If you don't know, you are just flapping about in the dark. It's my stake in the ground, and I can always reference back to the stake. It's easy for me when I know what's important, as it's an easy reference. The stake isn't fixed; it changes. As I change and grow, my reference changes. Either way I always have a reference."

Martin's advice for others is to put insights into practice to develop wisdom. Insight not lived, is knowledge; lived insight is wisdom. Wisdom is not knowledge, though it is shared as knowledge. "Wisdom", he adds, "becomes a part of your life, as opposed to an idea you recall."

Evidence of what's important

So how do we get to what's actually important for us? Similar to the 'scientific data gathering' you probably learned about during science class, to reveal what's important you'll be undertaking two steps which are to collect enough samples and identify what they are. There's a third step, to group them, which you'll use later, to reveal what is centrally important.

These will be explained in more detail later, though in brief they are:

1. Collect

You'll observe and record your experiences, specifically your reactions to events in your life, and pay particular attention to the actual story and description that you give to those events.

2. Identify

You'll decipher and decode your descriptions to reveal what it's about, what's important. This forms the base of your 'Value Stack'.

3. Group

Once you have collected enough information about what's important, you'll group and identify what each group is about, until a single word appears at the top of your Value Stack.

Trigger harvesting

As described above, we collect our experience in the form of events and our snap judgements or internal stories, in order to be able to identify what is important for us personally. I suggest using a journal with three columns per page to record your experiences. It's important to record our actual personal reactions, stories, assessments, interpretations, attributed meanings, or judgements, as they actually occur, as close to how we think them as we can.

Avoid writing what you think it might be about. You use the actual content of your complaint or story. This is because it is your actual story that reveals what's important. If you record what you think it's about, you'll identify your ideas of what's important. While ideas and concepts have their place and can be very useful, in this case we are looking for what is actual. The suggested layout is shown in the following diagram.

You record, as often and as practically as you can, whenever you react to something in your situation, the environment you're in, or with others. The reaction can be as quick as a moment, or something that endures for minutes or more.

To record the story in your mind, you're essentially capturing a narrative of:

- 'They're ... *(judgement)*, because they are/are not ... *(quality)*'
- 'I'm ... *(feeling)*, because they are/are not ... *(quality)*'

Worksheet for Identifying What's Important

Event	Story	About
Observable Facts	Attributed Meaning	Important for you
——— ——— ———	——— ———	———
——— ——— ———	——— ———	———
——— ——— ———	——— ———	———
I said/did... They said/did.....	"They're disrespectful"	Respect

Worksheet for identifying what's important

Carefully take note of previous experiences and list those where you felt any of the below. Also take note if you feel any of these as they happen. They can be everyday experiences—you experience them like this.

- **Anger.** When you experience *anger*, even in its lesser forms and even if it's just for a moment, such as frustration, annoyance, irritation, or slightly worked up about something. This suggests that you perceive that something important for you either already has been or is at risk of being compromised.

- **Judgement.** If you experience *judgement* or criticism of others or the situation. This suggests that you perceive that someone has been in breech of what's important.

- **Cynicism.** When you are ever *cynical* about something or someone. This suggests that you perceive something important in the present may be compromised, and it happens to have been compromised in the past.

- **Anxiety.** Whenever you feel *anxious* or afraid of something. Fear suggests that you perceive the possible loss of something important for you.

- **Upset.** In general, if you're *upset* about something. This suggests that you perceive that something important isn't happening or has been compromised.

To get close to the essence of the story you have, the meaning you attribute to the situation or person, pick any of these sentence stems.

Imagine that you're telling a close friend *'why it is like it is'* or *'why it's wrong'*. Record what you spontaneously thought and made the situation mean, not what you'd like it to mean, or think it means. The actual content of your meaning is what you want to capture, as far as practical anyway.

1. They're not ... *what?* (e.g. 'respectful') in which case, what's important is the personal version of 'respectful', which is 'respect'.

2. They are ... *what?* (e.g. 'impatient'). Then ask yourself what the opposite of that is. For example it could be 'patient'. In this case, what's important is the personal person version of what you identified as being the opposite of 'impatience', such as 'patience'.

3. I'm upset/angry/critical/cynical/judgemental with/of them because he/she/they:

   - Are/are not ... (e.g. undisciplined/disciplined).
   - Don't/didn't ... (e.g. clarify).
   - Are treating us/me with ... (e.g. disrespect).
   - Are being ... (e.g. insensitive).

4. What's missing is... What should be there is ... (e.g. dignity).

5. They don't have any ... (e.g. trust).

6. They don't have any ... because they're not ... (e.g. no respect because they are not inclusive).

In general, whenever you find a description that someone else *is not something that is virtuous* and uplifting, such as disrespectful, untrustworthy, impatient, undisciplined, then the word after the 'not' part is usually a good indicator. You 'flip' it. For example:

Description	*Opposite*	*About*
Disrespectful	Respectful	Respect
Untrustworthy	Trustworthy	Trust
Impatient	Patient	Patience
Undisciplined	Disciplined	Discipline
Unclear	Clear	Clarity

In addition, whenever you find a description that someone else *is something that is not virtuous* or uplifting, such as disruptive, vague, lazy, then you need to identify what for you is the opposite of that word and then convert that word into what's important for you personally. Another way to do that is to ask yourself, 'What is the described quality the absence of?' or, 'What's its opposite?' For example:

Description	Opposite	About
Disruptive	Harmonious	Harmony
Vague	Clear	Clarity
Lazy	Active	Activity
Complex	Simple	Simplicity
Blunt	Sensitive	Sensitivity

There are many more words available for download, with instructions in the conclusion at the end of the book.

Stacking what's important

Remember the continuum between concrete and qualitative? Our concrete events, the actual observable facts are, well, concrete. They are at the concrete end of that continuum. The quality that we reveal in relationship with that event is, yes, qualitative.

The aspects that we have so far identified as being important for us are the concrete ones—they are closest to concrete circumstance and actual life. Observable events are concrete descriptions, and our relationship with them reveals that they are the concrete elements of what is important for us. This is represented in the following diagram.

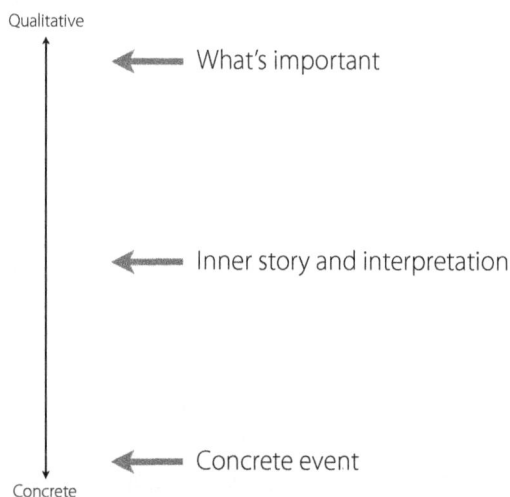

From concrete event to qualitative values

What we're going to do now is build the base of our values pyramid—our Value Stack. You can do this using paper and working with the qualities as a list, or use small post-it notes which makes resorting your qualities a little easier.

1. List

On a page, with one word per line, list all the aspects that your life has revealed are important for you. A real-world example of this is shown.

Attention
Embrace
Integrity
Equity
Justice
Adaptability
Generosity
Progress
Empowerment
Respect
Opportunity
Connection
Support
Hope

Example of 1st level of Value Stack

2. Sort

Now sort the list. Ask yourself: 'Which qualities seem or feel like they are similar and belong together?' Connect the qualities that, **to you**, are kind of the same. Don't be concerned about being right—just go with what seems right to you. Besides, you can always change it, though most rarely do. Update your list as your life reveals new aspects of what is important for you. This participant grouped her list as shown below.

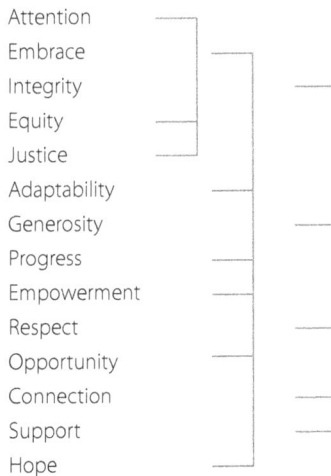

Attention
Embrace
Integrity
Equity
Justice
Adaptability
Generosity
Progress
Empowerment
Respect
Opportunity
Connection
Support
Hope

Example of sorting for 2nd level of Value Stack

Reorder your list according to your self-selected groupings.

3. Identify your second level

You'll now identify what each of your groups is about. You are going to identify a quality that describes and explains your group. The word you use might already be in your group, or it may be a new word. Your basic question here is: 'What's that group all about?'

Within your group of words, you might find a word that is a more abstract word than the others. For example, kindness seems like a more abstract word than achievement. Achievement you can almost see, whereas kindness is something that can only be experienced. Decide which word is a candidate for describing the group of words.

If none of them stands out in that way, of if that word does not work for you, then you ask yourself: 'What quality do I have when I have all of those qualities together?' Your answer is the word that describes that group of qualities.

The way you test whatever word you choose is: 'According to the way you experience and perceive things, can you have the higher quality without the lesser ones?' If the answer is no, then you have your word. If your answer is yes, then you need to find another word.

For example, in the worked example, the participant organised their qualities as follows. They saw that within each of their groupings was a word that described or governed that cluster—equity, progress, and connection.

Attention	
Equity	Equity
Justice	
Embrace	
Adaptability	
Progress	Progress
Opportunity	
Hope	
Empowerment	
Integrity	
Generosity	
Respect	Connection
Connection	
Support	

Example of 2nd level of Value Stack

4. Keep going until you have a single word

Keep following the process of the previous step until you have a single word at the top of your stack that describes what everything that's important for you is actually all about. In the example being used, the participant came to 'harmony' as their top word. When they wrote that, they said, "Yeah, everything that is important for me is all about harmony! Being in harmony with others, harmony with my environment, harmony with my own life."

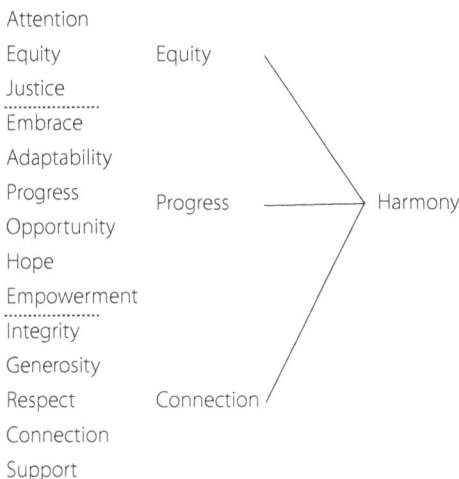

Attention
Equity   Equity
Justice
....
Embrace
Adaptability
Progress   Progress ———————→ Harmony
Opportunity
Hope
Empowerment
....
Integrity
Generosity
Respect   Connection
Connection
Support

Example of a complete Value Stack

Now let's take a look at that again from the perspective of the concrete to qualitative continuum.

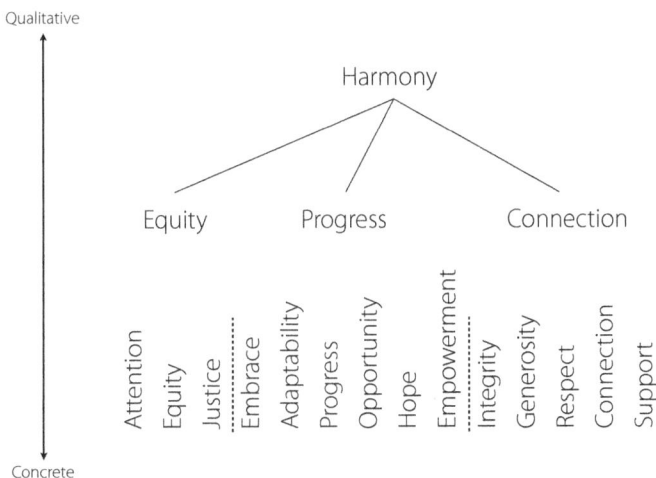

Qualitative

Harmony

Equity   Progress   Connection

Attention
Equity
Justice
Embrace
Adaptability
Progress
Opportunity
Hope
Empowerment
Integrity
Generosity
Respect
Connection
Support

Concrete

Example of a complete concrete to qualitative Value Stack

The aspects of what's important initially revealed through experience are distributed across the base of the pyramid or stack. By identifying what each group is about, the stack narrows until a single word is at the top of the stack. This is your 'Value Stack', it's what makes sense for you. It's not a universal, nor is there a right or wrong version of your stack—only more or less clarity about what's important for you, and what is centrally important.

5. Integrity check—is your value stack self-evident?

The way I interpret this stack is that for this person the following are self-evident:

- For equity to exist and not be compromised, there must be both attention and justice. It's not possible to have equity without attention and justice. Equity is created or diminished as attention or justice are created or diminished.

- For progress to exist and not be compromised, there must be embrace, adaptability, opportunity, hope and empowerment. Progress is created or diminished as any of its constituent aspects are created or diminished.

- For connection to exist and not be compromised, there must be integrity, generosity, respect and support.

- For harmony to exist, there must be equity, progress and connection.

- What is centrally important for her is harmony.

- Her recipe for creating harmony is increasing and ensuring that all ground level or front-line qualities exist or are experienced as existing: attention, justice, embrace, adaptability, opportunity, hope, empowerment, integrity, generosity, respect and support. Equity, progress and connection are not included, as they have been elevated since they are created through combinations of concrete qualities. The more any of these concrete qualities are established the more harmony she will experience, and, the more any of them are compromised, the less harmony she will experience.

- She now knows the factors that will create for her the experience of harmony. She can now do something about creating it, rather than continue to react to its absence. This is done through the more concrete, front-line values. For example, she can give attention or support to others.

- Since what was important was revealed through perception of behaviours and events that compromise what's important, as a minimum, the opposite of those behaviours would be perceived as the presence of what's important. In essence, she has her behavioural recipe for compromising harmony, and therefore for establishing harmony.

When I shared these points with the person who developed this Value Stack, she confirmed that all points were self-evident to them, saying, "It's as if you've just read my mind". To use an earlier analogy, hers is a cake called 'harmony' and to mix it she uses eleven concrete and tangible ingredients.

Likewise, review your Value Stack and ask yourself:

- Is it true for you that the more intangible and abstract qualities (the ones higher in your stack) require the more concrete qualities? This question ideally produces a 'yes'. The more abstract quality is dependent on the more concrete ones.

- To your way of seeing things, can you have the more abstract quality without any one of the concrete ones? This ideally produces a 'no' or at least an 'it would be diminished'. Does that make sense to you? The more abstract quality is dependent on the more concrete ones.

- Can you have the more concrete qualities without the more abstract one? This question ideally produces a 'yes'. The more concrete qualities are not dependent on the more abstract quality. The more abstract quality creates and shows up as the more concrete ones. Upward dependency; downward creation.

6. Update—refine with new experience

Life itself is never static. Our experience is always changing. The way we experience our environment changes. What's important for us changes. Over time, what was once important sometimes no longer even registers, and something that was never important starts to show up. Different aspects of the essence of who we are drawn out as we experience our environment differently. Your Value Stack is not static—it changes.

Many years ago 'belonging' was important for me. These days, it's not. I find that I do not react when someone tells me that I 'don't fit'. When I'm being playful, my response is "I know. That's what makes me so good at thinking differently." In contrast, 'dignity' is something that now registers more highly than 'respect' in my Value Stack, when many years ago it didn't even register at all.

Though at first we rarely change our Value Stack once we've created it, it pays to notice whenever our experience shows us that something new is important. Whenever we notice something new, add it to the Value Stack. It's useful if we periodically revisit our Value Stack, to notice whether certain qualities are no longer important.

Update your list as your life experience reveals new aspects of what is important for you.

At this point, many people consider their purpose to be the word at the top of their Value Stack. Using the above as an example, it could be someone saying that, 'My purpose is to create harmony for others'. In a sense, this is true, and the person would certainly feel a strong sense of fulfilment helping others to experience harmony. Besides, she has her own recipe for helping others to experience that quality. This can be and is, for many people, sufficiently fulfilling, as it appears that this is everything that we ever get upset about. It seems to be the thing that defines our experience; so why wouldn't it be what we are here for?

Years ago, I would have agreed entirely.

What's my message?

Whose life is it anyway?

While true that we might consider our purpose to be what is centrally important, in my experience, even if we were actively helping people to experience harmony, there is a good chance that we'd feel a little 'off'. Staying with what is centrally important is a bit like setting out to climb a mountain, finding a delightful, rewarding and wonderful view on the way up, and deciding to stay there without reaching the top. While exhilarating, it's still no substitute for reaching the summit. With a little more persistence, the summit will be reached. While the view near the top is what is centrally important, the view from the summit is your message, what you could say you are to bring into the world more consciously. Just as the summit gives context and further meaning to the view on the way up, our message adds context and meaning to what is centrally important for us.

Just as the different levels of what's important could easily be the basis for a sense of purpose, there are other, broader origins of a sense of purpose in the first place. The different origins of a sense of purpose are shown in the following model.

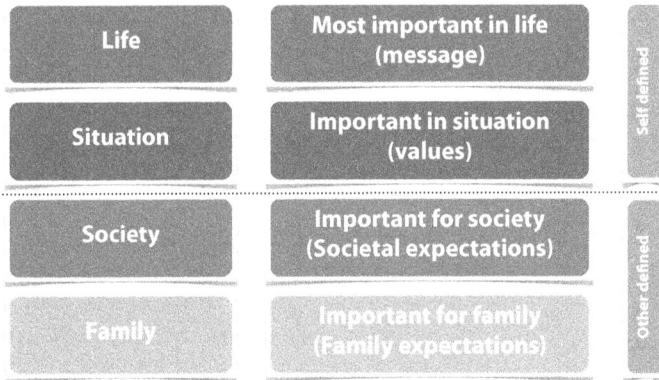

General origins of a sense of purpose

For most of us, we grew up with a sense of purpose defined by or given to us by others. The first stage is where our well-meaning families hand purpose to us. Though well intentioned, this usually started with what we received from our families as the message of what we ought to do with our lives.

The next stage is usually the sense of purpose given to us by our broader culture and society. We're influenced to take on and adopt what our culture defines as important. Most of us just take it all on board—at least for a while.

Eventually we might have had enough of others defining what we do with our lives and what's important for us. We might instead decide to define for ourselves what's important and what our purpose in life will be.

The next stage is all about the situation and what is important for us in the situation; and what our response will be. Indeed, it's all about what our response needs to be and our ability to respond. Our sense of purpose comes from responding to the need of the situation in front of us. We are the one that chooses if, when and how to respond. We are self-defining. This stage is about living through and in integrity with what's actually important for us.

Though this is often experienced by others as authenticity, on the inside it can often feel fragmented, like hopping from one thing to the next without a unifying thread that informs all of those activities. We define a sense of purpose at this stage according to what is centrally important for us.

The final stage is where our sense of purpose is derived from our own life itself. Specifically, from what is most important in our life. It's the unifying thread and theme that runs through our life, and as a result we are sharing that in service of others. Our message is the unshakeable foundation through which we orient our own lives, make our choices, and conduct our actions. It is at this stage that we realise that we have a message, a message that is derived from and revealed through our own lives.

The earlier stage of responding to the situation and knowing what is centrally important for us is a necessary and even essential preparation for living the theme and message of our lives.

Once we have identified what is centrally important for us, we tend to sense that we are getting close to what our life is about. However, the methods that got us this far will not be sufficient to take us the last stretch. Mountaineers climbing Mount Everest at first use their natural breathing. During the final stretches of their climb to the summit, they usually supplement their breathing with tanked oxygen. They use a different strategy. In a similar way, though we're still the one doing the work, we need a different strategy to reveal what is most important. Up to this point, we have used our in-the-moment experience to reveal what's important, and then gone through increasing abstraction to reveal what all of that is about, revealing what is centrally important. What's most important is revealed through particular significant and strong events or themes that we have experienced in or through our lives.

As you'll see, your message is what's most important, is what matters most, is what moves you, is what you get upset about and react to when it's compromised. Some of the benefits of knowing what your life is the answer to are:

- What really matters becomes like an inner guide for you, simplifying and clarifying choices and actions.
- Without knowing what's most important you can feel adrift on the seas of uncertainty and confused by the fog that seems to cloud every choice and fork in the road. Being clear on what you have to share and why can be like an internal orienting compass.
- Knowing you know what matters most can give you a clear sense of direction.
- What matters most is the direction. How you choose to create that are your goals.
- Life is a completely different experience when you understand what guides you.
- Knowing what's most important is a foundation in your life that you can never lose, nor can it ever be taken away.

Wounded messenger

For over 30 years I felt pain around the question of 'What am I here for?' as it remained unanswered. For whatever reason, that unanswered question was a particularly painful experience for me. I perceived that what I was doing in life was meaningless, and I felt empty. Whenever I met with someone who likewise was feeling at a loss to identify their calling in life, I would feel for them with a deep emotional understanding of how they felt and the dilemma they faced. The more often this happened, the more I noticed my desire to be able to help them in this way.

Earlier, when I said I had undertaken my own process to identify what my life is calling me to, I used my 30 plus years' theme of painful experience as the basis of how I revealed my calling. I laughed when I came up with 'help others realise their calling'. While that unanswered question was most certainly the most excruciating experience of my life, what I had not shared earlier was that I'd looked at all the experiences in my life that had been very painful for me, not just that thirty year unanswered question.

In my curiosity to explore more deeply and widely, I'd asked myself the same set of questions for other experiences in my life that I remember had been particularly painful for me.

- When I was young, my favourite pet dog died, and I was terribly upset. I felt engulfed by an emptiness, and I remember thinking that life seemed altogether pointless, that, with the passing of my dear dog, life had lost its meaning.

- I've had a few relationship break-ups in my younger adult years, including a divorce. During every one of those times I remembered how empty I'd felt, like there was nothing there, just an empty hole, and the deep sense of futility and purposeless I'd perceived. This is amusing for me now, but I remember declaring once to a friend, "Relationships are a meaningless waste of time!" I believe the exact opposite now though.

- A few times I've been in roles that were made redundant, and each time was I faced with the deep pointlessness of it all and the profound emptiness I felt.

"What is this?", I'd asked myself, noticing I'd had essentially the same perception and felt experience each time, even though the situations appeared to be vastly different from each other. 'How can this be?', I wondered. Then I had one of those amazing 'eureka!' moments. I realised that each time my pain was evoked because of the perceived absence of what was most important for me—meaning and purpose, and being full and filled. When I had perceived the greatest departure from what was most important, I'd experienced things to be the most painful.

The bigger the gap between the situation and what's important, the more painful our experience will be. The greater the perceived departure from what's most important, the more painful the experience. The greater the perceived departure from our essence, the more pain we feel.

I see the same pattern in others as well. For example, Katrina, called 'The Goddess of Teaching' by her students, has the message, 'Be worthy, feel secure'. Along with the situation of her Great Wound, she reviewed other very painful experiences in her life. Her situations and the way she experienced them were:

- When she was young, she perceived her mother as largely absent or otherwise unavailable. She remembers making it signify she was unworthy, and she personally felt very insecure.

- When a pre-teen and still at home, she perceived her parents often fighting. She interpreted this as not being good enough and that there was nothing that could be counted on.

- As an adult she spent time as an emergency teacher at a school that had processes perceived by her as treating students as objects. She changed the way they were being implemented. As a result, she was not invited back to the school. She took this as a rejection and as a confirmation of her unworthiness to teach, and felt very unsure of her future as a teacher.

Have you ever tasted a delightful cake that had icing so deep in texture and flavour that it simply enriched an already magnificent cake? This is what our message is like. Let's revisit that cake we've so far been collecting ingredients for and baking. All the qualities that are important for us are the ingredients of our cake. What is centrally important is the type of cake that those ingredients make. Our message is the icing that adds greater depth to, enriches and explains our already magnificent cake.

You are about to use a rational approach to a very significant non-rational experience to reveal your message, the unique service you're here to provide.

Take a look at your Value Stack. How does it feel for you when you experience a significant compromise of what's important? People usually say things like 'Sucks', 'Awful', 'Distressed', 'Upset', and 'Angry'. These are all different word variants for 'Painful'. The vast majority of people that I work with describe their feeling of a significant compromise of what's important to them as the experience of 'pain'.

We've been sensitised to the departure from what's important for us through our experience of the feeling of pain. It's experienced as painful to experience a gap in, a departure from, and compromise of, what's important. What was experienced as painful is what we've been sensitised to, and what we have been sensitised to is important for us.

Taking this to the extreme, we're most sensitised to what was and is experienced as most painful. What is most important is what we have been most sensitised to. What we have been most sensitised to has been and is most painful for us to experience. Therefore, what is most important for us is revealed through what has been experienced as most painful for us.

What is needed is the ability to decode our experience in a way that reveals what is most important, what we have been most sensitised to.

What was not made explicit during the creation of your Value Stack is that our experience of our environment, the relationship we had with the events in our life, is both a perception and a feeling. We used our reactive feelings as indicators and pointers to our perceptions. It was from our actual perceptions and interpretations that we elicited and revealed the qualities that are important for us. We are emotionally sensitised to those events in our life, and we tend to automatically perceive them in a particular way. Revealing our message follows a similar path.

From a feeling point of view, you'll be identifying what you are most sensitised to. You'll do this through identifying and then reframing what has been your most painful experience. From a perception point of view, you'll be identifying and reframing what you perceived was not there or was taken from you as part of that most painful experience.

This is represented in the following model. In relationship to our experience we have both a perception and a felt experience. Our perception can range from what's important being always available to never provided or taken away. Our emotional or felt experience can be in the range between what we are least sensitised to and most sensitised to.

Let's take a look at the four areas of the model. What we are least sensitised to, and has always been perceived as available, seems to just not be that important—it's unimportant. When we have what we are least sensitised to, together with a perception of something never there or was taken away from us, we have a scarcity perception. This is the opposite of what we would have wanted to perceive was abundantly available. When we have what we are most sensitised to, together with the perception of something always available, we have a painful feeling. This is the opposite of what we would have wanted to feel in that situation. However, when we have both what we are most sensitised to with what was never there or taken away from us, we have our message, though experienced and described, as its opposite—our message opposite.

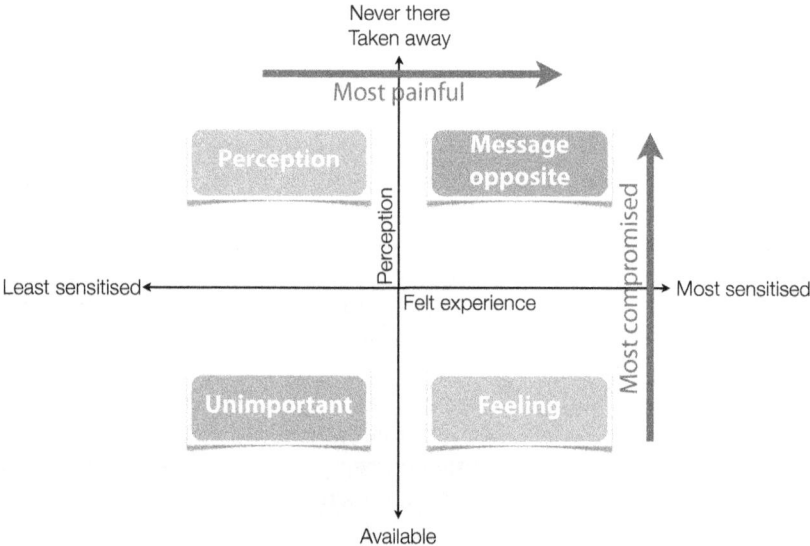

Experience as opposite of message

The feeling of when things were most painful and the perception of what was not there for us, reveals something probably outside of our current awareness. We are probably not conscious of this experience. As such, these are more of our unconscious revealers.

The interesting thing about sensitivity is that it tends to be universal. We're sensitised not only to an inner experience in our own lives. We're sensitised to an inner experience in anyone's life. What we are most sensitised to in our lives is also what we are most sensitised to in other people's lives, and what we are most sensitised to in life generally.

It's called empathy. We experience general empathy whenever someone else is experiencing pain; we understand that they're experiencing pain. However, we experience a more specific empathy when the pain that someone else is experiencing is similar to or the same as our own experience. We literally have a deep emotional appreciation of how they are feeling and of their circumstance.

I call the event(s) or theme in our life that we experienced as most painful as our 'Great Wound'. We very often feel greatly wounded by them, sometimes even defined by them. If this is the case for you, it is not the intent of this book to address that, other than to say our experience of our Great Wound changes as we actively work towards creating our message. What I do hope for you is to realise that your Great Wound may well be the source of meaning and fulfilment in your life.

As we'll soon find, our Great Wound was our experience of the greatest departure from that which was most important for us, a specific form of universal love. It was painful to experience that gap. This absence of love is what we are most sensitised to. It's also what we experience greatest empathy for when others are likewise experiencing that absence of love. Because it's our greatest empathic experience, I call it the 'Peak Empathic Response'. Our life has sensitised us to this specific absence of love, and when we decipher our Great Wound, we discover that we have the answer to that absence of love. It's called our message.

The evolution from Great Wound to Message is represented in the following model. Your Great Wound leads to your great sensitivity, which evokes your great empathy, which results in your Message. The centre of our Message is our Great Wound.

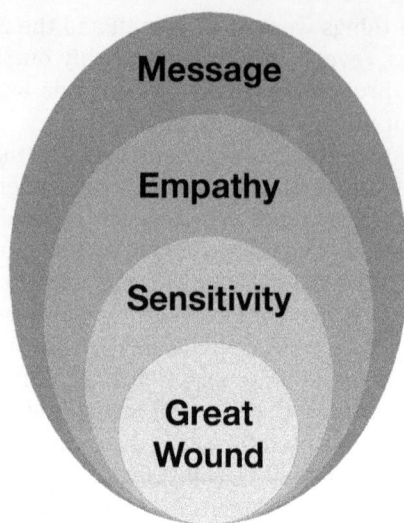

From Great Wound to Message

Zaheed's experience

Zaheed, to whom you were introduced earlier, reports a complete change regarding what for him was his Great Wound. "There is no wound any more", he says, "There is just a gift. There is just what I am here for. Maybe the pain was just how you had to learn the gift. I don't even think about the wounds. The wounds themselves have become irrelevant because I no longer experience them as wounds, only as gifts. Sure, something happened. It was painful at the time, but now all I remember is the gift. I am so grateful."

Flipping wound

As said earlier, there are two parts to the experience of your Great Wound and Message—perception and feeling. The process of identifying your message is:

1. Situation
2. Perception of Great Wound
3. Feeling of Great Wound
4. Decode perception and feeling
5. Message

This section is all about seeking to answer, 'I was *what* and felt *how*?' regarding our Great Wound, and then decoding that as your Message.

1. Situation

To identify the way you experienced the greatest departure from what is most important, recollect an event or theme in your life that was most painful for you. Focus on your experience of what happened, not on the details of what happened. If you have several experiences that are 'most painful' then, if you want, though it is not necessary to do so, you can follow this process for each of them. Doing such an inventory of your experiences may well show that you have tended to perceive and feel those types of experiences the same way.

2. Your perception

Your perception focus in that situation will tend to be on either of two possibilities. There are two primary ways to help you identify your perception in that situation, and within either there are two secondary ways—choose the one that helps you connect more easily with your perception. Your perception could have been regarding either:

    a.   Yourself, or

    b.   The situation

Find the words that have the most impact for you, that really 'bite' or sting to consider them. Considering the words you find, find the *one word* that stings the most.

    a.   *When your perception was about yourself:*

        Go with the option where you seem to just know your answer.

        i.   In that situation you perceived that you *were* what ... ?

           For example:

Purposeless	Unworthy	Disrespected
Insignificant	Powerless	Unvalued
Self-doubting	Excluded	Flat

        ii.   In that situation you perceived you *weren't* what ... ?

           For example:

Purposeful	Worthy	Respected
Significant	Empowered	Valued
Trusting	Included	Energised

b. *When your perception was regarding the situation or others in that environment:*

Go with the option where you seem to just know your answer.

i. In that situation you perceived that the situation was or others were what ... ?

For example:

Meaningless	Denigrating	Disrespectful
Exclusionary	Diminishing	Condescending
Disempowering	Scary	Unjust
Heartless	Controlling	Unworthy

ii. What didn't you have, was never given to you, or was taken away from you by the situation or others in it ... ?

For example:

Meaning	Elevation	Respect
Inclusion	Value	Significance
Power	Self-trust	Justice
Care	Choice	Worth

3. Your felt experience

Your emotional experience will tend to be through either of two possibilities. There are two possible ways to help you identify your felt experience in that situation—choose the one that helps you connect more easily with your felt experience. The two ways to identify your felt experience are:

a. How you felt in that situation, or

b. How you would have wanted to feel

Find the words that have the most impact for you, that really 'bite' or sting to consider them. In fact, find the word that stings the most.

a. You felt how in that situation?

For example:

Empty	Separate	Disengaged
Uncomfortable	Worthless	Ignored
Flat	Afraid	Disconnected
Unsupported	Trapped	Disempowered

b. **In that situation you would have wanted to feel how?**

For example:

Fulfilled	Included	Engaged
Comfortable	Worthy	Acknowledged
Energised	Courageous	Connected
Supported	Free	Empowered

4. Your message

Just as your experience has two parts, a perception / interpretation and a felt experience, your Message has the same two parts—a perception and a feeling. Your Message is the flip of your Great Wound.

Your Great Wound is the combination of:

a. Your perception of what you were in the situation, or what the situation itself, including the people in it, were (e.g. powerless or disempowering)

b. Your felt experience in that situation (e.g worthless)

For example, the overall experience of the Great Wound could be something like: 'In that situation I was powerless and felt unworthy'.

Identify what your overall experience is—perception and feeling. Take note of and write down the way you perceived that situation and how you felt in it.

Your Message is made up of their opposites:

a. The perception of what you weren't or what was not provided by your environment (e.g. empowered), and

b. What you would have wanted to feel (e.g. worthy).

On a page write the following and include what your answers are.

Great Wound:

Perception = ... (e.g powerless or disempowering)
Feeling = ... (e.g worthless)

Now just flip and take the opposite of both. Ask yourself:

a. What the exact opposite of that perception is

b. What the exact opposite of that feeling is

On the same page write the following and include what you identified as their opposites.

Message:

Perception = ... (e.g. empowered)
Feeling = ... (e.g. worthy)

Your message has two ways to be expressed.

    a.   Be *message perception* (e.g. empowered), feel *message feeling* (e.g. worthy), or

    b.   Feel *message feeling* (e.g. worthy), be *message perception* (e.g. empowered).

In this example the two options are:

    a.   Be empowered, feel worthy

    b.   Feel worthy, be empowered

Write out the two ways to express your message.

    a.   Be ... , feel ... .

    b.   Feel ... , be ... .

Now sit or stand upright, and say the two versions out loud at the volume of your normal talking voice, and notice which one resonates more strongly for you. Notice which one just seems or feels more 'right' than the other. Notice what your body does in response to both versions. Some indicators are a bigger smile, your eyes light up more, your heart lifts, your shoulders edge back expanding the chest, it just feels more congruent, or you just have a sense of knowing. When you say them out loud, you'll know which one it is. If they're both the same for you, then they're both good and just pick one as it makes no difference.

If you want, find a succinct way of saying your message. For example, it could be something like 'Feel worthy through empowerment', or even 'Worthiness through empowerment'. Avoid the temptation of your mind to elaborate or explain your message. Keep it simple, straight to the point, and succinct.

Then write out the version that resonates more strongly for you. Highlight or circle it if you like. Write your version of *'be empowered, feel worthy'*.

The following are actual examples of people's messages. It does not matter if they do not make sense to you. They make perfect self-evident sense to the people who wrote them.

'Care and be free'

'Be just, feel supported'

'Engagement through respect'

'Be valued and feel worthy'

'Feel connected through inclusion'

'Fullness through evolution'

'Have self-trust, feel courageous'

'Have choice, feel empowered'

Receiving what you give

Quickly ask yourself this: When interacting with others and you have been at your absolute best, is this, your message, what you have been helping people to experience?

Imagine different ways of acting on your message and notice how you feel and perceive doing so.

- You are actively helping people to directly experience your message for themselves
- You are helping people learn how to experience your message for themselves
- People leaving their interaction with you having experienced for themselves what your message says

Notice how you feel and perceive knowing that this is the case. For example, when Katrina was asked: "How would it be for you to know that you were helping people to know that they were worthy and feel secure?", she replied, "I would feel absolutely fantastic. It's wonderful to know that what I am sharing with others is my own life." She paused and added, "In fact, I'd know that I am completely worthy, and I'd feel completely secure."

So imagine vividly that in some way you were helping people to experience what your message says, and ask yourself how you'd perceive yourself and feel doing so. Answer for yourself, 'In helping others experience for themselves my message, I'd know that I am … (what perception?), and I'd feel … (what feeling?)'

This happens often. When actively in service of helping others experience for themselves our message, we experience for ourselves our own message. In helping others, we experience that ourselves. We are not seeking to experience for ourselves our message. We experience it as a result of helping others to experience it.

We'll often use different words for how we'd experience helping others experience our message, but invariably the words we'd identify are either variants of our message or alternative ways of describing 'fulfilment'.

A great teacher once said, "In giving we receive". I think that this is what he meant.

Looking at the opposite aspect of what you imagined above is also insightful. How would it be for you if you inadvertently caused people to feel the opposite of your message, to feel the same way as you did when you experienced your Great Wound? For example, when the same person above was asked this question, she said that they'd "think I was terribly unworthy and feel completely insecure about what I was doing. I'd be mortified."

Imagine that

Regarding our wound, we can never get rid of the fact that something happened. What we can change is the way we perceive it. Something happened. That's true. The meaning we gave it, wasn't. However, it did sensitise us to something.

While the way you perceived that situation might appear to be true, and you might even have been convinced that it was true, it wasn't. It never was. It didn't happen the way you remember it. It wasn't actually and objectively the way you perceived it. It was never the meaning you gave the situation, and it was never the meaning you gave about yourself. What is true is that you experienced that situation in a particular way. That was then.

It is because of that situation that you now know what matters most for you. You now know what your message is. You can now choose to provide that for others. You now know what will give you a deep sense of fulfilment.

What happens to the way you experience what you call your Great Wound, when you now know that it is the source of your message and, when you act on it, that it is the source of purpose, meaning, and fulfilment in your life? Is it still only a wound, or has it now also become a gift?

When you live the gift of the wound by helping others to experience your message, the way you experience the wound changes. Your former wound is now the motivation and fuel for what you are called to in your life because it evokes your Peak Empathic Response.

When I am actively helping people realise why they are here, and to create, in some way, their message, I have no uncertainty about who I am and why I am here. It does not even occur to me. This is true for others as well. This is something that will be true for you as well when you live it.

When you are so full of helping others experience for themselves your message, when you are so full of experiencing the receiving that comes with your giving, the fact that there was once a wound becomes irrelevant in the sense that it becomes something else. It has become irrelevant in its pervious sense. You have gone beyond your experience, you have gone beyond the wound and the way you experienced it, and yet have included what you have become sensitised to. Your wound has been transcended and included, and in doing so, the nature of the 'wound' has changed and become more of a gift.

Our Great Wound is what we have experienced in our life as most painful. It's also what we're most sensitised to in others. It's the human problem we care most about doing something about. It's the source of a profound sense of purpose and fulfilment. The situation happened, yet our experience of what happened changes. It can be the wound that defines us

—as the reason to avoid life or to participate with life. When our wound defines the reason we have for not participating, we might believe that 'forgiveness' for what happened is something we have to do to move forward. It's as if our 'lack of forgiveness' for what happened is holding us back. When our wound defines our participation with life, we remember what happened and appreciate how it has shaped us. We naturally have gratitude for how what happened has shaped us. When gratitude happens, forgiveness naturally occurs. When we receive the gift of what happened, we're naturally grateful and forgiveness has already occurred.

When we are truly living the gift of what we have been sensitised to, we might and often do say that there never was a wound. We might recognise that whatever happened led to something we care deeply about and gives us meaning and fulfilment when we act to create it. It was only ever a perfect gift that helped shape our life in the way it needed to be shaped. It was only ever a gift.

What, message integrity?

Now you are going to 'test' the integrity your message.

Self-evident

To you, is it a self-evident truth? Does it almost seem as though it's obvious? For many of us, it seems so obvious we might ask, 'Doesn't everyone see the world this way?' Are you convinced of the truth of your message? Hopefully you said, 'Yes'.

Central importance

Now write your message above the top of your Value Stack. Draw a line from the word that was at the top of your Value Stack and join it to where you have written your message. Consider the word that was at the top of your Stack, the word that described what was centrally important for you.

Ask yourself whether your message adds meaning to, gives greater depth and context to the word you had at the top of your stack? It only needs to make sense to you. Hopefully you said, 'Yes'.

Ask yourself, 'Can I have my message without the quality at the top of my stack?' In other words, 'To me, if I take away the quality at the top of my stack, can I have my message?' Again, this only needs to make sense to you. You may even see that the word at the top of your stack relates to and is required only for one aspect of your message. That's okay. Either way, hopefully you said, 'No'.

To you, if you remove the quality at the top of your stack, does one aspect or both aspects of your message also get removed? Hopefully you said, 'Yes'.

Empathy

How would it be and feel for you to know that the people around you were experiencing for themselves what your message says? How would it be and feel to know that you were the one helping them experience for themselves the form of love that matters most to you?

How would it be and feel for you if people around you were experiencing the absence or compromise of your message? Would you feel compelled, if you could, to do something about it?

When you've been at your very best with others, is that what they have experienced as a result of their interaction with you, or at least what you'd hope was the case?

Look again at your message. If you had an opportunity to help other people experience your message, to perceive and to feel for themselves what your message describes, do you in a way feel compelled to do so?

Could you choose not to? Could you live without doing so? Hopefully you just said, as people I have worked with have said, 'Of course not!'

Given the opportunity to help others experience my message, it would be absurd not to.

Love

Think of love in the universal sense, look at your message, and simply ask yourself, 'According to my definition, is my message necessary for there to be love in the universal sense?' Using the above example, it would mean 'Are empowerment and worthiness necessary for there to be universal love?' Hopefully you answered, 'Yes'.

If that question does not work for you, then ask it this way, 'According to my definition, can I have universal love without what this message says?' Using the above example, it would mean asking, 'Can I have universal love without empowerment and worthiness?' Hopefully you answered, 'No'.

Receiving giving

How would it be for you to be actively helping others to experience for themselves your message? How would it be to know that, as a result of their interactions with you, they experience for themselves what your message says? Imagine spending your days actively involved in creating this for others. What would you know about yourself and how would you feel?

Summarising the essence of what we have covered in this chapter, the pattern is:

1. You were in a situation or situations; something happened in your environment
2. You felt pain in reaction to that situation
3. You interpreted the situation in some way, you attributed meaning to the situation, you identified a problem
4. You flipped that interpretation and revealed your message, the answer to the problem you're here to give, the challenge to which your life is the answer

Later you'll ask yourself:

1. For whom does that problem exist?
2. How can I solve that or help them solve that for themselves?

The one lens

By now we know that:

- Our experience has shaped our life and what our life is the answer to.
- Our message describes an aspect of universal love.
- We have been sensitised to the absence of that love.
- We experience that the absence of this love is painful for us, in fact most painful.
- When life is most painful, we tend to experience it the same way.
- Everything that is important for us ultimately leads to our message and the aspect of universal love we have described.
- Ultimately, the absence of this love isn't just something we get upset about, it is the only thing we've ever been upset about.
- So far, we've spent our life not realising that we have been reacting to the absence, ultimately, of what matters most for us, our message.
- The way our life has been shaped is the way we perceive our life. Our message isn't just 'a' perspective; it's the only perspective we experience the world through. The world is perceived and experienced as the absence or presence of our message.

- Being aware in others of the absence of, or the departure from, the experience of our message evokes our Peak Empathic Response.

- Our Peak Empathic Response is our peak source of motivation to do something about it.

- Now we have the possibility and option to not just react to the absence of a particular aspect of love; we have the possibility and option to actively create it on behalf of others.

- Know it would be absurd not to.

How is this so? As we saw with our Value Stack, qualities towards the bottom of our stack are made up from a myriad array of different parts. Collectively those parts are needed for the more abstract or higher quality to exist completely.

It's like when white light passes through a glass prism and differentiates into all of its constituent parts, giving us the rainbow that we are all familiar with. To recreate white light would mean recombining all the colours of the rainbow. Without all the colours of the rainbow recombined, the white light isn't quite so white. It's off-white. White light differentiates as many parts. Those many parts recombine as white light.

The one differentiates as the many. The many reintegrate as the one.

Universal love is differentiated into its multitude of different parts. Each of those different parts or aspects recombines as universal love. Each one of us represents or is sensitised to one of those parts; it's the quality we're here to create our way. Together we recombine our collective message as universal love.

Personal love, together universal.

Some believe and would say that we became sensitised to what was most painful. This is a very common version of reality. This says that we are the result of our experience, that the perception and feeling we experienced came after and as a result of the painful experience.

Another, although less common, version of reality is that your message is the version of love that *you* came to create. Your message was already within you before you ever experienced it being compromised and as painful. This says that we came in with our message, and life provoked our sensitivity to it when we experienced departure from it.

It's for us to decide which of these we favour. It is simply a question of which came first, our Message or our Great Wound, and whether each of these versions of reality is partially true, or not.

Either way, the events in our life that were the greatest departure from what's most important for us were experienced as most painful. Because it was most painful, that experience is most useful for identifying what's most important.

What's my gift?

Is 100% natural truly good for you?

Justine's experience

Justine was born in New Zealand and is the eldest of three children. She's married, has a sever year old son, and readily acknowledges that her family is important. Having worked in marketing roles since completing her degree in Marketing and Economics, what she loves most about her work is the ability to make things happen. She loves gardening and is fond of her Wisteria bonsai. Justine is someone who cares and feels very deeply.

"Many years ago I saw a business coach", Justine explains, "and I realise that I was learning things that aren't me. For example, I am a very conceptual person and I was learning how to be very detailed and organised in a linear way. The expectation was to be well planned and organised. I did that for years and years, as that's what was expected for someone at my level. You learn that what you naturally do isn't how you are expected to do things; so you learn to stop doing what's natural and become some story of how you should be. I got the message that I shouldn't be conceptual, that I shouldn't be thinking outside the square, because that's not what you ought to do."

Not only does Justine realise that she was taught to be unnatural, she's clear about the toll of operating in an unnatural way. "We seem to have this belief that we should be talented at everything. It's just not true. We beat ourselves up for not being good in everything. It's just exhausting trying to be. It can be a bit horrifying to realise that you're not actually that good at something that you used to get paid to only do. I had to work twice as hard as anybody else to be any good at it, to actually pull it off. You just manage; you just make yourself do it."

"It's exhausting", she says describing what it's like operating in an unnatural way. Despite working hard all day long trying to meet the various demands of her job, Justine shares that, "I'd go home tired and with little emotional energy. It actually creates stress as it goes against who you are."

Commonly unnaturally common

Many people feel like Justine did and perhaps you can relate. Your concerns, like many others, could include:

- You're working hard at your work, but doing your work the way you're working is simply exhausting. For example, you might find analysis, creating structures, being innovative, or assertiveness, just hard work.

- You're conscientiously working to round out your weaknesses, as you've been advised would be good for you, yet no matter how much training and practice you perform, you find that things never quite seem to work when you work with your weaknesses. Things just seem to take twice as long and seem twice as hard than when you work with your strengths. For example, you might be great at working with people yet find driving results a struggle, or vice versa.

- You're good at your otherwise enjoyable job, but there are tasks that you just dread doing. You dread them because they are so hard to do. You don't enjoy them, and you'd almost give anything to avoid having to do them. You might even feel some guilt about hating those tasks. Yet out of your sense of professionalism and integrity, maybe even duty, you do them anyway. For example, you might be in a creative job and love the creative work, but filling in detailed reports seems to do your head in.

- You can do a particular task for a short amount of time, and not even very well at that. Once started, you quickly start to feel restless and perhaps even need to rest. You don't know why it seems so tiring. You might even think to yourself that you ought to be good at it. For example, you might be great at execution and getting things done, but the prospect of developing a strategic plan seems to take all the excitement out of your job.

- You can undertake a task, maybe even maintain it for a long time, but it just takes so much effort to do it. Though you can more or less do it, the standard just does not seem to be adequate. It's hard for you to feel engaged with that activity.

- Your job requires you to be good at many different things, but no matter how much you try, you just can't seem to nail a few of them. Though you might once have gone into the job full of hope and confidence, now your confidence seems to have taken a battering. You might even be thinking you're in the wrong job. Others might be thinking so too. For example, you're great as a teacher and the students love coming to class, they're engaged, and they're all making so much progress even parents are commenting. However, watching grass grow would be preferable to the requirement for you to be doing the analysis that is supposed to be enhancing leaning outcomes.

- You care about the work you do. You might even feel a sense of satisfaction, contribution and fulfilment in what your work is about, yet some tasks fill you with such dread that you could procrastinate all day not to have to do them. You're confused or perplexed about why you care about your job yet hate some of the things your job requires. For example you might be working in service of others, such as in a community service arena that supports local youth, and you love that work and the effects it has, and, while you know that promoting your programs and the financial support it generates is important, doing so feels completely unnatural.

- You can achieve a certain task easily and to a high standard even though it might be different from how others do it. You're instructed to do it a different way, perhaps for the sake of consistency, or because someone in authority decides it ought to be done that way. You're doing your best, telling yourself you ought to be able to achieve the same result doing it a different way, but no matter how much time and effort you put into doing it that way, it never seems to be done to the same standard, never to the same quality, and just takes longer to do. You even feel less satisfied in your work accordingly. For example, you work as an instructor and create terrific learning for participants through your facilitative style. You find the new instructional style personally off-putting, hard to do, and you notice a marked reduction in engagement in the sessions you run.

This is completely understandable. None of this is your fault. How could it be? Sometimes you just don't know why some things seem so easy, and others so hard.

What's going on though, is that we might have taken on the message that we're supposed to be good at everything, don't understand why we're not, and we're unsure about how we identify what it is that we are naturally good at. We might see that others are great at something and see ourselves as somehow deficient for not having the same ability. We either expect that we're gifted in everything, or we are in one or both comparison games—where you compare what someone else is great at to what you are weak at, or where you compare what you are great at to what others are weak at. This is represented in the following model.

To expect you to have all possible abilities is simply an unnatural expectation. This is what happens at the 'Possibilities' stage. For example, many parents have an expectation to be able to have a high powered career, a deeply intimate marriage, a loving and happy family, maintain their health, and to have the time and energy for everything that needs to be done, all at the same time, and all to world-class standard. Something will eventually give. For most it's just unrealistic and unnatural to expect great performance on all possibilities simultaneously. There's a lot of effort in trying to manage and maintain all of those different things simultaneously.

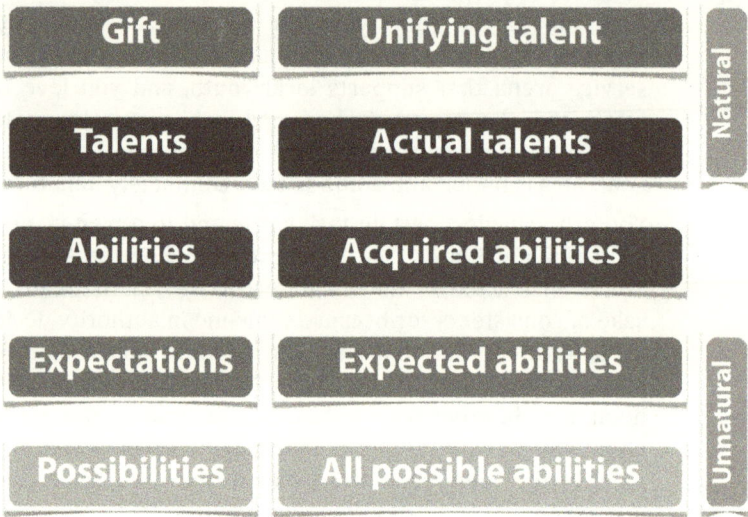

Gift	Unifying talent	Natural
Talents	Actual talents	
Abilities	Acquired abilities	
Expectations	Expected abilities	Unnatural
Possibilities	All possible abilities	

From unnatural to natural

Maree's experience

Maree loves travelling and experiencing new cultures, and has a passion for learning languages, e.g., Chinese, and more recently, French. Her love of animals, especially cats, is such that her friends call her 'The crazy cat lady'. She's someone who regularly points out what's great about others and has a knack for helping others feel positive about their achievements. She has recently gone from managing only herself to managing a team of 40 people.

Maree vividly describes the impact of operating in an unnatural way. "I spent years denying my real self and containing my playful nature and sense of humour. For a long time this has contributed to a belief that I'm not good enough and unworthy. I was trying to be something that wasn't natural, and bad at it, causing a lot of anxiety. It also drove a desire to please others."

Connecting with and accepting what was natural for her, explains Maree, "was a weight lifted off my shoulders, a new found freedom, feeling light and more at peace. I realised that I am not broken. I am me, and I am okay with that. For me, that was just a relief, a real shift in the love I have for myself."

She initially had a mixed response from colleagues. "Some were curious", Maree shares, "and questioned my behaviour, asking if I wanted to be seen as not being so serious and proper all the time. Some were surprised, perhaps a bit unsure of what was going on. Others were delighted."

Describing what's different as a result, she says, "Being more lighthearted is more natural for me. It's effortless. I am not thinking over what I should say before I say it, I just say it, and I get a better result. The quality of my relationships has improved. I get better connection with others, and I establish more trust more quickly."

The difference for Maree is that, "I'd much rather be playful and get results than be serious and get results. I had started to hate myself being in that more serious mode. I started to hate my job. By being more of myself, I am actually enjoying my work and connecting better with others."

The change in her experience of her work has been significant. "After all of these years of searching for the right job", she explains, "it was actually the change in myself, an acceptance of myself, that changed things. I'm now working in a way that is more natural for me. I am not battling with myself any more. I have more time to focus on what I want and how I am going to achieve them. I'm not worrying any more about being good enough, because now I know what's important and what's natural for me."

Describing her experience from which she derived her message, she says, "After all the anger associated with painful experiences in the past, I am actually now very grateful that I experienced them. They're a blessing. Now I understand the connection between that and who I am today. I previously thought my experience was a bad thing and meant I was damaged. Now I think the opposite. I know I am not broken. My anger is gone; just not there any more. The Great Wound is the great blessing. Because of the Great Wound I know more of who I am and what's important to me."

Maree's message is 'worthiness through significance', and in interacting with her it's no surprise that her Value Stack prominently includes connection and trust. Her advice for people exploring their life calling is, "Don't think about it too much. Get into action. You won't really get it until you do. The worst that can happen is you'll learn about yourself."

Naturally natural

We often try to be something we're not. This can lead to feeling like a fraud, out of depth and, feeling weighed down with self-doubt, concerned that others would eventually realise how bad we really are at things. We can feel like we're faking it—an impostor to ourselves. It can be hard to believe in our own competence when aspects of what we're doing seem unnatural for us.

In a task to be done, performing a role or doing a job, others have expectations about your abilities and we often have expectations about our own ability to perform in all areas defined by the task, role or job. This is the 'Expectations' stage. These expected abilities are often well beyond and outside of what we are actually able to do well. Even if you tried, you wouldn't be able to learn how to perform some of those tasks—they're so unnatural for you. You do your best anyway. Put simply, some of those expectations are not natural for you. Even though they're expected of you, they're still unnatural. For example, you might be great at driving results yet struggle to work with people and orient them together towards those results.

For example, Katrina, whom we met earlier, is superb in the classroom with a great ability for delivery. She's the first to admit that developing curriculum is a real struggle for her and is tiring to do. She acknowledges that some teachers get really excited about curriculum development, while it fills her with dread. Yet it's assumed by the education hierarchy that a great teacher will be great at both curriculum development and delivery. She is regularly expected to devote a huge amount of time towards curriculum development; something that requires what is for her an unnatural talent. The expectation to operate unnaturally results in her thinking about giving up on teaching; something that would be a great loss for her students.

Then you have your actual abilities and what you have learned and acquired the ability to do. They are not necessarily all natural for you, though you are able to do them. You know what you're naturally good at or have learned and acquired the ability to do reasonably well. You may even know what you're not naturally good at and what you have not managed to learn how to do well. You're doing a task, role or job, and manage the expectations around your abilities and learning. This is why delegation exists, to be able to focus on what you're good at and can do, while others that are good at doing other things do those tasks. It's more effortless all around. However, just because you're able to do something, does not mean that it is natural for you. Many of those learned abilities might have been as a result of your desire or someone else's instruction to improve a perceived weakness.

This stage is both natural—you're using natural talents—and unnatural—you've acquired certain abilities.

How effortless would it be to be primarily utilising your actual, natural abilities and talents? How would it be to be doing what you are doing according to what is a natural talent? What kind of results do you think you'd create, and what do you think your performance would be like as you were doing it? At this stage, you are working your talents. Because you're working your natural talents, they've become strengths. You are working what is truly natural for you, your natural abilities. It's far more effortless to do so.

Jay Niblick, author of *'What's Your Genius?'*, has done research involving 197,000 people, including 10,000 interviews. He says emphatically that everyone has unique talents, in that all of us are naturally good at certain things and not at others. When we're using our talents, we tend to do them well and enjoy doing them. According to Jay, we all have unique thinking and decision-making styles, and that research suggests that they are the results of genetics and experience. Our success in what we do depends on how aligned we are to our thinking and decision-making styles, our unique talents.

One of the standout findings in Jay's work is that no individual talent is more important for success than any other. Successful people worked their talents in roles that utilised them. Different roles, however, require certain talents more than others. Regardless of the role, if you're not using natural talents, your performance will be hindered. That's the difference.

The only limitation of the stage of actual talents, is that the talents still feel separate, somewhat fragmented. Even though you're naturally good at them, at least possibly so, there's no unifying thread that defines and explains them all. Realising the identity of your unifying talent is what the Gift stage is all about. It is knowing what your one unifying talent is that creates, gives rise to and shows up as all of your other talents. Your gift is the word given to all of your signature talents. When you work your gift in a given situation, you automatically work your other talents that are applicable to that situation.

It's kind of like strengths flexibility, the ability to be automatically responsible to the situation according to what you can bring to it.

Justine's experience

Justine, whom we met earlier, recently had a choice to shift to a role with a greater focus on using her natural talents. Though the adjustment to working through what's natural wasn't without its challenges, Justine's glad she made it. "You have to realise that part of that (acquired abilities) is just learned behaviour, and you have more to offer through what's natural." Speaking of what it was like to focus on her natural abilities and let go of what was acquired, she says, "There's a period of time where you just float as you try to get the balance right. Then something settles, and you get more comfortable with what's natural."

Greater clarity with what is natural helps Justine make decisions about her work. "For example", Justine explains, "not so long ago I was in a role where all my skills were useful, and an opportunity arose that required a higher degree of detail (an unnatural ability). I was not going to be able to offer that without a lot of effort. I discussed with the organisation how the role combined strategy development (natural) with detailed analysis (unnatural). Analysis just did not match my natural skills. We agreed that I was half of that role and could tolerate the other half given the right support. In the end the new opportunity didn't work out for me, though the conversations were very easy for me to have. It was very easy for me to come out at the other end of it remaining motivated, and still positive in the eyes of all the people that mattered. I am able to easily move away and into positions now where when people try to give me detailed work for analysis, I can comfortably hand it back or delegate."

Working to her strength has had a positive effect for Justine. "I go home with more energy, more emotional energy," she shares, "and I'm glad about the decisions I make."

Effortless and abundant

So how would it be if things were easier and more effortless for you to do, compared to other ways of doing things that are hard and effortful? Imagine spending your day doing things in a way that's just hard. How would you be that night? How would you be with those you care about? Now imagine spending your day doing things in a way that's just easy by comparison. How would you be different that night, and how would you be different with those you care about?

Imagine having a single way of doing everything in your life, a single way of functioning that just works for you. It utilises all of your talents. Compared to when doing things is hard, your single way of doing things is just easy for you to do. You might not be aware of what your single way of doing things actually is. You do things that way anyway. Doing things that way just seems natural. When you learn to use that approach well, you have an ability that's almost effortless, things work and you feel engaged with what you're doing. You can maintain that way of doing things for a long time. Your capacity for that seems abundant. Your one way of doing things has many specific forms, and those many specific forms are all different ways of your doing your one way.

I'll give you an example from my own life of what it's like when you're outside your gift. I can do analysis of data. Honest. I can do it for about 20 minutes, and then I fall asleep, I'm that tired. I feel like I need to put head to pillow. Moreover, I'm not very good at it either. I have learned to 'do analysis', but doing so is exhausting for me. I can do it—at huge cost. Analysis is so effortful for me, I can only do so for minutes at a time, and then I'm fatigued. I don't enjoy analysis either as it's such hard work for me. I once took a creative design job, only to discover that it involved mostly analysis. To say that I did not enjoy that role is an understatement. I dreaded going to work. Worse, I took my tiredness and frustration home with me. I lasted little more than a couple of months.

I am so grateful for people like my sister, who can do analysis effortlessly and for a long time. She has a talent with numbers and analysis. I do not.

Tim Roth, author of Strengths 2.0, cites Gallup research and says that when we're not utilising our strengths, we are six times less likely to be engaged in our job.

Everyone is naturally gifted in some way. You are gifted in some way. You may not know in what way. When you do things according to your gift, you do them naturally and spontaneously. You've always had your gift. You usually default to it as your approach to life. If you're operating outside your gift, then what you do is tiring, perhaps exhausting.

Our culture tends to value what is scarce and effortful; with things generally rising in value the more scarce it is seen to be. Our culture tends not to value what is abundant and effortless. Indeed, our culture tends to take for granted whatever is abundant and effortless, even dismissing it as worthless.

You're more than likely in the habit of giving attention to what is hard to do, not easy to do. As such you may not even recognise what your gift is. You might even diminish or even deny your gift. That you may not recognise your gift does not mean that your gift is not there. It just means that it is currently unrecognised or unknown to you.

Your gift is often overlooked because it requires such little thought or effort to use it. Your gift is different from a learnable skill. Virtually everyone can learn to drive a car, though not many have the natural ability to become a formula-one racing car driver.

Your gift is so easy and so default, you probably haven't paid much attention to it. It's just the way you naturally try to do things. Unfortunately, as we tend to not pay much attention to our gift, they can very easily remain unknown and underdeveloped. Others notice though—it becomes known to them, and they pay attention. Listening to what others notice is one of the primary ways you'll get information about what your abilities and strengths are.

Having a gift tells you nothing about how well your gift is being utilised. It can be expressed in a useful way, or it may be expressed in a way that is not useful. What I mean by 'useful' is whether you're getting the results that you are after. When your gift is not being used usefully, you're not getting those results so easily. Your gift can be used to push people away—and I have done that many times in the past—or your gift can be used to bring them closer.

Here's an example from my own life. When I was a young adult, as happens to all of us, my relationships would occasionally experience some conflict. I'd want to create closeness and my approach was to better understand what was going on in those situations and with the woman I was seeing at the time. As paradoxical as it sounds, at the time I did not know that insight is something that I do naturally, especially insight into others. When conflict happened in those relationships, without realising and unbeknown to me, I'd apply even more insight into those situations. Much more insight. Wanting to create deeper understanding, I'd go about it all wrong and not create the results I was after. I would see patterns and share things with my girlfriend that were factors behind whatever was happening, I'd offer causal insights into what was happening for my partner. I'd do this even when there wasn't conflict, just in normal day-to-day living. Little did I know that this was generating the opposite effect to what I wanted. Doing this was tending to push them away. It was not bringing us closer. I invariably became an ex-boyfriend, and would be told by my ex-girlfriend that they didn't want to be with someone who understood them before they did, and that they didn't like me knowing what they had not yet shared. After this happened several times, I realised that I was the common factor—that I was the one person making the same mistake many times. It took me a while, but I eventually realised that volunteering insight into others, when they have not asked for it, tends to have the effect of people backing away. These days, I help people through processes where people choose to come to know themselves more fully.

We're always having some sort of effect on others in our environment, whether we're aware of it or not, and that effect is in part our creation. The effect you have can be creating what you want, or it can be destroying what you want. Either way, you're always creating something. The effect that we create is determined by how we show up in life. As in my personal example above, when you're thwarted in life you apply your gift even more.

Some examples of this are:

- Katrina's gift is rapport, and she does rapport even more whenever she feels that life is not working the way she wants.

- A senior manager, whose gift is collaboration, will tend to automatically react with more collaboration when he feels thwarted. He does not always immediately appreciate that a different style, such as direction, might be more appropriate for the situation.

How do you do?

What you are gifted in, by itself, is not intrinsically motivating. For example, Katrina is gifted with rapport, yet she does not find certain types of gatherings of people at all interesting. Sometimes it's quite the opposite for her, and she has absolutely no interest in participating. While she can do rapport effortlessly, it's not by itself interesting for her. However, once she's involved in helping people to know that they are worthy and feel certain, she's interested, activated, and motivated. Another friend, Lucy, is a gifted artist who is enthusiastic about depicting people in a particular way. She has zero interest in drawing landscapes, buildings or flower arrangements. In her words, "Nothing could be less interesting for me."

Your gift, by itself, is 'So what?' It's just the way you do things that works best when it works. The 'So what?' is answered when your gift is applied to what's most important for you. It's important to identify your giftedness so you can deliver on and create what's most important in a way that works best for you. Put it to work in service of what is most important for you, and you have a method that is most effortless for helping to create what's motivating. When your giftedness is used well by you, it most effortlessly produces the results you want to create in your life. When what you want to create is your message, then your gift is being used for what is most important. Your giftedness becomes your default method for delivering on and creating your message.

You do not necessarily 'see' people's talents. You can see talents at work. In a way, you can see and experience the concrete, tangible expressions of talents—yours and others.

When a talent has been worked to a point of consistent high performance, then you have, as Tim Rath says, a strength. A strength shows up as your practiced talents. Strengths are inherent capacities that have been practised enough to deliver consistent performance and manifest energy efficiently.

Talents are the more concrete expression of your gift. Your gift, being intangible, is a more abstract, qualitative description. This is represented in the following diagram that shows talents, strengths and gift along the concrete—qualitative continuum.

Qualitative

⟵ Gift

⟵ Talents
Strengths

⟵ Skills

Concrete

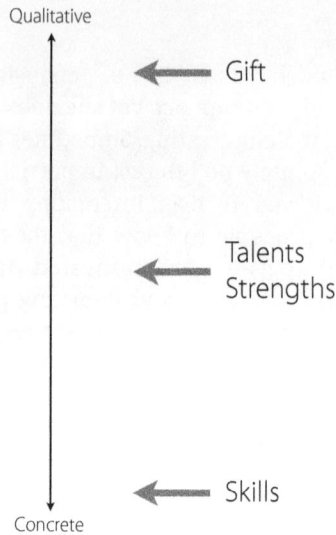

From concrete skills to qualitative gift

Your gift is a talent that's abundant and effortlessness. It also happens to be your default approach to your life. It's the way you do what you do. It's the way you do you.

To know whether you are expressing your gift skilfully, simply ask yourself whether you are getting the results and performance you want or know you can achieve? Only you'll know the answer. If not, then in general, you are either not skilfully utilising your gift, or you are operating outside of your gift and not using your gift at all. Not getting the performance and results you want in your life does not mean that you do not have a gift. Other factors are involved.

It's not what you think

Many years ago I had a key insight into how to identify your innate qualities. It's an insight that I want to share with you. It forms the basis of how you reveal your gift to yourself.

I was working as a manager of seven other people. Eighteen months into the role, someone from Human Resources approached me. They informed me that I had been formally accused of 'bullying' one of the people who reported to me. One of the things I liked about where I was working at the time is that they had a very strong series of policies that worked to uphold and protect dignity and safety in the workplace. I couldn't for the life of me think of a situation where I might have acted in a way that someone else would have deemed as 'bullying'. I was shocked and curious. This had come completely out of left field.

When I asked about the basis of the accusation, I was told that I could not be told the details as we were now following a formal grievance process. When I asked why there had not been any conversation with me about this matter before a formal charge, I was told that it was "because of the severity of the accusation". The HR person then advised me to seek legal support and representation. I did not act on his advice and chose to represent myself, as I suspected that the accusation was a way to deflect other issues.

What I had not realised about this organisation was that bullying accusations were assumed to be true. In our culture when someone is accused of an unsavoury crime it is often assumed to be true and their reputation is forever ruined. It's called 'trial by media', and I see it occurring very often in Australia and elsewhere. Similarly, I seemed to be being treated as guilty simply because of the accusation.

The hearing had a mediator, the woman who had accused me of bullying, and a senior union representative who was there in support of the accuser. During the preliminaries the reportedly catastrophic effect of the critical bullying incident was read out. This was the first time I'd been informed about the basis for the stress leave she'd been on. It was made clear that I was answerable to having caused this effect. The presumption, once again, seemed to be of my guilt.

The woman who had accused me of bullying was asked to describe what happened, what it was that had precipitated the bullying charge. With her head facing the table, sitting silently for some twenty-seconds, she finally said, "He's big!"

I couldn't help myself and said, "I'm big. That's it? You cannot accuse someone of bullying based on their physical attributes. That would be prejudice." Bear in mind that I am 200 centimetres tall, or six foot six. She on the other hand is a lot shorter. I was feeling irritated at being told I was a bully for being tall. The mediator asked me to refrain. The mediator told her that there needed to have been an actual event where my behaviour met the criteria for bullying. She was asked, "Was there an actual event?" to which she replied, "Yes." Again holding her gaze to the table, she said, and I kid you not, "He's big, and he's got a deep voice!"

It is true, I am tall, and yes, I do have a relatively deep voice. I was feeling a mixture of annoyance and confusion. Then, sternly pointing a finger towards me, she yelled, "And he agrees!" At this point, all feeling of anger evaporated, and I could feel for her obvious distress. My anger became empathy.

Later, still feeling for her distress, I very much wanted to fathom how being tall and having a deep voice could be perceived as 'bullying'. I knew that there had to be a way of making sense of it all. I stayed with the question of how someone could perceive my physical attributes as an aggressive and inappropriate expression of power. Then I had another 'eureka' moment. She was experiencing something in me as excessive and as compromising something important for her. I already knew that safety was important for her, but "what is she experiencing in me?" I wondered. "Ahh, bullying is the aggressive misuse of power." Remembering that friends have sometimes said that I have a powerful presence, and that as her manager there was already a power imbalance, I speculated that she perhaps perceived power in and assigned to me as excessive and therefore it made sense that she would judge me as a bully.

While my accuser was great at rapport, she certainly would not be described as a powerful woman. She also had concerns with a female member of the team that did inhabit a high level of personal power. It made sense to me that when a person with a very high level of energy of a certain quality interacts with someone with a very low level of the same energy, they would very easily perceive that difference as either a bad thing and excessive, or as a good thing and want it.

I could see that, as our gift is our default approach to our life, we would have an automatic response if ever we perceived that life was thwarted in some way. We naturally and automatically would apply even more of what is effortless, abundant and innate. We would naturally apply even more of our gift, perhaps even excessively so. That would very easily lead to others perceiving us as excessive, not helpful, and dysfunctional.

Appreciating innately

That was a key insight—what's innate in us is not always appreciated by others or even functionally expressed. It could just as easily be experienced as a good thing, or as a bad thing. It all depends on how the energetic differential of our gift is experienced.

We're not always expressing our gift in a way that is useful, beneficial, and functional, particularly from other people's perspective anyway.

Therefore, both favourable perceptions of your gift as well as unfavourable expressions of your gift are all expressions of and indicators for what your gift actually is. As such, your gift is revealed when your capability is most effortless and the availability of that quality is abundant.

This is shown in the following model. When things take much effort and you're utilising a quality that is scarce, it'll be exhausting. When you're using a quality that's effortless, and yet you're utilising what is scarce, it can be the experience of peaks of ease, though it cannot be easily sustained. When you're using a quality that takes effort together with abundant, it can seem that what you're doing is sustainable and yet it is tiring. However, when you're utilising a quality that is both most effortless and abundant, things are sustainably easy for you. It's your gift.

Abundant

Talents

Sustainable
Tiring

GIFT

Availability

Judgements

Effortful ← Capability → Effortless

Exhausting

Peaks
Easy

Scarce

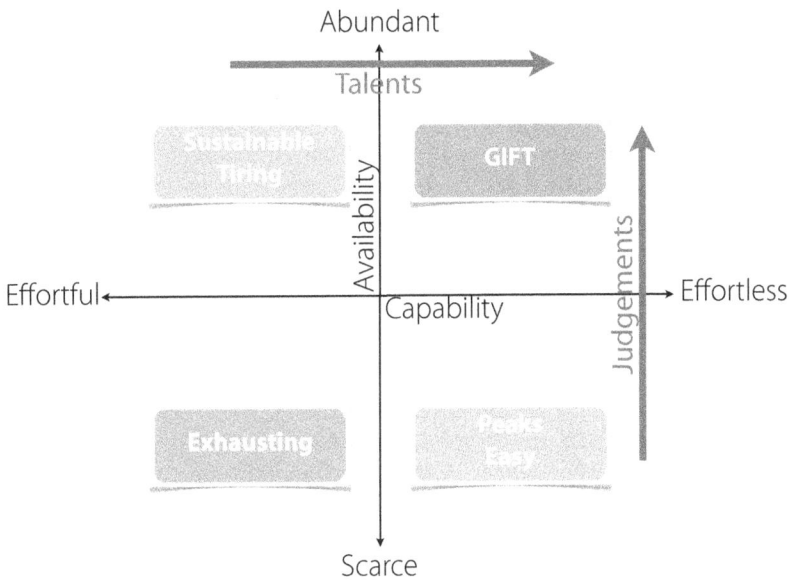

Our gift is abundant and effortless

When you were working to create your Value Stack, you gathered information about how you perceived your circumstance. The more information you gathered, the broader and more relevant your Value Stack. To reveal your gift you'll be using a similar approach. This time though, you'll be including the perceptions of others as additional clues. You'll collect information in two areas:

1. What you are aware and conscious of

2. What is outside of your current awareness and aspects that you are not conscious of

Energy has different forms. The amount of energy is simply its ability to do or enable things to happen. Heat, electricity, light, sound and movement are all different forms of energy. They can all cause things to happen. Electricity enables the television to work, the light to give off light. Light enables you to be able to see when it is dark.

Energy can potentially be released and harnessed from such forms as coal, natural gas, wood, diesel fuel, wind, and solar. These are forms of potential energy, because something has to happen for the energy to be converted and released. For example, a book sitting on a table has potential movement energy, which is what it will have if it is pushed off the side of the table.

In another example, water stored in a dam is a form of potential energy. The higher the water level, the more water pressure at the bottom of the dam. The amount of water pressure in pipes that come out from the bottom of the dam is much higher than in pipes that come from the top of the dam. It's the same thing when you go under water—at a certain depth your ears can sometimes 'feel the pressure'.

Think of your gift as an energy source that you have access to an abundance of. Others by comparison, who do not have the same gift, do not have access to the same amount of the energy that you do. It's as though yours is a dam that is deep and large. Theirs is a dam that is shallow and small. You can call this difference between the amount of energy between you and others as the 'energetic difference' or 'energetic differential' between you and others. Different people will experience this energetic difference is in different ways—some positively, others negatively.

To identify your gift, you will primarily be using the way people experience this energetic difference with you. There's a difference in levels of your gift quality between you and others that you interact with. There are several elements of extremes of perception involved that can help create a great deal of clarity. You'll look for feedback that indicates how that difference between you and others is perceived. Remember that feedback tells us much more about the person giving it than it does about anything else—in their feedback people are revealing what they see. As such you'll be looking to gather information that relates to the different aspects of the dynamic between yourself and others:

1. When others regard your gift as a bad thing or excessive— they'll tend to judge your character or your behaviour. A gift overused or otherwise perceived as excessive will tend to evoke character judgements. For example, when I was judged as being a bully.

2. When others regard your gift as a good thing and desirable— as they perceive the need, they'll tend to ask you for it. For example, I have a friend who is infectiously enthusiastic, and I will seek him out when I'd like to feel more enthusiastic about what I'm doing.

3. When friends regard your gift as a good thing and want to learn how to bring it into their lives—you'll tend to mentor them. A friend, Matt Church, who says that this is 'frientoring', introduced me to this term. For example, a good friend of mine is automatically and effortlessly supportive of people, and years ago I had him mentor me in the art of being supportive.

4. When you judge others as being deficient in a quality such that if they had more of it their lives would be better—many years ago I used to complain that, "If only people had more insight into their lives, they wouldn't have the problems they're facing..."

The gift of quality reaping

You'll gather information in five areas to help reveal your gift. Not all of them will be as applicable for you as other areas will be. I've observed that different people have an easier time identifying information from some areas more than others. In addition, like many others, you might appreciate how your gift shows up in many different ways through your life. The five areas are:

1. Others' character judgements of you
2. Others' requests for your help
3. Your mentoring of friends ('frientoring')
4. Your judging of others as deficient
5. Your concrete talents

1. Others' character judgements of you

Those judgements don't even need to be current. When people get angry with you or judge you, what do they judge you for? With people that you're comfortable asking, you can deliberately harvest their perceptions by asking, "When you think I'm excessive, what do you call how I'm behaving? You say that I'm being overly what?" List the judgements you uncover. Examples of some judgements might be such things as anal, pedantic, aggressive, detached, effusive, blunt, impulsive, perfectionist, compliant, reclusive and naive.

Ask yourself what quality must be there for someone to perceive you that way. What quality are you manifesting when that person perceives you that way? What quality, when perceived as excessive or dysfunctional, might show up that way? What is the positive quality or attribute that can show up that way?

Using a 'perfectionist' judgement as an example, say regarding each judgement: 'It's not that I'm a *perfectionist*, I'm just *particular*'. Take note of what you uncover. Examples and possible translations are shown in the following list.

Judgement	*Quality*
Dominant	Assertive
Disrespectful	Playful
Disruptive	Enthusiastic
Arrogant	Self-promoting
Pedantic	Precise
Aggressive	Assertive
Effusive	Expressive

Blunt	Direct
Impulsive	Excitable
Compliant	Considerate
Reclusive	Autonomous
Naïve	Non-judgemental
Serious	Focussed
Anal	Detailed
Emotionless	Objective
Controlled	Disciplined
Process-driven	Methodical
Scattered	Creative

2. Others' requests for your help

When people want access to what is abundant and effortless in you, they'll ask for it. They will often nominate the talent quality that they are looking for when they request your help. When others ask you for your help, what are they asking for? For example, they might be asking you for such things as enthusiasm, generosity, strength, passion, creativity, calm, wisdom, pathways, insight, new meaning, analysis, and perseverance.

Ask yourself what people ask you for. This is especially applicable when people nominate the talent quality they want. Ask yourself what quality of yours they are seeking to access. You can ask those who know you: 'If you were ever to ask me for help, what do you think I'd be good at or I am already good at helping you with?' Be careful to separate any values that are identified from the skill you use to produce it.

Examples and possible translations are shown in the following list.

Request	*Quality*
Finances	Analysis
Planning	Sequence
Action plan	Pathways
Understanding	Attention
Support	Empathy
Motivation	Enthusiasm
Alternatives	Creativity
Insight	Wisdom

3. Your mentoring of friends (frientoring)

When you're mentoring friends—frientoring—in particular ways, what are you mentoring them with? For example, it could be around such things as planning, getting things done, organising, sequencing, rapport, communication, and mood setting.

Ask yourself what you are mentoring people in, what do you help people learn? It does not matter if it is something you have formal skills in or not. What matters is that people are voluntarily learning from you, and you are helping them. Identify what you are helping people learn and then ask yourself what quality is showing up in you. What is that mentoring topic about? What quality are others receiving from you? You could ask those who know you: 'If you ever wanted to learn something I'm good at, what would you want to learn?' Be careful to separate any values that are identified from the skill you use to produce it. Examples and possible translations are shown in the following list.

Mentoring	*Quality*
Project planning	Sequencing
Speaking	Conviction
Communications	Clarity
Getting things done	Drive
Connecting	Rapport
Mood setting	Aesthetics
Facilitation	Insight

4. Your judging of others as deficient

Just as others can perceive your gift as excessive, you might judge others who lack your gift as being deficient. When you complain about and judge others as being deficient in a skill quality that would solve their problems, what do you complain about? What do you complain about when you say something like: 'If only they had more ..., their problems would be solved!' For example, you might complain that others have such things as a lack of insight, discipline, drive, sensitivity, directness, or direction.

When you complain that others are deficient in a certain skill, what do you complain about? When you complain: 'If they stopped being so ..., their problems would be solved and they'd get on in life!' that suggests the opposite of a quality that you may inhabit. When you complain: 'If only they were more skilled at being..., their problems would be solved!' that suggests the actual quality you may inhabit.

There are two ways we tend to focus our complaints:

- If only others *stopped being* ...
- If only others *were more skilled at...*

Go with whichever version works better for you. From there, identify what quality you are describing. Examples and possible translations are in the following list. Then ask whether it's true for you.

Stopped being...	Quality
Disorganised	Organisation
Disruptive	Support
Selfish	Consideration
Lazy	Discipline
Closed	Openness
Unmotivated	Drive
Blunt	Sensitivity

Were more...	Quality
Organised	Organisation
Supportive	Support
Considerate	Consideration
Disciplined	Discipline
Open	Openness
Driven	Drive
Sensitive	Sensitivity

5. Your concrete talents

What are your concrete talents, what are you good at? It could be in such things as planning, engagement, analysis, making things, creativity, communication, aesthetics, decorating, or event management.

Ask yourself what your concrete talents are? What are you good at? When you get employed, what abilities is your employer getting as part of that exchange? You could ask those who know you or work with you what they regard as the talents you just seem to be naturally good at. Examples are in the following list.

Talent	Quality
Project planning	Organisation
Working with people	Engagement
Making people comfortable	Rapport
Interpreting data	Analysis
Anticipating effects	Patterns
Making and fixing things	Dexterity
Environment setting	Arrangement

Decorating	Aesthetics
Getting things done	Achievement
Generating ideas	Creativity
Communication	Clarity
Business improvement	Sequencing

As true as self-evident can be

Remember the continuum between concrete and qualitative? Your concrete talents, what others observe about you and what you observe about others, are your observable aspects and are, well, concrete. They are at the concrete end of that continuum. The qualities that reveal these perceptions are closest to concrete because they were derived through perception of your concrete abilities.

You'll now follow essentially the same process you did to create your Value Stack. Where you used what's important for you for your Value Stack, for your Gift Stack you'll be using the qualities that you just identified.

What you're going to do now is build the base of your gift pyramid—your Gift Stack. You'll start with the qualities you just identified at the bottom of your pyramid, and go through the same process of 'What quality is created by those?' until you have a single word—your gift—at the top of your pyramid. In practice you can do this using paper and working with the qualities as a list, or use small post-it notes, which makes resorting your qualities a little easier. The following description is for working with the qualities as a list.

1. List

On a page, with one word per line, list all the qualities that you just identified. If the same quality shows up multiple times, just write it down once.

2. Sort

You'll now sort your list. Ask yourself: 'Which qualities seem or feel like they are similar and belong together?' Connect the qualities that, **to you**, are kind of the same. Don't be concerned about being 'right', just go with what seems right to you.

This is your Gift Stack, and it need only make sense to you. Besides, you can always change it. Most people I have worked with never change their groupings. Though they do update their list as their lives reveal new qualities.

Now reorder your list according to your self-selected groupings. An example of a grouped list of qualities follows.

Analysis
Considered
Evaluative
Flexible
Perceptive
Rapport
Openness
Inclusive
Light hearted
Peaceful
Conservative
Relaxed
Flexibility
Empathy
Attention
Organised
Outcome-focus
Action-orientation
Big picture
Perspective
Clarity

Example of 1st level of Gift Stack

3. Identify your second level

You'll now identify what each of your groups is about. You are going to identify a quality that describes and explains your group. The word you use might already be in your group, or it may be a new word. Your basic question here is: 'What's that group all about?'

Within your group of words, you might find a word that is a more abstract word than the others. For example, empathetic seems like a more abstract word than inclusive. Inclusiveness you can almost see, whereas empathy is an experience. The more abstract word is a candidate for describing the group of words. Remember that what maters is what makes sense for you. There are no universals here.

If none of them stand out in that way, or if that word does not work for you, then ask yourself, 'What quality do I have when I have all of those qualities together?' or 'What quality is created when all the qualities in that group exist?' Your answer is the word that describes that group of qualities.

The way you test whatever word you choose is: 'According to the way you experience and perceive things, can you have the higher quality without the lesser ones?' If the answer is no, then you have your word. If your answer is yes, then you need to find another word.

In the worked example, the participant organised their qualities as follows. They saw that within each of their groupings was a word that described or governed that cluster.

Analysis	
Considered	
Evaluative	Flexible
Flexible	
Perceptive	
Rapport	
Openness	
Inclusive	
Light hearted	
Peaceful	Rapport
Conservative	
Relaxed	
Flexibility	
Empathy	
Attention	
Organised	
Outcome-focus	Action-orientation
Action-orientation	
Big picture	
Perspective	Perspective
Clarity	

Example of 2nd level Gift Stack

4. Keep going until you have a single word

You keep following the process of the previous step until you have a single word at the top or most abstract end of your stack. That word describes and defines what all of those qualities are about.

In the example being used, the participant came to 'Collaboration' as their top word, as their gift. When he wrote that, he said, "Yeah, everything I do is collaboration." In having known him over a year, I couldn't have imagined a better word. His approach to everything is to bring people together in service of a common objective. He naturally succeeds in getting people to choose to participate, contribute, and work together. Guess how awesome he is as a manager and leader within his organisation when he utilises his gift well! When he is not at his best, he reports that he is accused of being too collaborative. When he is at his best, he has an amazing ability to create collaborative environments. His completed Gift Stack follows.

```
Analysis
Considered
Evaluative              Flexible
Flexible                                        ╲
Perceptive ·················                      ╲
Rapport                                           ╲
Openness                        ╲       Connect
Inclusive                        ╲     ╱        ╲
Light hearted                     ╲   ╱          ╲
Peaceful                           ╲ ╱            ╲
Conservative            Rapport ·                 ╲
Relaxed                                            ╲
Flexibility                                         Collaboration
Empathy                                            ╱
Attention ·················                       ╱
Organised                                        ╱
Outcome-focus    Action-orientation ·           ╱
Action-orientation ················    ╲        ╱
Big picture                             Progress
Perspective                            ╱
Perspective         Perspective ·     ╱
Clarity
```

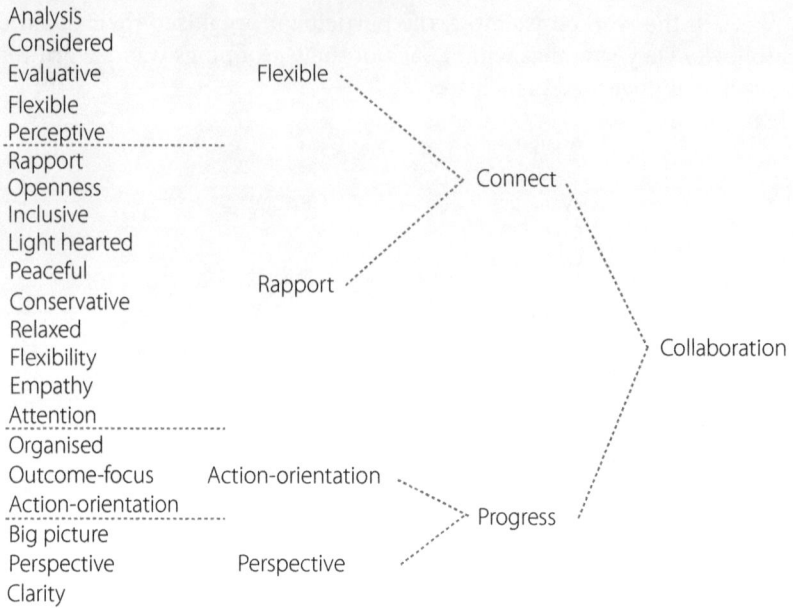

Example of completed Gift Stack

To give you an idea of just how unique to you your Gift Stack is, another person, who also happened to work as a senior manager, had a Gift Stack with many of the same and similar qualities. The way they organised and made sense of their Gift Stack was as different as the two people themselves.

His gift is 'Visionary', and he most certainly is. His approach to activity is that he creates a vision of what he wants and how he is to achieve it, and goes at it from there. His staff readily come on board with where he'd like them to focus their attention. Even he reports that when he is not at his best, he'll be accused of being too impractical and 'pie in the sky'. When he is at his best, he has an amazing ability to muster people around a common goal and purpose. His completed Gift Stack follows.

Focus
Discipline
Organisation   Drive
Drive
Direction
Consistency
Direct
─────────────
Honest   Honest
Transparent
─────────────   Integrity
Pattern recognition
Context   Context
Objective
─────────────   Visionary
Clarity
Confidence   Insight
Insight   Pathfinder
Knowledgeable
─────────────
Detailed
Methodical   Intelligent
Intelligent
Logical

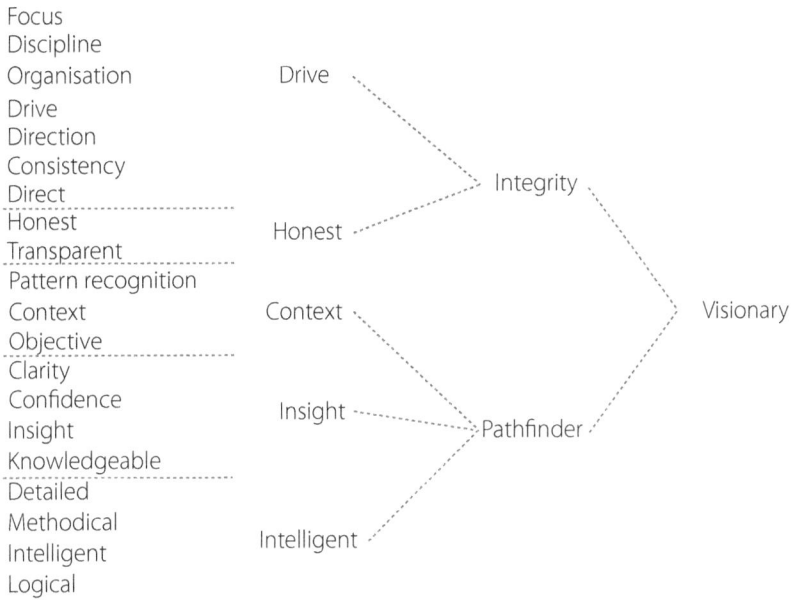

Example of completed Gift Stack

5. Check your gift stack is self-evident

As you did when you created your Value Stack, check for consistency. This means to review your Gift Stack and ask yourself:

1. Is it true for you that the more intangible and abstract qualities (the ones higher in your stack) require the more concrete qualities? This question ideally produces a 'yes'. The more abstract quality is dependent on the more concrete ones.

2. To your way of seeing things, can you have the more abstract quality without any one of the concrete ones? This ideally produces a 'no' or at least an 'it would be diminished'. Does that make sense to you? The more abstract quality is dependent on the more concrete ones.

3. Can you have the more concrete qualities without the more abstract one? This question ideally produces a 'yes'. The more concrete qualities are not dependent on the more abstract quality.

Life is most effortless when you are living through your gift.

Can I be of service?

Many find it useful to create their personal 'service' statement and 'life mission' statement. Just as you wrote out your message earlier, you can now add a few words in front of your message. Again, keep it succinct, and avoid the temptation to elaborate or explain.

Service statement

For your personal service statement, which describes what you 'do', put a few words in front of your message that describe what you are helping others to experience. Your statement can begin with 'I'. Here are some examples:

- I help people feel energetic through empowerment.
- I create engagement through respect.
- I enable actualised calling.
- I help people feel connected through inclusion.
- I help people feel cared for and be free.

Mission statement

Your mission statement is essentially: GIFT in service of MESSAGE. Your gift is how you achieve your message for others. Here are some examples:

- With vision I help people feel energetic through empowerment.
- With rapport I create engagement through respect.
- I illuminate actualised calling.
- With creativity I help people feel connected through inclusion.
- I lead people so they feel cared for and are free

Try this out for yourself and find a short, succinct phrase that resonates for you. It's important to keep your phrase succinct, almost short enough to be a t-shirt slogan or bumper sticker on your car.

Reminder

A short statement also makes for a simple reminder. We all occasionally forget who we are and why we're here—I think that's part of the inevitability of being human. I suggest you find a reminder that works for you.

For example, I wear a bracelet with the words, 'Illuminate actualised calling'. It also prompts great conversations when people ask about it.

Adam's experience

Adam did what many, if not most, of us do when we 'think about' our message and then rewrite it. When we first worked together, Adam came up with, 'Using insight to help people be clear and feel certain'. I then let him know his mind might 'play around' with the words in due course.

After a few days of thinking about it, he'd made it, 'To support others to be clear and feel certain, via the articulation of deep insight and the practice of skilful means'.

Asked to reconsider a simple-as-possible form, he changed it again and settled on, 'Supporting others to feel clear and confident using insight'.

Adam shared that though 'certain' arose at first, he later found that 'confident' resonated more strongly for him. For him 'confident' as a word 'feels the most right'. For Adam, both 'certain' and 'confident' are equally valid—just as being and love are equally valid. The test is simply whichever one resonates more strongly for you, literally which one has your heart lift more when you say it. I learned this test from Donald Epstein.

Each of the three versions that Adam created feels different for me. Notice for yourself whether each of Adam's versions seems or feels differently for you, and if so, how:

1. Using insight to help people be clear and feel certain.
2. To support others to be clear and feel certain, via the articulation of deep insight and the practice of skilful means.
3. Supporting others to feel clear and confident using insight.

After this process with Adam had finished, the two of us spoke about another perspective that was clear for him that's related to this example. Like many with a mindfulness practice, Adam was aware that there were 'healthy' and 'unhealthy' ways his mind could play around with the words. The resonant shift from using 'certain' to 'confident' is an example of a healthy shift, for the reason explained—it felt more right. Adam recognises that the second version was his thinking mind talking in unhealthy ways.

Similarly, it pays to be mindful that there may be unhelpful elements of our minds that play below our own level of consciousness and might creep into and persuade us to edit our message.

Keep it simple

The point is to keep it simple and not over-thinking it. I find it most effective for most people to keep their phrase to the words that showed up for them. If, as in Adam's case, you find replacement words that resonate more strongly for you, then use them.

Either way, you use what is effortless for you, your gift, to support the creation of your message. That's what you can do. That's how you'd go about doing what's important. In that way what you are here to create and the way you go about creating it are congruent. We will explore this topic in greater depth in the 'learn' stage.

Permission to self

You have now completed the 'identify' stage of the Stages of Actualisation. You did this by exploring your own life, the available information, and ways to interpret your experience. This next stage is the 'permit' stage of allowing for and accepting that you have a message—of giving yourself permission.

Stage	Focus	Be
Being	Be	Grateful
Actualise	Result	Activated
Transform	Method	Convinced
Learn	Discover	Curious
Permit	**Allow**	**Accepting**
Identify	Explore	Honest
Denied	Accept	Open

Permit stage of the Stages of Actualisation

Several years ago I was working with a group of people, helping them realise their calling. Every one of them had profound insights and, as we have covered already so far, realised their message and gift. This was when I thought that my message was 'Fulfilment through realised calling'. It was this situation specifically that helped me to refine and change my message.

A few weeks after the session where they realised their message, I touched base with them. Only a few of them had done anything with their insight. A few of them had taken tangible action. For most, their insight and revealed message, and the program, were now nothing more than a pleasant memory. This reveals far more about me than it does about them, but I was stunned. I'd felt satisfied a few weeks earlier with the program and their messages. All the participants were congruent with what they had come to. I simply could not comprehend those that had not acted. For a moment I perceived their 'action' as 'not good enough' and then felt guilty about how I had judged their behaviour. They were, as always, free to choose for themselves what action they take, if any.

I did not realise then that I had a particular assumption. I grew up with friends who whenever they decided to do or had deep insight about something, they'd immediately go headlong into doing it. If they didn't yet know how or they didn't yet have the skills, they'd know what their first action was—go get that knowledge, go learn how. They just did it, and kept at it. I took this approach for granted.

Curious, I asked this group of recent participants about their actions and how they came to them. Then out came their 'reasons' and I was suddenly presented with something important for them that I had taken for granted and completely failed to address. The ones that had not yet acted all felt some pain around not having done so, and I could see how I had contributed to their sense of pain. That I felt about an inch tall is an understatement. Mind you, being an inch tall is no mean feat for someone 78 inches tall!

What I'd done was a little like putting a blindfold on someone, taking them to a place far from home, spinning them around, pushing them over, and then giving them the instruction to find their way home. I realised I'd let lose a group of people who had one of four approaches to taking action. Since then I have created a general roadmap which will be covered through the remainder of this book. Even then, the same four patterns emerge.

1. One group, like the friends that I had grown up with, take their message by the horns and start taking action the moment they know their message. They start learning about their message, how to communicate it, and how to create it. They simply invent a starting point and get started. They give themselves permission. They don't mind if there is no path. They make one.

2. Another group are simply unsure about where and how to get started. They have the intent to act, though have not given themselves permission. They tend to get frustrated with not knowing where to start. They need and are looking for guidance about what actions to start taking. They want at least some advice about where to put their attention, and why. They want some form of general roadmap for their journey towards living a life they are called to. Without that guidance, they don't take concrete actions. They need to know the starting point. They have a condition for permission called 'a known roadmap'. They don't give themselves permission to take the path unless they know they are on an established path.

3. The third group experience active blocks to taking action. They have the desire to act, though do not yet have the intent to act. They tend to get frustrated with their inability to start or persist. They have beliefs and stories that run counter to any desire they may have for taking action. If they wait too long, the insight that they had gets shelved and so too does any chance of taking action. They need an alternative way of making meaning about things that gives them a better story, a story that supports them to act, rather than a story that they use to persuade themselves not to act. They need the ability to get to the starting point. These people seem stuck in a belief that they cannot or will not walk the path, even though there's a part of them that wants to.

4. The final group don't even have the desire to act. Revealing their message and giftedness is experienced as an activity they had that remains without action. They're happy to keep their insight an intellectual exercise. Some of them actively want to talk about and discuss the process they went through, thinking that talking about it is somehow the same as doing something about it. Talking about doing is not the same as actually doing. No amount of talking about the work that needs to be done around my house is going to get it done. These people don't even want to walk the path.

Waiting to reveal your source

In a very real way, our calling is our essence. It's the essence of who we are. To act on our calling ideally means to use our gift in service of our message, to put our essence to work and to make our essence visible.

Notice what happens for you when you start to consider acting on your 'message'. Many hesitate when the following sorts of things happen.

- **Some disbelief.** You're excited about your insights into your message and gifts and things are making a whole lot more sense. Somehow though those insights seem like they're someone else's, or otherwise do not seem real. Even though you know more of who you are, you still somehow feel restrained.

- **A desire to defer action.** Though deeply moved by your experience, life still goes on, and you feel the pressures of life bearing down on you. While what life is calling you to is important, those other pressures seem more immediate and urgent. Because they're more urgent, you decide to put off acting on your message until those urgent matters are dealt with.

- **Some doubt.** You'd love to get right on to create a life of meaning. However, it somehow seems so big an undertaking that you have a niggling uncertainty about whether it can be done. The need seems so large that you're unsure about what difference you could really make, if any.

- **An all-encompassing scope.** Certain about bringing yourself into the world more consciously, you feel daunted or burdened by a sense of the huge responsibility for changing the world.

- **Delegating to others.** You like the idea, prospect and possibility of helping others reorganise their life according to what organises yours. While you could imagine someone like Oprah Winfrey or Tony Robbins doing that, you can't see yourself doing it. It seems like it's really up to someone else.

- **An apparent values conflict.** You know that you're here to uplift others in your unique way, and when you imagine doing so in some way, you feel an inner conflict, like something's being compromised.

- **A uniqueness expectation.** You're enthusiastic about stepping up and showing the world who you are, yet seem a little concerned that you don't have a unique way of achieving that, as you expect that your contribution needs to be unique.

- **A forecast life change.** You're clear that you're here to step into what life is calling you to be, though the picture you have of what that looks like seems very different from the life you have now. You might even think that this means you'll need to change your job or even your career. There's a part of you that's concerned about changing your life that much.

- **Imagining others' thoughts.** You recognise and appreciate the way your life has been shaped. The mere thought of sharing that with others has you feeling like you'd be artificially puffing yourself up and being arrogant. You can't help but imagine that you'd experience disapproval and rejection from others.

- **A desire for getting it perfect.** You'd like to respond to what is most important, and because it is so important for you, you don't want to get it wrong, ever. If you were to get it wrong, you might even imagine that you'd be the cause of others experiencing the opposite of your message, the very thing that was most painful for you. Your noble desire to get it perfect has its companion concern of not wanting to get it wrong.

- **Some regret.** You'd like nothing more than to serve others in a way that you're most passionate about, though all you can see is what seems to be all of that lost time and those countless missed opportunities for having made a difference.

What's really going on though is that we don't always really know how to get to the action that matters. We don't always know how to work through what appears to be thwarting us. We don't necessarily know how to generate a motivation for action that's greater than what seems to be holding us back. We don't always know how to perceive and give meaning to our experience that serves us in the best way.

This is completely understandable. Moreover, it's not your fault. This happens to everyone, not just you. There's a common journey for people. Rightfully, we start out relying on other people's advice. In a very real sense we're told what to do by external authorities. When we endorse or sanction their advice and direction as the thing we choose to do, we generate a sense of motivation. This motivation is externally derived. Even when this externally derived motivation appears to work, there's another, hidden story. When we have endorsed the externally derived direction and turned it into our motivation, we have a motivation that is internally generated. We converted what was external into something internal. This natural process is demonstrated in the following model.

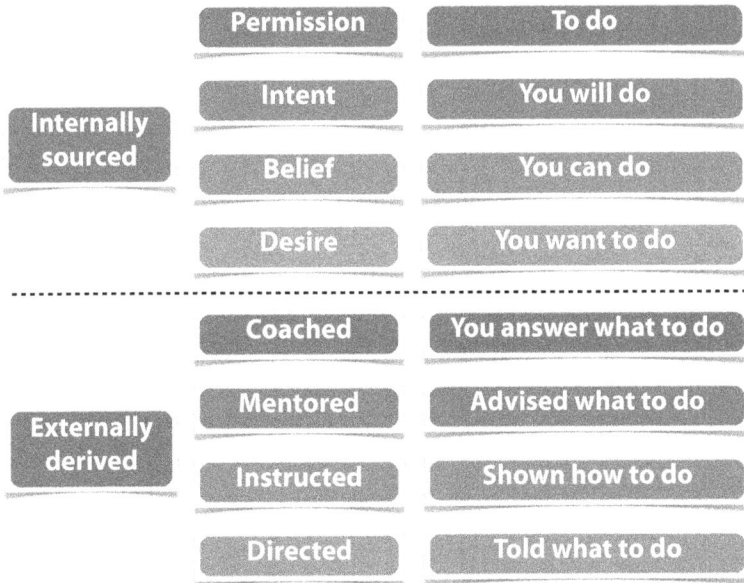

Internally sourced	Permission	To do
	Intent	You will do
	Belief	You can do
	Desire	You want to do

Externally derived	Coached	You answer what to do
	Mentored	Advised what to do
	Instructed	Shown how to do
	Directed	Told what to do

From sanctioning others to giving ourselves permission

When we don't know what to do or how to go about something, or feel unsure about our ability to do so, our motivation is usually to seek out guidance on what to do. Ideally we are told what to do by someone who already knows. It's the same as when we start a new job or go somewhere new. We usually don't know all the specifics of what we are meant to be doing, and what we really need is direction. We might have motivation, but until we know what we're meant to be doing, it's hard to get started. Knowing what to do releases our motivation in to action. When we agree with what we're doing, we endorse it, and it becomes the focus of our motivation.

Once we're told, our motivation tends to move to wanting to know how. We usually need to be given instruction and shown how to do something and even given the opportunity to do it ourselves as part of our learning. In the process of learning from our instruction, we would have endorsed what we were learning or else we would not have learned it. We sanctioned it as a way of doing something.

Once we are proficient and know how to do what we need to do in the situations we're in, we're likely to realise that we're in situations that are more complex than those to which we're accustomed. We're moved from being able to deal with the complicated, and now need to know how to adapt to the complex. For most, a spreadsheet and modern car are complicated; people and ecosystems are complex. We're not likely to be familiar with the nuances of these types of complex situations, and our motivation tends to be to get access to sound advice. In this case, it can be important to have mentors in the field in which we seek to become more capable. The right mentors offer sound advice based on their years of experience that we ourselves don't have yet. The moment we endorse their advice, our internal motivation is made active.

After receiving advice, we usually realise that we have a sense of knowing what we need to do and how to do it, but aren't always clear of what we know. Our motivation turns to finding our own answers and finding someone who can help us do that, a coach. A great coach is skilled in eliciting from us and clarifying the answers that we already have. Once we know we have the answer we seek, we have endorsed our own answer and get to work.

While all of these are important and beneficial, they are all initially based on external assistance. At the right time, all of those external forms are entirely right and appropriate. However, even when initially derived with external assistance, our motivation ultimately was internally sourced.

Regardless of what form that external source was, before we endorsed what actions to take and how to do it, we had some form of desire. A desire for what we want to do or for the result we want. We only take action because we first have the desire for doing so. Others can be very helpful for igniting that desire within us, but that desire is always within us. Before we get up and fetch a glass of water, we have a desire to satisfy our thirst or to remain hydrated. Very often, for actions that we are habituated to, our desire is outside of our awareness. We just know that we want a glass of water. However, without desire, no action can or will take place.

We can have all the desire in the world, but before there can be any form of action, we must have the belief that we can. For everyday activities and activities that we are habituated to, our belief is already 'yes, I can'. Our belief isn't even questioned. It's already outside of our awareness. The moment we say, 'I can't' we're right. If we ever said, 'I can't get a glass of water' which might happen, for example if you're very sick, then in that moment, it's not possible. The moment we believe that we can, action becomes possible. Possible, but not yet assured of happening.

Intention to take action is what comes next. Without the intention that we will take some form of action, we won't. Our intention might be outside of our awareness, particularly for actions that we are already able to do. Just before we act, we have the intention for doing so. Before we got up and fetched a glass of water, we had the intention to do so. Sometimes we know what our intention was once we've done it.

And yet, even with the strongest of intentions, some people still do not take action. They haven't yet given themselves permission to act. We learn at a very young age to ask permission to do anything. We ask permission from authority figures—first our parents, then teachers, then the person in charge.

For example, have you ever been in a job where you were in the habit of asking your boss for permission to do something, even though you've done it many times and are already good at doing it? Have you also had the experience of your manager's saying to you: 'You don't need to keep asking for permission. Just do it when you know it needs to be done'. In a sense you're being given blanket permission. Permission still came from outside of you.

We start seeking permission outside of ourselves. For many, eventually this becomes an internal process of still waiting for 'someone' to give us permission. We don't realise that we ourselves need to give permission. As long as we are waiting for or seeking permission, we don't yet have it. Without it, there's no action. It's easy to give permission to ourselves as a result of externally derived guidance. It's not always so easy to do it for ourselves. However, do it we must.

Those who have no hesitancy to act have no hesitancy giving themselves permission to act. It is as simple as giving yourself permission to do the best you can when you do it—permission to be the best you can be right now.

Are you prepared to give yourself permission, in some way, to help others experience your message for themselves?

The stories we tell

Many of the concerns I hear are outlined below. Truth is that I have told each of these stories to myself at one time or another.

'This means I'll need to change what I do in my life, career or job'

No, not at all. What you are creating in your life can stay exactly as it is now. Realising your message does not infer or assume that what you are doing in your life needs to change. If you choose, the way you do things in your life might change to include your message and utilise more of your gift. That is entirely up to you to choose. Guidance on how you can adjust how you do what you do is covered in the later sections of this book.

For example, a project manager realised that fostering trust with those she works with not only delivered better projects, it also helped her feel greater fulfilment through creating a way of working where others she worked with experienced higher levels of her message. In another example, a manager whose message is 'engagement through self-trust' trusts and shares with those with whom he interacts, why it is that he trusts them. His trust in others supports their ability to trust themselves, and increases engagement as well.

Knowing our message can also clarify and add depth and meaning to what we are already doing. For example, Lucy, a gifted artist, thought that relationship was most important for her, and she thought she should become a counsellor. When she discovered that her message was around 'freedom' she realised that in her art she was already depicting her message. Her art, as she describes it, depicts the source of freedom, which to her is within each of us. In her words, she depicts through her art what is for her a particularly intimate personal relationship. She went from being in doubt about whether her art was relevant to what's important for her, to being even more committed and enthusiastic about it.

Knowing our gift and message can help inform and clarify life, career and job choices. Knowing our gift and what matters, we can evaluate whether certain choices will utilise more or less of our gift and produce more or less of what matters.

For example, one person couldn't decide whether to work for a consultancy that advised other organisations on creating sustainable change, or to work for such an organisation creating sustainable change. His message is 'fullness through evolution', and he clearly saw that working for an organisation would give him greater scope to create that experience for others.

Our message can easily be the way we do things, our primary method for achieving what we create. For example, when I'm working in a 'leadership development' role, my method is all about authenticity and purpose being central for most effective leadership.

A CEO whose message is about empowerment rightfully seeks to empower his workforce. Doing so is fulfilling for him and helps produce extraordinary results.

Along with the way we do things, our message can also become the result we want to create. For example, in this book and the programs I run, I am explicitly focussed on purpose and life calling—it is the explicit result that many people are after. In another example, that CEO might at some point choose to become an authority on 'personal and organisational empowerment' and mentor other CEOs on the art and science of empowerment.

We don't have to change anything. Doing something is our choice. If we take this on though, as a result of our own choices, our life may change. As people participate in the creation of what their life is the answer to, many choose to change certain aspects of their lives. This is a self-evident choice—not something they felt they had to do.

'This means that I have to create something completely new'

Not at all. There are many examples of people who have not created anything new, and are great at doing what has been done before. We don't need to create a new form of carpentry to be a great carpenter. Smiling at people and complimenting them on what they do well are not new. We've been doing that for millennia. Katrina's a woman for whom smiles and compliments are her way of helping others experience within themselves her message of 'worthiness'. For her, that's enough. The way we create our message can simply be our way of doing what's been done before. It can be as simple as smiling at people.

Most new ideas trace their history to other ideas. Even when things are new, few innovations are truly unrelated to anything else. Most creation and progress is based on existing circumstance and truths, albeit a reorganisation or repackaging of accepted truths in new ways. New ideas are usually related to established ones. Vinyl records existed before compact disks. Music existed on physical disks before they became purely electronic. Music players existed before the iPod. Music was played on music players before they were played on phones. Telegraph existed before radio, and radio before wireless. The idea for the engine carburettor came from the old perfume bottles with the squeeze bulbs. New methods have their foundations on other methods.

Even a commonly quoted saying about iterative innovation is based on earlier versions. In the seventeenth century, the scientist Isaac Newton made the statement, "If I have seen further, it is by standing on the shoulders of giants." I used to think that this was a unique saying. Five centuries earlier in 1159, John of Salisbury records Bernard of Chartres saying, "We are like dwarfs on the shoulders of giants, so that we can see more than they, and things at a greater distance, not by virtue of any sharpness of sight on our part, or any physical distinction, but because we are carried high and raised up by their giant size." Millennia earlier, in Greek mythology, the blind giant Orion carried his servant Cedalion on his shoulders. So where exactly did Isaac Newton's statement originate? What Isaac Newton said was a new way of saying what had already been said.

As we'll learn later, familiarising ourselves with what is already known regarding our message is a great place to begin.

'This means that I'm responsible for changing the world'

No. Your way, your choice. We always start with one person. That changes their world. That changes the world.

You choose the number of people you interact with and reach. In its concrete form it could and often is something everyday, such as a parent, artist, a senior manager, an athlete, or teacher. Your purpose is always important and you have an important role and contribution to make, no matter what number of people you touch. You might already be in the perfect situation for the expression and creation of your purpose. For example, you remember the CEO whose purpose is 'empowerment'. To him, to be actively involved in the empowerment of his staff is completely fulfilling. We need to be responsible for what we can create; not for changing the world.

Having a message does not mean that we are obliged to be operating on a world scale like Nelson Mandela, or Mother Teresa. Some people automatically turn their range of responsibility into something they feel overwhelmed by. Smiling at someone, complimenting someone on what they do well, showing trust in someone, being friendly, listening when someone speaks, and asking someone for their wisdom, do not require the whole world to be changed. Either way, the person on the other end of those actions is influenced in some way. When we act, someone's world is changed.

Just make the range of your influence with people something that you're comfortable with. Our range might start with one other person. Indeed, your range will always start with one other person—you. After that, there's always the first person that experiences for themselves aspects of what our message is about. When we are feeling happy and interact with others, someone is always the first person to experience us that way and be affected in some way. That's a start of just one other person. Can you be okay with and do that?

'This will cause a values conflict'

In part, this is why we created our own Values Stack. At the bottom of our values stack it can seem that values might be in conflict. Assertion might appear to be in conflict with dignity. It can be a challenge to know which value is appropriate in a given situation. Imagine for a moment that for someone, assertion and dignity together create respect. Imagine that for them, to show respect is to assert your view in a way that maintains the dignity of others. When it's actually about respect for them, assertion and dignity are no longer in conflict because they have a value that unifies them. When we are living a value that is higher up our Value Stack, the values that are included in our higher value are no longer in conflict. This is because to live our higher value, we must be living the values that create it. In the above example, to live respect, the person will more than likely be living assertion and dignity. At the top of our Values Stack, there is no conflict at all, as all values are already being included.

Whenever there's a perception of a values conflict, just identify the higher value that includes them both. After that you can come up with a concrete way that that embodies and creates that higher value.

'I'll do something later, once other things are done…'

If true, then we've just prioritised other things as more important. This can be completely the appropriate thing to do. However, many of the suggestions that will be made later describe how we can incorporate aspects of what is most important for us into what we are already doing. We can start now. We do not have to wait. Our message and whatever else we are doing do not need to be separate aspects of our life. Indeed, one of the easiest and simplest ways of incorporating our message into our life is to include it into what we are already doing, as a way of living our life. Remember our CEO whose message is 'empowerment'—it's their perfect method for achieving their tangible results.

Conversely, 'I'll do it later' can also be a wonderful procrastination strategy. I can always put off something if I choose to make something else more important. This can be a bit like saying, 'I'll lie down until the thought passes…'

However, what's it going to be like for us to know that we're putting off what is already most important for us, especially when aspects of our message can be easily included with our life as it is now?

'I'm not good enough'

Good enough for what? Take a moment and ask yourself 'I'm not good enough to … (what)?' Identify what it is that you think you're not good enough for.

- Is level of impact what you're not currently good enough to achieve? It's too much to assume that others must experience your message totally and absolutely, that they must experience 100% of what your message says, especially in your first attempt. Some people expect perfection on their first attempt. It's as unrealistic an expectation as it would be to expect that you could win the 100 metre final in the

Olympics without any training. Progress is iterative. We all start at our own version of a low base. Without developing the skill borne of effort and adjustment, there's no steady improvement. Rather than say, 'I'm not good enough to win the Olympics!', say, 'I'm good enough to talk and walk'. Rather than measure success according to affect on others, which is outside of your complete control, are you good enough to act in a way you choose? Are you good enough to smile, compliment, or trust someone? Are you good enough to read a book on empowerment, self-esteem, or trust-building? Focus on what you can do—not what you can't. Focus on the action you can take—not what you expect other people's experience ought to be straight away.

- Are you assuming an overwhelmingly large number of people? Imagining getting out of bed tomorrow and, without any preparation, interacting with a thousand people so that they experience for themselves the qualities described through your message. That's just unrealistic if that number is overwhelming. Then you've just got too many people as part of your starting point. Can you start with one, or one at a time? Are you good enough for that? If you'd like to start with more than that, what number of people do you consider yourself good enough for? When I'm trying out something with people that's new for me, I usually start with one other person at a time, then I quickly move to working with small groups at a time, before I make it public.

- Are you assessing yourself against some absolute standard? Since when does anyone get out of bed and, without any effort, instantaneously become the best in the world at something? If you haven't done the work to become world-class and you're assessing your current ability according to someone else that is world-class, that's just unrealistic. Your ability changes week to week, day to day, hour by hour, moment by moment. In this moment you have a certain capability for doing something. The only realistic assessment of performance is to assess your performance according to what was possible when you did it.

- Are you comparing yourself to someone else? You cannot be someone else. Nor can you do what they do the way they do it. You will never be a satisfactory version of someone else—at best, you can be a mediocre version of them. What you are best at is being you. Only you can be the best at being you. No one that's ever lived or ever will live can be better at being you than you. While you might surpass someone else's ability at something, you'll never be able to be them. Olympic records always get surpassed. The new record holder isn't trying to be the previous record holder, though they may well have been inspired by them. These others that, 'you're not good enough to be'—how about you change that so that, 'they're good enough for you to be inspired by'.

'I'm too broken'

Why? Ask yourself and complete: 'I'm too broken because … (why)?' This is usually answered with variations of your own Great Wound. It's as if we say to ourselves: 'I'm broken because I'm wounded'.

I used to think that I had no right to help others with their purpose because finding my own sense of purpose had been so elusive for me. I now realise that this is precisely why I can and must help others.

However, while it may seem that you are wounded, you are not actually wounded. You had an experience or experiences that were painful at the time. You, as in the essence of '*you*', are not wounded. Nor are you broken. You never were. What if the very thing you think makes you broken is the potential source of your own fulfilment? What if it makes you perfect for what you're here for? Whatever the experience that was painful for you at the time, it can be experienced in one of three ways. Many thanks to Donald Epstein for helping me to deeply appreciate these three levels of awareness.

1. **There is only the wound.** The wound is as I perceive it. It defines me, who I am, and what I am capable of. I am broken because I am wounded. This wound was done to me. I am helpless to do anything about it. In other words, I am not responsible for my life. The wound is. I want to avoid that pain at all costs.

2. **The wound is a gift.** Something happened, it is true. However, the way I interpreted that event is not true—it was just my perception then. Living the story I created then and propagating it through the rest of my life does not serve me or those I care about. Moreover, whatever happened then is not happening now. I can choose to live my life through what I thought of as a wound, or I can accept that it has shaped my life in some way, and sensitised me to what I feel motivated to create. I choose to live and to move towards what it is that I do want in life. What was once painful is now transformed into something that I want to create. For that I consider what was once a wound is also a gift. I am not responsible that something happened, though I am responsible for the meaning I give it as I am responsible for my life.

3. **There are only gifts.** I am who I am—and who I am was shaped by the factors, pressures and experiences throughout my life. All of that was perfect preparation and shaping for who I need to be right now in life. I cannot be who I am without all of those experiences. Without all of that, I cannot be as perfectly ready for my next action as I am now. I have only gratitude for how my life has been shaped. I am what life has shaped me to be.

'I'm not worthy'

Worthy of what? Ask yourself and complete: 'I'm not worthy of ... (what) because ... (why)?' Usually this is a variation of 'I'm not worthy of my message'. 'Surely someone else is more worthy!', we might think to ourselves. 'Not worthy' is simply not a helpful story or way of thinking about things. You are worthy—you always have been. You are worthy of your message, because it's the message you have.

If you think that you're not worthy because you're not confident in your abilities and are not perfectly skilled in taking action, there are these things to consider:

1. Confidence has nothing to do with your circumstance or experience.

2. A perceived constraint can easily become your next action or goal. For example, if you have a rule for being confident such as, 'I can be confident when I've had experience', then go and get experience.

3. If your concern is that you're not perfectly skilled, then who is? If 'perfectly skilled' means no possible room for improvement, then there is no one on the planet that's perfectly skilled at anything. It's just another form of comparing ourselves to a mythical 'perfection' that does not exist. Developing skill takes time and practice. Just because you don't think you're at a particular skill level, just remember the word 'yet'. You're not at a particular skill level yet.

'I don't know enough'

This is another belief addressed through the word 'yet'. You don't know enough yet. I disagree with you though. You already know a great deal, though you might not be aware of what you know. This will be covered in more detail in the section 'Who'd know you knew?'.

In addition, whenever we say we 'can't' do something, there's usually a 'because' that comes after it. This is simply a way of seeing what appears to be an obstacle. It's as if we say, 'I can't because of this obstacle'.

Since that apparent obstacle is what is perceived as the current cause, it is the very thing that needs to be achieved next. The source of our 'can't' becomes our next interim goal.

For example, 'I can't buy a house because I don't have enough for a deposit', indicates two goals:

1. The end goal is to 'buy a house'
2. The interim goal is 'have enough for a deposit'

So if we ever think that we can't because we don't know enough, then we know what we need to do next, which is 'know enough'. Either way, how do you get to know about anything? If you don't yet know, go learn what you can.

'I couldn't possibly make a difference'

Does it make a difference when you make a difference for one person? When you think of the whole, it can easily seem that our efforts make no difference. However, can you make a difference with those that you meet? You already are making a difference. Do you have friends? If you do, then you have already made a difference in their lives in some way.

The best story to make a point here is an adaptation of 'The Star Thrower', part of a 16-page essay by Loren Eiseley (1907–1977), published in 1969 in The Unexpected Universe. The story has been widely modified, and a version I've had on my fridge for years follows (source unknown):

An old man had a daily habit of walking along the beach in the light of the early morning. One night, a storm had passed over and the next morning he saw a person off in the distance bending, moving and spinning like a dancer. Coming closer he saw a young woman. She was not dancing, but was reaching down to the sand, picking up a starfish and gently throwing it back into the ocean. She would then move on and do the same with another starfish. Along the beach, the old man saw, were thousands of starfish.

Approaching the woman, he asked, "Why are you throwing starfish into the ocean?"

"The sun's up, the tide's out, and if they stay on the sand they'll die."

"But there are miles of beach and starfish all along it. How can you possibly make a difference?"

Just as she had been doing all morning, she bent down, picked up a starfish and threw it into the sea, saying, "It made a difference for that one."

'The answer already exists'

Sure, an answer might already exist. 'An answer' is not 'the answer'. Someone has already figured out their answer to something. That's great, but what's your version? As Oscar Wilde says: "Be yourself; everyone else is already taken."

This objection has a focus on a solution that already exists out in the world, and it is assumed superior to anything inside of you that is not yet outside of you. Can anyone else do your smile better than you? If you look at people teaching success principles, very little of what they teach is new. What they do though, which is completely new, is that they do their version of success principles, and they do it their way.

It does not matter if someone else has done something similar. No-one else has done your version, your way. Only you can do your life your way.

Moreover, no answer, especially when it comes to we complex humans, is ever perfect. In archery, the bulls-eye is a large red dot. Hitting a bulls-eye does not mean that you've hit the exact centre of the red dot, only that you've hit the red dot. Even a bulls-eye is slightly off from exact centre. However, slightly off still wins the gold-medal.

That some answers are more effective and inclusive than others in some contexts does not mean that other answers are wrong or ineffective. That said, you've been sensitised to the absence or presence of a quality your whole life. You know already whether something aligns and resonates with your message quality or not. You already know what factors enhance or diminish your message qualities—just look at your Value Stack. You might not be aware that you already know.

'I've missed my chance'

A chance for what? A chance to make a difference in the lives of others? How can that be so? It might well be true that your past is not as you would like your future to be. Even if that's the case, your past is not necessarily your future unless you choose it to be. The decision of yesterday does not need to be the one you make today. At any time you can choose to create a different future for yourself. You always have the opportunity to make today the day you decide for a future that you choose.

Have you lost your chance to act today? If not, then you have not missed your chance to make a difference. As Anna Quindlen said, "The life you have led doesn't need to be the only life you have."

'I'll be disapproved of and rejected'

Maybe, maybe not. Can you be sure? So what? So approval and acceptance are important for you—you can still do what you do, even if that's different for you, and maintain and grow approval and acceptance. This is especially true if you decide that the approval and acceptance you can give to yourself is what really matters.

Fear is simply the anticipation of something important for us being compromised at some time in the future. Even if you are concerned about others' response to you, you can do a few things about it:

1. Include people important for you in your journey.
2. Test your future forecasting assumption with others. 'If I go and try x,y,z, what would you say?'
3. As Theodor Seuss Geisel (Dr. Seuss) says: "Those who mind don't matter and those who matter don't mind."

'I'll fail'

What people call failure is usually, 'not getting the result I want in the time I want'. Every action is slightly off. Every action slightly misses the mark. However, as a result of continuous corrections, the result is achieved.

Would you call the pilot of an international flight that lands on time at its destination, a failure? That plane spent at least 90% (some would say more than this) of its time slightly off course. However, because of continuous monitoring and adjustments, the plane arrives as it should. Interestingly, it is because of the awareness that the plane is slightly off course that enables the pilot to make an adjustment. Even when you pick up a glass of water, your hand makes slight course corrections on its way to the glass. Are you a failure for making corrections, or are you a success for picking up the glass? If you literally stopped whenever your hand made the first course correction on the way to the glass, you'd never reach it. As Robert H. Schuller said, "Failure doesn't mean you are a failure; it just means you haven't succeeded yet."

So in this regard, it does not matter what we intend to do. The guarantee is that we will always be slightly off on the way to achieving our intentions. We've just tried to measure success too early, and are turning the inevitable 'slightly off' into a personal judgement. It is because we can perceive that we are slightly off regarding achieving our intentions that enables us to adjust our actions, thereby making success more likely. As Denis Waitley said: "Failure is only a temporary change in direction to set you straight for your next success."

Sometimes we blame ourselves for not anticipating things that show up along the way. That'd be like saying that we ought to have known in advance what the lottery numbers were going to be. To judge ourselves on what was only knowable as a result of taking action is to make a mistake in perception. This is confusing foresight with hindsight—making the 'hindsight-foresight fallacy'. We can only act on what we know, and it is not possible to know everything. Every action produces more information and increases what we know. That new information further informs the next action, and so on. Sure, things may end up taking longer than we anticipated or forecast. This only means that there has been a delay in time compared to what we forecast. Nothing more.

Without trying, nothing happens. Not trying will guarantee that success never happens. There cannot be success without trying. Michael Jordan knows this. He said, "I can accept failure—everyone fails at something—but I can't accept not trying."

'I don't have any interest in doing anything about it'

That may be true. There are, however, a few things to consider.

- Give it a go and see what happens. Act on helping others to experience your message, act on making it the focus of your attention, and notice how you feel in response and how they respond. Ask yourself whether you'd be motivated to experience more of this. Give yourself permission to discover intrinsic motivation.

- What problem large enough is worthy of you? For example, the problem of how to best help others know what they are here for, was a problem big enough for me to give myself to. For many others, how to best help others experience what your life is the answer to, is a problem sufficiently big that's worthy of them to answer. Find your own version.

- What range or number of people is big enough? It might be that helping a few people or limiting yourself to the city you currently live in does not generate sufficient motivation. Invent a challenge big enough to be interesting, but not so big to be overwhelming. Keep increasing the number of people you're making a difference to in a positive way or increase the geographical reach, until you find something that you feel motivated about progressing towards and acting on.

Kate's experience

Kate is a very pragmatic, down-to-earth, and caring person. The second of five children, she's lived in Melbourne her whole life. She is currently studying full time for her Masters of Social Science, along with her existing Bachelor of Business, Graduate Diploma in Applied Finance and Investment, and Graduate Diploma in Financial Planning, all of which were completed while working full time. She loves spending time in her garden and relaxing with friends. Her experience is a great example of a significant shift regarding uncertainty and how a change in attitude towards 'failure' changed things significantly.

"I can't actually control the future", she says, "I can make choices, I can act, I can learn, I can do it all over again." She admits that she used to invest much time and energy trying to be certain of the result of any choice; that she used to seek to avoid uncertainty. For Kate, "Uncertainty was scary. Uncertainty," she explains, "was tied up with anxiety of not knowing what's going to happen. What others would regard as an exciting prospect I'd regard as a dangerous prospect. If you don't know what's going to happen then anything could happen. It might turn out in a way I didn't expect or don't like; so I shouldn't take the risk. It would seem like too much of a risk. I used to spend a lot of time in the early hours wondering about what bad things might happen."

"It has now flipped into a positive", she shares, "I don't know what's going to happen, but that's okay, as something good might happen, or if something unexpected happens, I can make a new decision and make a new path."

The change for Kate was realising that she always can choose her next action. "It's not possible to know exactly what's going to happen", Kate smiles, "so worrying about it is a waste of time. I can do something and see what happens." Far from being fatalistic, she's emphatic that, "This isn't just acting in a blind way; it is still acting with a purpose in mind, but being open to what I could not anticipate."

She shares that, "In the past, if the path or outcome was unknown, I'd regard it as unachievable. To not have options was to feel stuck and incapable. For something to be achievable, the outcome and path had to be known. This is impossible, as I have discovered."

In the middle of making a career change, she has realised that, "Clarity comes from doing. It opens up possibilities – volunteer work, an internship, working overseas, return to study, or something I haven't yet thought of, who knows. One of those things will fall into place, and when it does, I am ready for it."

Kate is far from being idle about her position of possibilities. "It's not just about waiting for something to fall into my lap," she explains, "as I know that I need to help make them happen."

For Kate, choice and capability go together. "Knowing I have the freedom to choose is really exciting. Any one of a number of exciting things might happen, but either way, something exciting will happen. With no choice I feel incapable. With choice I know that I am capable of responding to whatever happens."

Interestingly, her message is 'Be capable, have choices', and it is delightful to see her just living it.

Immunity to permission

One of the conditions for flow is to have a challenge that is neither causing anxiety nor boredom. There are two ways to reduce the experience of anxiety when presented with an anxiety-producing challenge.

One way is to focus externally and reduce the size of the external challenge. This is done by breaking down the overall challenge into smaller challenges such that the next challenge no longer produces anxiety.

Another way is to focus internally, reduce the anxiety being experienced, and increase our ability to be okay with the experience of anxiety. According to Robert Kegan and Lisa Laskow Lahey, authors of 'Immunity to Change', when we desire change we often inadvertently get in our own way and sabotage ourselves. We know we're getting in our own way when we are inexplicably unable to reach or act towards an important goal. According to Kegan and Lahey, our inability to act is not a failure of skill or willingness to pursue our goal, but our emotional immune system that seeks to protect us from anxiety.

All of us have a 'brilliant anxiety-management system' designed to reduce or remove anxiety, which shows up as an inability to progress towards a goal due to an assumption that we are not aware of. Our assumption is that if we were to take certain actions then that will cause us to experience bad things—we'll experience pain. Our proposed and conscious course of action threatens our unconscious assumption. So in spite of ourselves, we find ways to avoid the threat posed by possible action by not acting on it. Our anxiety managing system assumes that if we seek to create change we will experience pain.

Sometimes our desired change provokes anxiety in us as a way to protect us from experiencing a forecast, though usually unknown, painful result. We can seek change in our life and, unknown to us, another part of us sees that as likely to produce pain. When that happens, we have an inbuilt and counter-opposing force working against that proposed change. Our emotional immune system wants to immunise us from pain. The greater the perceived risk of pain, the stronger our immune system.

I've found that our greatest pain is our Great Wound. As such, the painful result that our anxiety management system most seeks to avoid is a repeat of our Great Wound. Our emotional immune system becomes stronger the more likely our unconscious perceives a repeat of our Great Wound.

For example, imagine your Great Wound is around 'being unworthy and feeling uncertain'. Imagine too that the way you interpreted it is unknown to you. Now imagine the prospect of taking action, or instigating some change in your life, that, unbeknown to you, is perceived to directly threaten a repeat of your Great Wound? How likely do you think you'd be to take action? Do you think that part of you would be motivated to ensure that there was no repeat of your Great Wound?

This part of us that is motivated to ensure that there's no repeat of the experience of our Great Wound is a force that runs counter to the action and change we seek. That motivation to avoid anxiety is our counter-opposing force.

The functioning of our emotional immune system is something that usually operates outside of our awareness. We are unconscious of it. We cannot change what we remain unaware of. Whenever we want to change things we are unaware of, the first thing to do is to become aware of it. Doing so returns us again to the position of choice. Whenever something shows up that has the effect of no action being taken, our emotional immune system is in operation and has been successful on countering any desire for action. Many of the above reasons and objections are simply other ways our emotional immune system shows up. The first task is to simply observe our immune system in operation, to observe our concern about a repeat of the experience of our Great Wound. Observe it in operation, check and test whether the assumptions being made are valid, and make a new choice.

The point is that there are two ways to respond to an anxiety-producing challenge:

- **External.** Csíkszentmihályi says that anxiety interrupts flow. So we need to reduce the external challenge that produces it.

- **Internal.** Kegan and Lahey say we can reduce the anxiety-producing pattern of our internal emotional immune system by observing it in operation and testing its validity.

I say, do both.

Power source

Many people believe that they don't have the power or authority to take action. They are usually referring to their belief that they do not have the formal authority that is given by whatever role, at work or in life, they have. While this may be true for some roles, we each have other sources of power. I like to think of power and authority having four aspects. This is adapted from the Integral Model developed by Ken Wilber. There is a dimension of power that ranges between personal and group. There is a reality that ranges between external and internal. This is shown in the following model.

When you have power that is both internal and personal, you have personal power, something inherent in you and your awareness. You could say that you are self-empowering. The external reality of that personal dimension is when you have personal power that is self-authorising. You authorise yourself; give yourself permission to act.

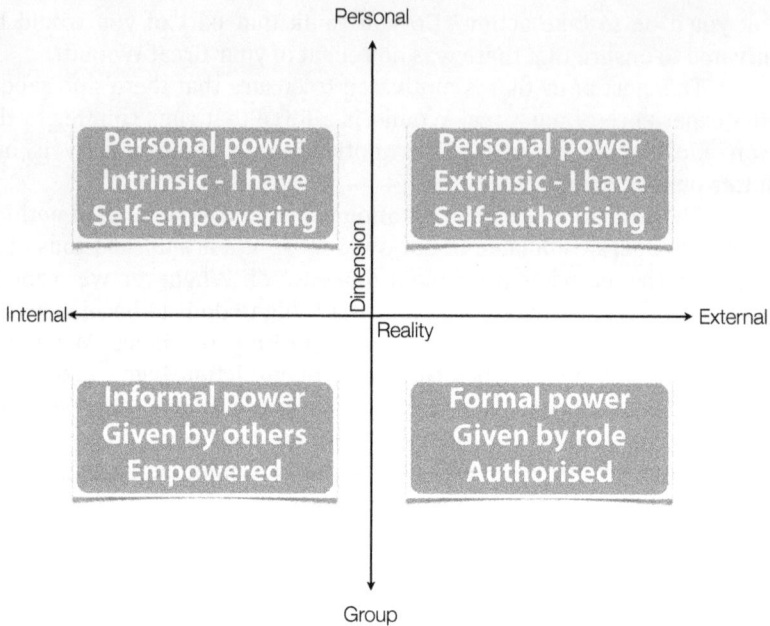

```
                        Personal
                          ↑
                          |
  ┌─────────────────┐     |     ┌─────────────────┐
  │ Personal power  │     |     │ Personal power  │
  │ Intrinsic - I have │  |     │ Extrinsic - I have │
  │ Self-empowering │     |     │ Self-authorising │
  └─────────────────┘  Dimension └─────────────────┘
                          |
Internal ←────────────────┼────────────────→ External
                       Reality
  ┌─────────────────┐     |     ┌─────────────────┐
  │ Informal power  │     |     │ Formal power    │
  │ Given by others │     |     │ Given by role   │
  │ Empowered       │     |     │ Authorised      │
  └─────────────────┘     |     └─────────────────┘
                          |
                          ↓
                        Group
```

Our four interrelated sources of power

When things are internal to a group of people, you have informal power that is attributed to you by others. In other words, you are empowered by others. The external version of that is when you have the power formally assigned by your role. You are authorised by your role to act.

We always have these four sources of power. That we have them to varying degrees, and that they can change over time, is a different story. The more of each of them, the more power we have overall. The less we have of one, the more important the other aspects.

When I was young, the local police wore uniforms. We gave the police a certain amount or power simply through their role. Whenever a police person asked, we'd respond. They were authorised by their role, and we gave them power accordingly and empowered them to enact their role. In a similar way, because they're politicians, we gave politicians a degree of power to act on behalf of society. We authorised and empowered the clergy on matters of ethics. We empowered our teachers to run the class in large part due to the role and the formal authority of their role. We'd often not speak with the senior manager for the same reasons.

These days, much has changed. I had a friend who was formerly a police officer and another who was a teacher, and they left in large part because their role no longer carries the same degree of power—people no longer empower them, no longer vest as much power to their role as they once did. Though still authorised, they are no longer empowered.

While being empowered and authorised are dependent on others, and can certainly serve you when you interact with others, you cannot control them, only influence them. Others decide whether to give you formal and informal power, and decide how much to give to you. Any formal power is vested in your role, usually due to the formal authority of the person who appointed you to the role. Others give any informal power to you, usually due to the way you interact with them.

What you do have control over is how self-empowered you decide you are, and how self-authorising you choose to be. Both of these are a decision you make. Only you can make that choice.

Can you give yourself permission to be self-empowered and self-authorised?

Perturbed

Perturbation is another way of describing the stories we tell ourselves that have the effect of creating inaction. As described in the introduction, experiences in your life are fuel for your transformation. With those experiences come emotions. Every emotion is an evolutionary impulse, fuel for action that can lead us towards becoming the person we're here to be. When the pressure of our experience is uncontained, it produces anxiety and we resist the transformation that the pressure is creating. One of the prime ways we resist is through the stories and beliefs that we tell ourselves—our emotional immune system. Life experience is seeking for us to take ourselves to a new way of being in the world, and those stories and beliefs have the effect that we don't take the action that would enable that transformation to occur.

Resistance to our own choices is just our own stuff. We can be aware of our own stuff or unaware of our own stuff. Either way, it's our own stuff. As a friend, Catherine Taylor, is fond of saying, "Who's going to win, you or your stuff?" You have a choice, in the end, about who's going to win: you and your life, or your stuff? Who's going to win—you or your emotional immune system?

Liberating permission

My favourite passage about giving myself permission is beautifully expressed by Marianne Williamson, from her book, 'A Return to Love'. This quote is often wrongly attributed to Nelson Mandela.

"Our deepest fear is not that we are inadequate. Our deepest fear is that we are powerful beyond measure. It is our light, not our darkness that most frightens us. We ask ourselves, who am I to be brilliant, gorgeous, talented, fabulous? Actually, who are you not to be? You are a child of God. Your playing small does not serve the world. There's nothing enlightened about shrinking so that other people won't feel insecure around you. We are all meant to shine, as children do. We were born to make manifest the glory of God that is within us. It's not just in some of us; it's in everyone. And as we let our own light shine, we unconsciously give other people permission to do the same. As we're liberated from our own fear, our presence automatically liberates others."

Change changes things

Your life is what you're here for. Eventually there is no avoiding the way your life has been shaped.

The difference between insight and wisdom is experience. It's the experience of applying the insight. The difference is action. It is important to start the process of moving from insight to wisdom.

It is important to act on the impulse of your message and what you are here for. Those who succeed in any endeavour get started. In some way. Any way.

Otherwise your insight will remain a pleasant memory. It'll sit on the shelf of pleasant memories of what could have been.

Some will get right to it, like a racehorse when the gate opens. Others might ask: 'Now what?' and need a little support. Either way, consider acting on creating your message, and even doing so, will evoke certain stories and beliefs for some people. Some call these obstacles. They're your immunity system at work.

Completely committed

When you apply what you know, life will begin to look different. Start to make small commitments with yourself. A true commitment has four parts for it to be complete:

1. **Who** (you)
2. Is doing **what**
3. By **when**
4. To what **standard**

As a simple example, I have made a commitment to give my partner a brief, 'present' hug when I get home. All four parts are here:

1. Who: me
2. What: hug with partner
3. When: upon arriving home
4. Standard: be present

My partner lets me know if I drop the standard I have committed to and am distracted. A fifth part is about how to make reminders.

You don't have to be perfectly skilled to start. You need to start to become perfectly skilled. Developing skill requires continuous practice of small steps. Like the plane that continually adjusts towards its goal, success is the result of continuous incremental corrections. Every action and subsequent correction is a choice. Every choice we make creates our own future.

With intent

There's a difference though between who you are now and the future you that has already created, in some way, more of what you are called to. It's called the difference between the current you and that future you. Who you are right now might decide on some concrete ways to be in service of others, and the future you has already done and created them. From the perspective of the future you, the current you hasn't yet, and the future you already has.

We grow through our experience. Perturbation describes how we can transform through the pressures we experience. That transforming can be in some small way, or a large way. It all depends on the pressures we experience. From the perspective of the transformed version of you, those pressures were necessary for the transforming process to occur. Indeed, you could not have become the transformed you without those pressures you successfully adapted to.

What's not so readily known about perturbation is that those pressures can be by accident or by design.

For many people, their experienced pressures are regarded as accidental—they happened. Those pressures happened, and we were shaped and transformed in some way. If we don't realise this is a transforming process that we are experiencing, there's a good chance we'll resist them and the transforming that's possible. That pressure remains until the transforming process is finished. That's transforming by accident.

Another option is transforming by design. That's when you intend to create an experience that's likely to produce transforming and perturbing pressures. You may or may not know that you'll grow and transform as a result. The point is that you can decide to create for yourself those transformative pressures.

To transform with intention is as simple as:

1. Deciding on a transformed or future version of you that is different in some way from who you are now.
2. Acting on it.

The easiest way to do that is to decide to create something that you currently regard as personally challenging. A challenge is simply the perception that something we're considering doing will produce internal pressures that we've not adapted to and overcome yet. If you had already adapted to them, you wouldn't consider it a challenge. It'd be easy. This is the basis behind the old saying of, "Do something every day that scares you." Doing something that scares you is a challenge. It's a challenge because you're experiencing internal pressure, and if it's a big challenge you aren't yet sure of your ability to rise above that pressure. We transform in some way as a result of doing so. Virtually all leadership development research points in part to the importance of significant challenges that the leader adapted to successfully.

Think of some significant challenges that you've had in your life. Though challenging, what did you get from those experiences? How were you shaped in a positive way? That's what perturbation is. That's perturbation at work.

You've transformed when you've achieved something that you currently regard as challenging. The current pressures of that challenge are shaping you into the future version of you that has already achieved that challenge.

The challenge you choose will present you with experiences and pressures that can be the fuel for your own transformation. Your future will be largely the same as your current situation when your decision is not a challenge and is within your current abilities. Where you decide for a significant challenge, the future you might well be different.

If your challenge is successfully navigated, the size of the challenge is a good indicator of the transforming effect that the challenge will have on you. The bigger the gap, the more you need to grow to surmount it. The bigger the challenge, the more the future you is different from who you are now. While the essential you is changeless, how you show up in life changes.

The transformed version of you required those shaping pressures. In the same way, when you decide on a challenge, the future version of you will require you to have become the person capable of having made it happen. In that way, the challenge has been surmounted, and the pressures of having done so have been integrated and you've transformed in some way.

While your living a life that's more fulfilling requires you to act, you choose the concrete form of your action. You decide whether what you choose is a challenge for you or not. If your choice of a concrete form of what your life is the answer to, is a challenge for you, your own life will ask you to become the person capable of having made it happen. Once you've achieved your challenge, your challenge is behind you, and your chosen future is your past.

The version of you—future you—that has created that contribution which you've chosen that you're here to make, is a different version of you from the one that seeks to create it. Between the two is the challenge you set for yourself. To create that contribution you choose will require that you become that version of you that has created it.

Knowing this can help you to deal with the inevitable obstacles that show up along the way of meeting the challenge. You may experience what you think are obstacles, but they are only 'obstacles' to the version of you that has not yet figured out how to surmount them. Once on the other side of that perceived obstacle, it becomes just something else that had to be dealt with along the way towards the successful completion of your intention. Your obstacle is simply a small challenge that's part of your bigger challenge. That obstacle is simply another part of that transforming pressure. Challenges within challenges, within challenges. The obstacle is a 'blip' to the version of you that already knows how to deal with it. The future version of you knows that the whole challenge and that obstacle were necessary. So in a way, that obstacle was simply there to help you become that future version of you that your future requires. In the process of surmounting that obstacle, you grew, you changed.

That process of becoming that future you, that process of being transformed though the pressures you experience, is 'change'. The interesting thing about change, is that, 'change changes things'. That's another one of my tautologies. As you change, you show up differently in life. As you show up differently, others may experience that as pressure. As others experience new pressure, their lives have presented them with fuel to transform. They're undergoing perturbation.

Along for the journey

Living your life as called and growing through the challenges you create for yourself may introduce changes to some of your priorities, as to where you put your attention and to your relationships. As you change, your environment will be influenced to change. Some will roll with it. Some may experience changes in you as something that's challenging for them to adapt to. If it's perceived as too much of a challenge, it's seen as uncontained and some may even resist. However, you can reduce the pressures that you are experiencing by removing the perceived sources of those pressures.

If I have a vested interest in not changing, in not transforming in some way, in not growing somehow, I'll resist changes in my environment. If you're in my life and you start changing in a way that I experience as pressure, I might have a vested interest in your remaining the same to avoid the pressures I'm experiencing. I might resist your changing.

Change is effortless and instantaneous, though working through the perceived barriers to change takes effort and time. Change requires that you show-up differently. Can you be okay with others possibly feeling uncomfortable around you as you begin to show up differently and fly higher? Are you prepared to be seen for who you are? Some people may seem to be invested in your not changing. It's important to have an open and honest conversation with those close to you about change so you can fly together. More than likely they're concerned about losing the person they care about or about undergoing the changes that your changing evokes. Love them regardless.

How are you going to remind yourself of your calling and your actions? How will you support yourself? What can you do? What will you do? How will you support yourself to give yourself permission?

Bring those you care about along with you on the journey. You can support each other and help contain the transforming pressures you're experiencing and have it successfully become fuel for your own growth.

Learning about your calling

You have now completed the 'permit' stage of the Stages of Actualisation. Giving yourself permission was the decision you made that moved realisation towards action. You did this by allowing your experience and accepting yourself. Next is the 'learn' stage. In the process of learning about, to mastery of, a given skill or topic, the focus is on discovering new things by being curious about it.

Stage	Focus	Be
Being	Be	Grateful
Actualise	Result	Activated
Transform	Method	Convinced
Learn	Discover	Curious
Permit	Allow	Accepting
Identify	Explore	Honest
Denied	Accept	Open

Learn stage of the Stages of Actualisation

Shu who?

If you have participated in learning, then you're more than likely familiar with at least a few of these types of situations and experiences:

- You'd like to learn about a particular topic or develop a new skill, but seem constrained in your ability to participate in your own learning.
- Whenever you think about learning you remember how tough it was during your school days being forced to participate in subjects you just didn't get, and seem to never find the motivation you need.
- You'd like to learn and grow, yet seem unsure about where best to put your time, energy and attention.

- You get well into a topic that at first you thought was interesting, yet eventually and frustratingly your interest drops over time until it seems to stop altogether.

- You attempt to learn certain topics or skills, and it just seems so tough and hard that you give up in frustration.

- You've already learned a topic or skill and are motivated to further develop, yet the next step seems somewhat elusive, and you're unsure about how to take it.

- You've learned a lot of theory about a topic, and you've found it useful, yet feel restless and want to get into action and apply what you have learned.

- You've participated in learning yet seem somehow struck by its lack of relevance for you, and it seems hard for you to keep engaged.

- You seem to be learning about things in general and find it hard to know how to directly apply what you have learned into your life.

What's really going on though is that we don't always appreciate the evolution of knowing about and developing expertise and mastery of a topic or skill area. As we know about any subject or develop a skill, including with our message, what we know and how well we can perform evolves through identifiable stages.

About 15 years ago I spent several months in Tokyo, Japan. I was working with IBM at the time and was brought there as a subject matter expert and was there to increase the skill of people there. I couldn't quite understand why the people I was working with would, the way I saw it, take what I said at face value. They'd just receive and take as true what I had to share. One of the people I'd become friends with was different though. She'd receive what I'd share, do it, then immediately apply what she'd learned to another situation. Confused by this, I asked her to help me understand what was going on. She told me about Shuhari. She told me that most of the people I was working with were Shu, learning the basics of what I was sharing. She was Ha, already knew about what I was teaching and was interested in innovative applications. Because I'd come from overseas, I was assumed to be Ri, someone already fully skilled in my topic and free of the constraints of what I was sharing. I was impressed with the elegance of that way of thinking. For example, I could see my own early years as an engineer in the aerospace and defence industry had followed the same trajectory.

The journey from learning to optimal performance is shu-ha-ri. It roughly translates to learn-detach-transcend. It comes from Aikido and is a way of thinking about learning and developing skill in any area. It illustrates the three levels of learning we go through for a given skill or area of knowledge.

What is assumed though is that there is already a desire to learn. It's assumed that motivation is already there to begin with. Placing desire first, it becomes desire-learn-detach-transcend, as shown in the following model.

Transcend	Learn thru unhindered creativity
Detach	Flexible innovation of learning
Learn	Learn and practice the basics
Desire	Motivation to learn topic or skill

Stages of mastery

Without the desire to do something, nothing happens. Your desire is your motivation. It's your 'why'. Along the way towards whatever you desire your motivation might start to drop, and when it does you'll meet what many people call obstacles. To persist and follow things through, you need motivation big enough to keep you going, though not so big that it causes a level of anxiety that's demotivating. You need a big enough 'why'. Without a big enough 'why' you will simply not have enough motivation. Without that, it can be difficult to initiate action, a chore to persist with action, and a challenge to complete what you started. The more passionate you are about your 'why' the more likely it will inspire and motivate you.

What if you just made your 'why' the very thing that you are already most passionate about—your message? How motivating is it to fulfil your deepest inner drive, your message, and to do it in a way that's most effortless and effective? What if you made your 'why' your message and the reach of people who will experience it. From the front of my fridge, my 'why' announces itself to me many times a day.

Once we have sufficient motivation, comes the learning. In learning anything new, we need to learn and practise the basics. It's all about the learning. We learn about and follow the established skill or knowledge area, the form, as it is given. At first, we don't question, we just learn and do as the form is taught. We concentrate on learning the applicable principles and information. We practise the way of applying the methods as given. In martial arts, this is the role of repetition. It is repetition that enables us to take what is at first taught externally, and internalise that knowledge and skill. Following the form without modification lays a solid foundation. Once it has been internalised, the foundation is solid, and learning has been achieved.

Once learned, once the foundations are solid, we can start to branch out. Rather than just following the prescribed practices, the reasons for each method and principle are questioned. We hold the original learning less tightly and start to detach from it. The underlying theories and principles behind the knowledge and techniques become known. Information from other sources is integrated. The original rules or staying true to the form are now seen as guides, and real-world exceptions require variations of the form. This is a flexible application and innovation of the original learning. Starting case by case, the rules are eventually seen from both sides—useful and limiting. New rules might even need to be created. Once customisation has become the new norm, the stage of detachment has been achieved.

When detached from the original form of learning, we can reach a level of departing from the form altogether where we're unhindered in our creative adaptation of our skill and knowledge. We transcend and leave behind the original form of learning. We're no longer learning from others, but from our own practice and application. We adapt what we've learned and create our own approaches to circumstances. At a certain time, the rules are left behind in that they are no longer thought about being applied or not applied. The needs of the circumstance determine the response. We think originally and try out innovations in real-world situations. We might even create our own methodology that's more effective in meeting needs. This new methodology becomes the new platform for other people's learning. This new platform, with its knowledge, skills, methods and rules, is then shared or taught to those that seek to learn the new form.

Sensitised sensitivities

You'll never know you know unless you give yourself permission to know. When people realise their message and have given themselves permission to have their message and to act on it, their consideration moves to what they know about their message.

This is especially the case when people launch headlong into seeking to create their message and bypass the learning stage. I've noticed that the following sorts of concerns get shared about levels of knowing about one's message:

- **Don't know.** You've realised your message and think that you don't know anything about it. You might even have a sense of disbelief about your message and the possibility that you already know a lot about it. You sit down to write down what you know about your message and nothing seems to happen.

- **Already known.** You're excited about your message and the possibility that you might have something unique to offer. You want to take action of some sort. However, it seems that everything about your message is already known by others, and that it's hard to find how you could add value along with what's already known. That can seem quite disheartening.

- **Not unique.** You know a lot about your message and you have a way of interpreting and explaining your topic that's new. However, you can't seem to move beyond the feeling that you know a lot about what others know, and feel a sense of dissatisfaction that you've not yet produced what you uniquely know. Others may even see you as an authority on what others have created.

- **Insufficient.** You know a lot about your message and what others have created in relationship to it, yet when you consider utilising that pool of knowledge, you only seem able to be critical of whatever others have had to say about it. It doesn't matter what someone else has to say about it, they're either wrong or have missed the mark.

What's really going on though is that we don't appreciate the evolution of knowing about a topic. What we know about any subject, including our message, evolves through identifiable stages.

Evolution of what you know about your message

Adapting 'shuhari' in the sense of it being about what you know, is shown in the following model. All of these stages are important and useful. If you want to continue to higher stages, then the pathway is through, and includes, the previous stages.

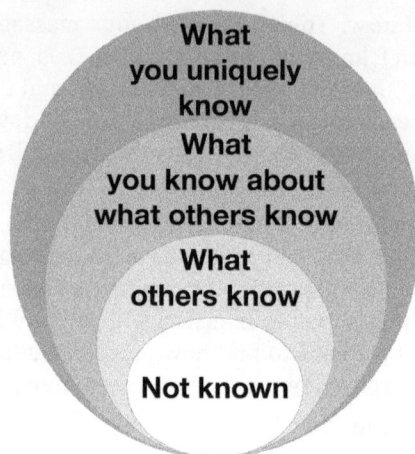

Evolution of what you know

At first we don't consciously know anything about our message. Some even use their perception that they don't consciously know as justification for not going any further.

If you want to know and learn about your message, a good place to start is with what others know. This is the next stage that has a focus on what others know. At this stage you're basically a student of your message. For example, Katrina, a high school teacher whose message is about 'worthiness and feeling secure' is motivated to learn about the current pool of understanding about self-esteem and confidence. All new knowledge, understanding, and knowing about any topic, including your message, always includes what others have known about it. Evolution of any topic includes what has come before. To do that though, you need to know some of what is currently known. This is your foundation and the bridge to what you know that others don't.

You're not just a student of what others know and to limit your learning to that. That's one purpose. You're also learning about what others know to help you realise that you know things about what others know. This is the next stage of knowing what you know about what others know. This is the stage of being able to add something to a topic based on what someone else had produced and had to say about it. To do this requires that you know what others have to say and do about your message.

Eventually you might realise that you know things that are just unique about your message. Its aspects, ways of thinking, ways of approaching, ways of creating your message that no-one else has thought about. This is the next stage. It's what you uniquely know. It's your unique contribution to the topic of your message. For example, Katrina, who by account of her students, is great at creating engagement in her classroom.

Her approach to engagement is completely unique. If she managed, in a sense, to reverse engineer and identify how she was doing that, she'd realise her unique contribution to 'creating engagement in the classroom', and more than likely to the general topic of 'creating engagement'. The truth for her, though, is that she's creating 'Be worthy and feel secure'. The consequence of her doing that is phenomenal engagement.

Fine-tuned sensitivity

Can you see in the pitch black using only your natural eyes? No—though you can see where there is light. What we see with our eyes is within a small portion of the electromagnetic spectrum called 'visible light'. The light bulbs you have at home produce visible light. That's why you can see at night when they are on. We cannot see in the dark.

Infrared and ultraviolet are outside of our normal visual range. Some animals can see using the infrared or ultraviolet part of the spectrum. Some birds, reptiles, and insects such as bees, can see near-ultraviolet light and use that ability for detecting food, mating, and navigation. For example, reindeer rely on ultraviolet light to spot some of their food. The familiar ultraviolet insect traps attract small flying insects. At night, snakes can sense the infrared emitted by other animals.

However, there is finely tuned equipment that enables people to see in the dark. They are called night-vision goggles that seem to show up in most spy movies these days. Even though we would normally consider something pitch black, there are still invisible portions of the electromagnetic spectrum that are available. We just don't normally see them because we do not have the equipment for doing so. Night-vision goggles use some of these normally invisible portions of the electromagnetic spectrum and convert them to a visible form, enabling someone wearing them to 'see' in the dark.

With the right equipment, you can see something others cannot. Someone with that finely developed equipment can see something that is not visible to people who do not.

If you'd spent 150,000 hours developing sensitivity to something, do you think you'd be good at detecting it? Do you think you'd be good at detecting its nuances? How quick do you think your equipment would be at detecting the presence or absence of whatever it was? I think your equipment would be more finely developed than anyone else's. Your ability to express and share that is another matter.

Your sensitivity training

K. Anders Ericsson was the Conradi Eminent Scholar of Psychology at Florida State University, in Tallahassee, in July 2007, when he published research in Harvard Business Review, titled 'The Making of an Expert'.

Correlating excellence with hours of practice, in a study of three groups of students at the Berlin Academy of Music, he discovered the elite group of students had all put in approximately 10,000 hours of practice. It seems that Anders Ericsson is the person who developed the 10,000 hour rule.

He researched his finding in other areas of expertise, and found that it proved valid in all of them. Other researchers, applying his finding to other areas of expertise have found the rule to prove true. Those who have achieved excellence by training for 10,000 hours include musicians, scholars, athletes, trainers, artisans, chess players, and business people.

A common belief is that athletes became Olympic and world champions because of their innate talent alone. The 10,000 hour research shows that success and mastery that reaches elite levels of performance is almost totally a function of 'deliberate practice'. Talent is by itself potential. Potential unused remains potential. To achieve elite performance requires working and improving that talent over 10,000 hours of deliberate practice.

Now guess what? You already have finely tuned equipment. You most certainly can already see what others without your sensitivity cannot. If you're an adult, you have more than likely spent 10,000 hours many times over finely tuning your equipment and sensitivity. It's your message.

Your message is not just a perspective you have on the world; it's the only perspective on the world. As said discussed earlier, the way your life has been shaped is the way you perceive your life. You've spent your life perceiving the presence or absence of your message qualities. If you're in your 30s, then you could say that you've spent 150,000 plus hours experiencing the world through your lens, sensitised to the absence or presence of what's most important for you. While this was not 150,000 hours of deliberate practice, much of this was time developing and fine-tuning your sensitivity to the qualities of your message. More than likely, you just didn't know that you were developing finely tuned sensitivity to it.

If 10,000 hours is elite, then what's 150,000 hours? With that amount of development fine-tuning your sensitivity to your message qualities, you'd be far better than most at detecting its presence or absence. Moreover, you'd detect subtleties and fine nuances that others simply would not see. They just don't have the equipment for your message. You do. They have the equipment for their message. Through sensitivity to their absence, you know what qualities are necessary for your message, you know when those qualities are present in a given circumstance, and you know the extent to which they are present. You know what, when and how much they are absent. If you know the extent to which something is absent, albeit largely unconsciously, you'll also know the extent to which they are present.

You could say that you have unconscious mastery many times over regarding the presence or absence of your message. You can't not already know a great deal about what's most important for you. It is inconceivable to me that you could spend that amount of time and not know anything. Not knowing you know is different from not knowing.

My view is that, as a result of your sensitivity to your message, who better to know the strengths and limitations of current knowledge on your topic? Who better to know what resonates with your message, or not? Your message is your genius. A genius for expertise in your message —knowing what works and what will not. You already know a lot about it. If you want to follow this through, then you can share your genius with others.

Who'd know you knew

Considering the process you used to create your Value Stack and Message, you already know:

1. The behaviours that compromise what's important at the concrete end of your Value Stack. You used them to reveal your perceptions that you used to create your Value Stack.

2. When you take the opposite of those behaviours, you have a set of behaviours that creates what's important at the concrete end of your Value Stack. This is a good place to start for how to create what's important. You have at least your current version of what it takes.

3. You know the qualities that must be present for the qualities at the top of your Value Stack to be created. As such you know your formula or recipe for creating or destroying it.

4. You already know a lot about how to communicate your message. Your values stack extends from concrete to abstract. Think of communication like being on an elevator that extends from the concrete ground floor all the way to the abstract top floor. As such, you can communicate with people who want the ground floor, concrete version, and those who want the top floor, abstract version. When you have the felt experience of your message, what does that felt experience create? When you have the perception of your message, what does that create, what do you have? If you organise your answers from concrete to abstract, then you have the makings of your ability to communicate what that all means to people, from ground floor to top floor.

Matt's experience

As an example of the last point above, Matt's message is 'Energetic through empowerment'. For Matt, 'empowerment' is described by his Value Stack, and he is able to communicate what he means all the way through to specific behaviours and his front-line values. He wanted to be more effective about communicating his meaning of 'energetic' with his staff.

I asked him, "What are you when you're energetic? What words come to mind?" He immediately replied with the following: responsive, engaging, thoughtful, creative, happy, productive, motivated, compassionate, and helpful.

I then asked him to order those words from the most concrete to the most qualitative. He then produced the following order.

Qualitative

Energetic

Compassionate

Thoughtful   Engaging

Responsive

Motivated

Creative   Happy

Productive   Helpful

Concrete

Example of creating a communication stack that started with 'energetic'

Some people have a concrete preference, and others a more abstract preference. For Matt, his ordering of words from concrete to abstract established his ability to communicate what 'energetic' means for people with different preferences. For example, he can on the one hand say, "energetic means to be productive and helpful" and on the other that, "it means to be compassionate."

I was grateful to learn from someone who knows a great deal about what it means to be energetic. He'd helped me appreciate 'energetic' in a new and richer way.

Knowing more

For many, just knowing and applying in their own way is enough. I know people who are brilliant in using other people's material for helping others in particular ways. Their way of being in service of others is best through using what others know and have created. They are brilliant with application. For others, using only what others have created is not enough. If you want to be unique in your message topic area, just knowing about what others know is not enough.

This is more fully highlighted in the following model. Any of these ways of knowing your message topic can be entirely right and appropriate for you when it's true for your way of doing things. My thanks to Matt Church for helping to clarify my thinking on this.

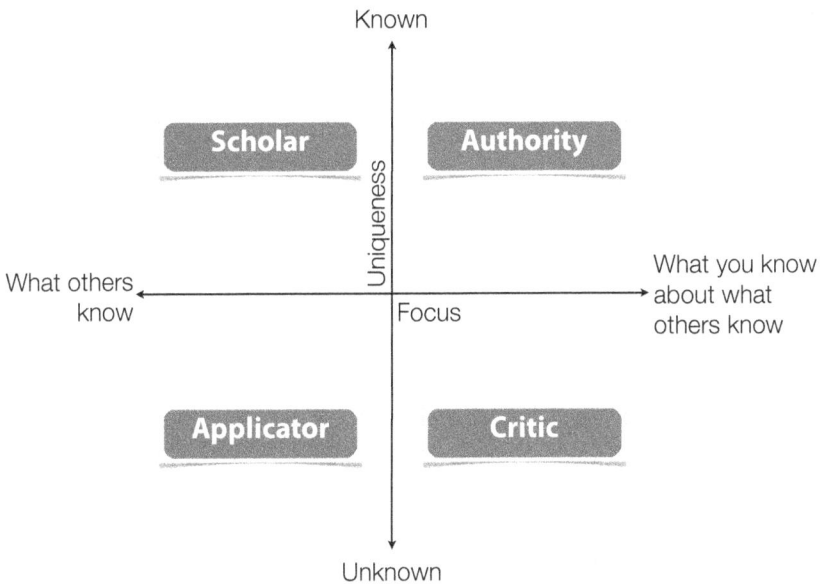

Varieties of expertise model

Applicator

When your focus is on what others know and does not include any of your unique contributions, you are effectively a student of that topic and know how to apply what you know. You are learning and have learned about your message topic. Your focus is on application of what you know. One of your gifts might be in being an outstanding student and in application of knowledge. You know you're operating as an applicator because you're learning about and applying your topic, and the source of what you know is from others. You're an applicator when you are applying what you have learned according to the methods you learned.

To learn what others know about your message and become an applicator:

1. Get the authoritative books on your message and read them.
2. Get to know the material of established authorities on the topic.
3. Participate in training on your topic.
4. Find a mentor or teacher who already has much experience with it, and learn from them.
5. Put into practice what you know.

Scholar

When you know what others know deeply and you bring a uniqueness of integration and your personal interpretation to the topic, you're a scholar, scholar in the sense of someone with deep knowledge and interpretation of a subject. You are a 'scholar' when you know your topic well and can add a sense of unique interpretation to it.

To develop as a scholar regarding your message:

1. Know your topic as per 'student', and know it deeply.
2. Develop your ability to communicate the subject.
3. Give instruction to others and teach what you know to others.
4. Identify your unique interpretations of the subject.
5. Harvest examples of those interpretations making a greater difference than existing ones.

Critic

If your uniqueness on the topic is not known and your focus is on what you know about what others know, you're able to comment on what others have created. Usually this is in what is deficient or incomplete about what others say. In essence, you're evaluating the relative merits of what others have done. You're a critic in the true sense, able to evaluate others' work. The way I use 'critic' is to mean a person who judges, evaluates, or analyses others' work and performances. I do not use it to mean someone who acts as a 'faultfinder', which is just pointing to what is wrong with something or someone.

To develop what you know about what others know is essentially the same as doing a literary review:

1. Read through and have exposure to what other people know and what their methods and applications are. Think about and take note of where you consider they have it wrong, and why you consider that to be the case. Alternatively, ask

yourself, 'They've said … and what I know is …?' If you can, back it up with some sort of evidence and a story. Matt Church describes this by saying that what you are doing is reviewing someone else's work and saying, 'Yes, but…'

2. Read through and have exposure to what other people know and what their methods and applications are. Think about and take note of where you consider they are incomplete. They have it right—just not far enough. Make note of what you consider is the more correct version. Alternatively, ask yourself, 'They've said … and what I know is …?' Matt Church describes this by saying what you are doing is reviewing someone else's work and saying, 'Yes, and…'. He also suggests that if you can, back it up with some sort of evidence and a story.

Authority

Very often someone can be both a scholar and a critic. Such a person may even be regarded as an authority on the topic as it currently exists.

When the focus is on what you know about what others know, you're focussed on what others know, and you know what's different from and in addition to others. When you add your uniqueness on the topic, what it is that's completely new, then you're a creative authority on your topic. You start to know that you are a creative authority on your topic when you start to come up with new information, new methods for application, or completely new insights or ways of interpreting the topic.

You have added to the topic of your message when you have done any of the following:

1. Provide a new way of interpreting that topic.
2. Identified an enhancement or a new way of applying what others have created.
3. Identify what you know to be, or seems to be, insufficient about what others say, and what is needed to make it even more correct.
4. Identify what you know to be, or seems to be, deficient about what others say, and why it is that what others say is incorrect.
5. Create what is completely new and unique

To develop your capacity as a creative authority on your message topic requires all the previous skill areas and builds on them:

1. Learn your topic, as per the student.
2. Become a subject matter authority as per the scholar.

3. Become skilled at identifying deficiencies and incompleteness as per the critic.

4. Identify innovations in content, meaning and method relating to your topic, creating adaptations of existing ways of thinking about, doing and experiencing your message. These are improvements on how things have been done before.

5. Be alert for your creative impulse which when followed can lead you to create new ways of thinking about, doing and experiencing your message. These are departures from how things have been done before.

6. Answer why your message is important. What are the benefits of someone experiencing your message qualities?

7. Answer how your message qualities are created, diminished and the stages between.

   - What factors must be in place to create it? Your values stack is your guide. The items of what's important at the bottom of your values stack are the conditioning factors, filters, constraints for delivering on what's centrally important and your message.
   - What factors when present diminish it? Your values stack is your guide.
   - What factors must be in place to create the optimal version of that?
   - What's the peak version of that? What do you call it?
   - What's the other, worst end of that? What do you call it?
   - What are the natural stages between the two ends of worst and peak?
   - What do you know about the stages of your message?
   - What do you have when you have the felt experience of your message, what does that felt experience create? If you organise your answers from concrete to abstract, then you have the makings of your ability to communicate what that all means to people.

Actually potentially actual

Does talent matter? Yes. Should you give up if you don't have elite performance? Absolutely not. Your gift, if not actioned, remains a potential. It moves from potential to actual through working it into high performance.

Jay Niblick conducted his research in part to identify those key characteristics that separate exceptional performers from the rest. The key finding of Niblick's research is that exceptional performers do two things:

1. They know and understand what their natural talents are.
2. They are in alignment with and apply their natural talents, incorporating those talents into what they do.

The point is that exceptional performance is available for all of us. You need to know what your talents and gifts are, and use them.

Your gift, your natural talents are your innate ability to do something. It can be physical or mental. It explains why you have an easier time with certain activities and subjects than others. Some can do sports more easily, others get abstract ideas more easily. Your gift still needs to be worked; you still need to learn how to convert potential into actual. Your deliberately learning and developing particular abilities that are suited to your gift do this. A gifted swimmer demonstrates their gift after learning the strokes, kicking off and doing turns, and doing much intentional practice. They still had to learn certain abilities, like the applicable stroke, to actualise their gift.

As both Tim Rath and Jay Niblick both point out, it is difficult indeed to develop ability unless you have some natural talent to begin with. Training and development is not the answer to a lack of natural talent. Lack of natural talent is only ever a weakness in the context of a role that requires it. You don't have a weakness; your ability to perform the expectations of your current role is weaker than the role currently demands.

If you want to develop your natural gift and talents towards the elite end of your performance, then heed the research of Anders Ericsson. He says that the most successful have a different history of practice, called 'deliberate practice', being an activity of intention and effort intended to improve their performance that builds on their natural talent. Elite performers in any activity continuously work to improve and innovate. Ericsson suggests that 10,000 hours of deliberate practice are needed for elite performance. This may sound a lot, but if your gift shows up as a talent for training, and you train four days a week, 40 weeks a year, and are continually adding improvements along the way, then in nine to ten years you'd be at the 10,000 hour mark and more than likely considered to be a master trainer.

Imagine what a master trainer would be like when the topic they are training others in happens to be the message they're here to share. Now imagine what it'll be like when you have developed elite performance in your gift and you are using that to help others know and experience what your life is the answer to.

Work what works

Knowing your talents, your gift, how you prefer to make decisions and where they fit best, leads to greater performance and success with less effort. Your actions and success are more effortless. This applies to anything you do. Tim Rath suggests, and Jay Niblick shows, that the people regarded as most successful in their area of endeavour worked their talents and put themselves into situations where their success relied most heavily on their talents. They made sure that their aspirations and choices depended on what they do well. When people align everything they do with what they are naturally good at, Jay says that they become geniuses at what they do, a genius with how well they perform due to their natural talents. This can be from making things, to cooking, socialising, strategy, art, and empathy. The requirement is to know your natural talents, your gift, and how to utilise them more effectively. As Jay says, any role can be done at a level of genius performance. That is as true for a cleaner as it is for the rocket scientist. All roles have nobility when you do them at a level of your greatest performance.

Being talented is one thing. Doing the work that enables superior performance, including mindset and visualisation, is another. No amount of sitting on the couch is going to develop a talent into strength and then into superior performance. Unless of course it's in couch sitting that you want to develop elite performance.

There's a huge difference between working hard through your talents and working hard through what is not your talent. Either way you're working hard. One of them is successful and most effortless. Working hard through what is not a talent is like banging your head against a brick wall—eventually you realise that it is you who are doing the head banging, and you choose to do things differently. As Jay Niblick and Tim Rath describe, when the best performers faced a skills or abilities gap in their role that reflected something that was not a talent, rather than seek to change themselves and develop a weakness, they changed their role in some way. They changed it so that it relied more on their strengths and less on what was a weaknesses in relationship to the role. This does not mean that they never chose to develop and acquire new skills. Just that when they did, they knew that it was not their natural talent they were using.

The key is to choose something that relies on your using what you do naturally well and then to keep getting better at it through deliberate practice. Learning what your talents are and how to use them for greatest effect still takes much time, effort and energy. Elite performance takes 10,000 hours of deliberate practice even for the gifted.

Jay's research shows that the best performers know their talents and act according to them. By doing that they achieve the greatest performance in what they do. In other words, the most successful do not invest most of their energy trying to improve what is not natural for them. They invest most of their energy becoming more skilled at what is natural.

This means that to deliver your best performance in any area, you need to know what you're good at and act in alignment with it. To know your talents, to know your gift, is to be self-aware. To act according to your gift is to be congruent—be self-aware and congruent.

As Jay Niblick and Anders Ericsson point out, the most successful and highest performing continually strive to improve within their talents, within what is natural. It is deliberate practice that leads to continuous improvement. The best performers invest time learning to be better at using their natural talents. In other words, the best performers continually learn to better apply their gifts. Tim Gallwey, author of 'The Inner Game of Work' and considered the father of self-awareness based coaching, seems to agree. He says that self-awareness is the starting point for improved performance. Awareness is the easy part. After that comes deliberate practice to improve. That takes effort. As the old saying goes, it's 1% inspiration, 99% perspiration.

In other words, to reach your top performance:

1. **Know**—be aware of your talents and gift

2. **Use**—be congruent, acting in alignment with them, using your gift to achieve your best performance

3. **Improve**—continuously improve, deliberately practising to use your gift for greater performance

A way to represent this is in the model below. In the beginning, you have access to others people's insight and experience about how best to use your gift. It's their wisdom, though to you it's your knowledge. When you act on that knowledge, you are deliberately practising what you know. When you use your gift you have the experience of using your gift and the performance created by doing so. For many, this is enough.

If you want to continue to improve your performance and how skilfully you use your gift, then insight is needed. This insight comes through self-awareness. Experience and knowledge, alone or together, do not provide insight. When you think about or reflect on that knowledge and/or experience, you'll derive some insights about them. Insight put into continuous practice and experience with awareness of what would improve—both produce greater performance and the wisdom that comes with it. To achieve that performance and wisdom requires self-awareness and deliberate, continuous practice.

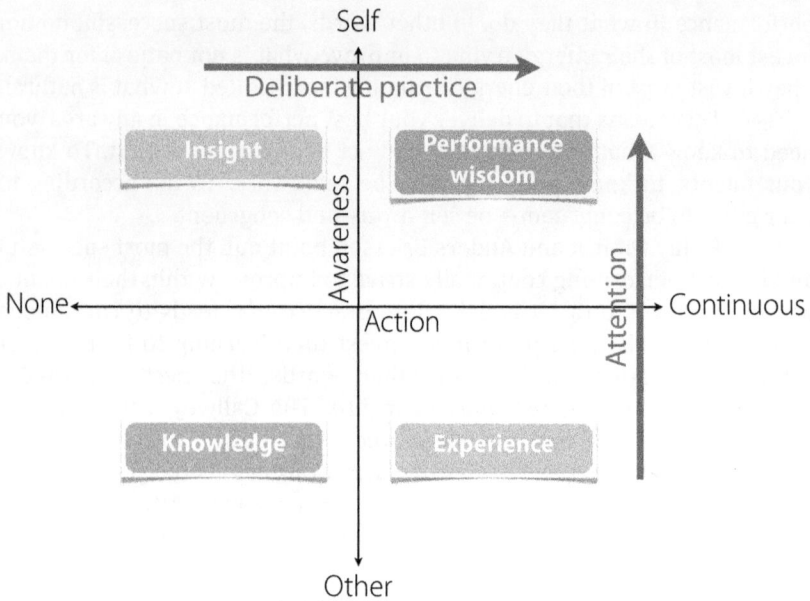

Performance wisdom model

Deliberate practice involves improving the strengths you already have and extending the reach and range of your talents. If I keep doing what I do the way I do it, my performance will stay the same. Doing it the same way and spending more time doing things the same way produces the same performance. It does not produce performance improvement. So you need to try things differently, you need to innovate your methods in some way. Deliberately practice on ways of doing what you do that go beyond your current level of competence and comfort.

Mind you, what many call 'natural improvement' that comes from practising, for example, the scales on a piano, is a progressive adaptation and improvement that comes with deliberate practice.

To make best use of deliberate practice, a well-informed coach or mentor can be a great guide, not only in helping you develop superior performance, but they can help you coach yourself. This is especially true when you are at the level of performance where you primarily learn through your own deliberate practice.

Innovating on its own isn't enough. It's a myth that you get better when you just do the same things the same way. Any innovation needs to be an improvement on the previous way of doing it. This is where feedback is important. You have to be alert to, seek out and get feedback. The closer in time your feedback is to when you did it, the better, as you can more quickly put into place corrective action. The sooner you realise that a change is needed in the way you're practising your piano scales, the sooner you can implement it and improve your performance.

A variation in performance that you observe or experience is a form of feedback. A simple form of deliberate practice in your area of knowledge is to be curious about and to incorporate what you learn from those variations.

Finding someone else who is already skilled in your area can help accelerate your learning and development. Moreover, once you are already at a high standard, a good coach or mentor can help you to become your self-coach. Self-coaching can be done in any field, and means to pay attention to anything unexpected that happens. Those unexpected events either improve or decrease your performance. You then do more of what increases performance, and work to avoid whatever decreases it.

I enjoy group workshops and I get curious every time someone asks a question or lets me know that they're confused. Their question or confusion is a form of feedback. I discover something whenever it happens. I ask myself: 'What did I do or not do that produced that question or confusion? What can I do to prevent that from happening again?' I then put that into practice next time around and observe the effect of having done so. If it's an improvement, I keep it. Other times I deliberately harvest feedback from people. A really simple way to do this is to work one-to-one with people, as they are far more likely to share their spontaneous questions and confusions. This is not to say that I am perfect at doing what I do, but this approach keeps me continually improving. It's my deliberate practice.

In the professional field, to lift performance as a manager and a leader takes discipline for continuous application. Sudden improvement happens rarely. Continuous incremental improvement is what works. Large change is the result of continuous small adjustments over time.

Developing your performance requires courage and patience, courage to be outside your comfort zone, and patience for the time it takes. There are no shortcuts to the time spent in deliberate practice.

Performance develops

Keys to developing greater performance:

1. Do it for reasons that are important for you to keep you motivated
   - For example, your motivation might be to get even more effective creating your message

2. Learn to use your gift
   - Learn about your gift and get started
   - Take specialised training to perfect your gifts and talents
   - Practise; invest time cultivating talents into strengths
   - Notice your performance
   - Notice how it feels for you doing it

3. Develop your ability to realise your potential
   - Keep doing it
   - Learn from the learned, such as a coach or instructor
   - Develop new abilities that allow you to make real more of your talents and gift
   - Ensure your role utilises more of your talents than not— or adapt it to do so
   - Establish appropriate structures that allow you to direct your talents towards your goals

4. Practise deliberately
   - Keep looking for ways to grow beyond what you can already do
   - Apply your gift in different ways in different situations
   - Ensure you get feedback
   - Get help from coaches, mentors, trainers or others who have enough expertise to act as such
   - Innovate on how you do what you do

5. Become your own self-coach
   - Have courage to be uncomfortable, and patience for the time it takes
   - Strive to be the best you can be; continually raise the bar of your performance standard
   - Look for variations and unanticipated events, as they give you clues for raising your performance standard
   - Learn from and adapt to those events in a way that increases performance

No doubt about it

Jay Niblick says that you can, if you want, achieve genius level performance—your best possible performance—in the area of your natural talents and gift. This is your 'how'. Similarly, you are already sensitised for and can, if you want, achieve genius level expertise—your best possible performance—in the area of your message. This is your 'what' and 'why'.

When you combine the two you can, if you haven't already, eventually achieve:

- Genius level performance
- Genius level message expertise

Developing genius level performance and expertise takes much time, energy and effort. That can seem daunting, especially as that can seem like a long way off into the future.

To be on your way to developing your genius, you're creating along the way. To persist in that journey, it's important to love what you do and why you're doing it.

Csíkszentmihályi describes that people seem happiest when they are in a state of flow—when they are completely involved with an activity. The involvement in the activity is such that nothing else seems to matter. The flow state is intrinsically motivating—there's reward in doing that activity for its own sake. Mihaly says that the flow state can happen while involved in an activity that comes from having skill and a challenge that causes neither anxiety nor boredom. He also says that true happiness involves the continual challenge to go beyond oneself as part of something beyond ourselves. There's every reason to think of your skill area as your gift, and the challenge to be how you can help others experience the solution to a problem otherwise known as your message. That challenge —your message—also happens to be something beyond yourself.

However, in some areas of your gift, with one or more of your talents, you'd have as a minimum a good level of performance already. You are already performing well in some areas of your life. In the area of your message, as shown by the creation of your values stack, you already have a good level of expertise for your message. There's a good chance you already know more about it than many others around you. Your good is already good enough.

You have already, as a minimum:

- Good enough level performance
- Good enough level message expertise

Your own life includes your gift. Your own life has revealed to you and includes your message. Your gift and message are the unique essence of your life. Your own life already includes both. To create your message most effectively you use your gift, and do so in a way that others experience for themselves the qualities that your message defines. You're already good enough to get started. If you want it, great can come later when you've done the work. Though you'll only start getting there by getting started, something you are already good enough to do.

You are already good enough to start sharing with others what your own life is about.

Learning for message creation

The previous chapter focussed on one aspect of learning—learning about your calling. There's another aspect to the learning stage that's necessary before continuing to the creating stages—learning about creating your message. It's about how your message becomes the results you create. Understanding how qualities are produced is important for creating your message and will help inform your choices.

People are often confused about the types of results they're getting. Perhaps you can relate to these common situations:

- You're doing what you do to the best of what you know how, even doing it to a high standard. Yet no matter how well you do it, others don't seem to appreciate what you're doing, and sometimes even complain. For example, Joann was relatively new to her organisation and was in charge of putting in place a new I.T. system. By all accounts she implemented it successfully and she was even satisfied that she'd involved all the relevant stakeholders. However, there was much resentment towards her from the staff because of her 'lack of engagement'.

- You know a lot about your field of expertise and might even be adept at diagnosing problems in what is widely regarded as a very complicated topic. Yet no matter how expert and predictable you are in that highly complicated skill area, even seeing many otherwise complicated issues as quite simple, people's unpredictable responses remain quite a mystery for you. For example a forensic accountant is adept at sifting through financial records of an organisation to identify any inconsistencies in where the money went. Yet his expertise was outweighed by his being 'difficult to work with'.

- Even though you're good at what you do, using your talents and delivering great performance, you often have the sense that you can't get anything right. You forever seem to become aware of things that you somehow 'missed'. You might even have been blamed by others for not having foreseen certain things, and you cannot understand why you didn't and can't seem to manage an appropriate response when others act that way.

- You might be great at what you do and applying that to what matters, and yet seem to have difficulty identifying if it's really working for you—you don't know if what matters is what's happening.

These types of experiences make perfect sense. If you can relate to these examples, none of them is even your fault. What's going on is that most people have never been made aware and therefore do not readily know:

- How to receive and interpret feedback in the best way
- No matter what you do there are always two different types of results
- There are different types of situations we deal with
- It's not always easy to identify when we are truly 'doing our thing' in the optimal way

Clarity on these four points will better inform how you can go about and create your message.

Setforward setbacks

Hindsight isn't foresight.

After the September 11 attacks on the World Trade Center and Pentagon in the USA, some people were accused of being negligent and incompetent for 'failing to realise the obvious', that someone learning to fly a plane without learning to take off and land was possibly someone planning a terrorist attack. Curiously, none of the people making these claims was busy before the attacks in promoting the obviousness of 'learning to fly a plane without learning to take off and land = terrorist plot'. People had observed this happening, and yet the full significance did not register with everyone—until afterwards.

What was 'obviously significant' after the event, was relatively insignificant before it. How does this happen? Humans are great at pattern matching. We'll recognise a face decades after meeting someone. We can easily recognise what certain information means when we've experienced it before. However, what about when we're exposed to a combination of information that we've never met before? With three pieces of information there are six possible ways of making sense of them. There are six possible patterns. With ten pieces of information, there are 3.6 million possible patterns. With 15 pieces of information, there are 1.3 million million possible patterns. Once we know what a certain pattern means, we have a tendency to expect that we 'ought to have known it all along'. It's the equivalent of telling ourselves, once the lottery numbers are announced, that we ought to have known what they would be before they were drawn. It's just not a realistic expectation.

We have turned what we have learned from looking back into the past, into an expectation of what ought to have been known back then.

Learning from the past is hindsight. Forecasting into the future is foresight. The problem is that we have made what is called the 'hindsight foresight fallacy'. We have confused hindsight learning with foresight expectation. Once a pattern is known, we often make the mistake of expecting we ought to have known all along. Regardless of whether this interpretation is given to us by others or we give it to ourselves, this is unhelpful feedback. Often, we only have access to information after the act, and not prior. We have access to information only once it is available. We can know what something means only once we know what it means.

It was not a failure not to know what was unknown before it was known. People who confuse hindsight with foresight will call it a failure. It is simply new information that became known as a result of people acting in some way. That new information was simply feedback.

Complexity thinking says that a complex system cannot be fully known, and that we can learn of a complex system only through interacting with it. There are three parts to this—the person acting, the broader system, and the information that gets produced as a result. If we look at this more closely, we can never objectively know everything there is to know, as what we know is always limited and finite. All we can do is act based on what we know at the time, and interact with our environment. This action and interaction produces more information in numerous ways:

1. First, you act in some way. Say you see your friend yawn and you ask if he is bored, as that's what he usually does when bored.

2. Your action is new information for your environment, which then responds to your action in some way. For example, upon hearing your question, your friend tells you he is simply thirsty.

3. The response from your environment is new information for you. This response you get from your environment is feedback. For example, you tested what you originally thought was your friend's boredom, and the feedback revealed that it was something else entirely. Your initial assumption was off the mark. You could say that your original test of 'is he bored?' failed, as it was refuted. However, you could say that it could only have been refuted by your interacting with him, and as such is a success as it produced feedback as new information.

4. That new information better informs your next action. For example, you get your friend a glass of water.

So are you a failure for having made what turned out to be a wrong assumption, or are you a success for testing your assumption and adapting accordingly? What is true is that you can only make corrective actions by knowing you are off target, you can only know that you are off target by being off target, and you can only be off target by taking action towards your target. In other words, what we often call failure is simply the new information that comes to hand as a result of moving towards our goal. It's not failure; it's feedback. Just as there can't be feedback without taking action towards your goal and trying, there can't be 'failure' without trying. As such, the only real failure is not trying—not taking action towards your goal.

The inevitability is that new information will show up as an indication of how far you are off from your goal, and therefore the extent to which you need to take a different action that takes you forward to your goal. You feedback forward, or 'fail' forward towards your goal. That new information was the required feedback that enables you to actually achieve your goal. Without feedback, there's no adapting, there's no achieving the goal.

That new information is simply the gap between the intended and actual result. If you'd known that gap in advance, you would not have acted in that way. Any adjustment is due to a perceived gap between intended and actual. The more quickly you can become aware of the need for adjustment, the more quickly you can adjust. In other words, to achieve your goal fast you need to adjust fast, and to adjust fast you need to 'fail' fast. The smallest adjustments are the fastest—so make continuous small adjustments on your way towards your goal.

The need for adjustments might mean that the goal is not achieved as quickly as you might have hoped. Therefore, there is no failure—only a delay in time.

Justine's experience

Justine, whom we met earlier, describes what it's like to shift to a more adaptive way of acting. "I'm getting more comfortable making mistakes, because I know I am going to learn from them. I realise that if I don't take action, I won't learn. What used to be called a 'mistake' was needed for the learning to happen."

Comparing previous and current attitudes, she shares, "I'm not inhibited from doing things by the fear of or even the perception of failure. There's not even such a thing as failure. What's different for me is risk-taking, which I don't even see as risk-taking any more. There's just more action, sooner. The idea is to just keep going. Act and adapt. You can experience and adapt as a normal state of living. 'Adapt' works much better for me than 'learn'."

Twice what you expect

You always have two results

Most of us think of results as something concrete. However, that's only one type of result. There is another.

When I get home and give my partner a hug, she feels connected. Though it's a simple thing, I know it's important for her. Notice, though, that my taking action towards a goal (hugging my partner) produced two results. The concrete or visible result was 'the hug'—anyone observing that situation would observe that a hug happened. What they would not see was the qualitative or invisible result of her 'feeling connected'. Mind you, my intent and goal is that she feels connected, and I do that through the hug. I achieve a qualitative result through a concrete action.

My qualitative goal is 'connected' and the concrete goal is 'hugged'. My method is 'a hug'.

As another example, when you have a concrete goal for drinking a glass of water, doing so will satisfy some thirst. The concrete result was 'drank a glass of water'. The qualitative result was 'thirst quenched'.

When you were creating your Value Stack, you interpreted your qualitative experience based on other people's actions. Regardless of what their actions had as a result in a concrete, tangible way, it had a qualitative result in you.

The point is that every concrete action will always produce two results:

1. Concrete result

2. Qualitative result

This is especially the case when your concrete actions involve and therefore affect others. Regardless of what you may intend, every action sends a message. Your actions are experienced and interpreted by others, and that interpretation is the message that they receive. You cannot see the message they received. The message that they receive is the qualitative result.

We cannot work on results directly; only on the factors, methods, and actions that produce results. Whatever the concrete and qualitative result we have in a given situation, they are the inevitability of those actions in that situation. How do we know the results that we were going to get? Because they were the results we got. The qualities that others perceive imbue the methods you used, influence and help to shape the qualitative result achieved. This is represented in the following diagram.

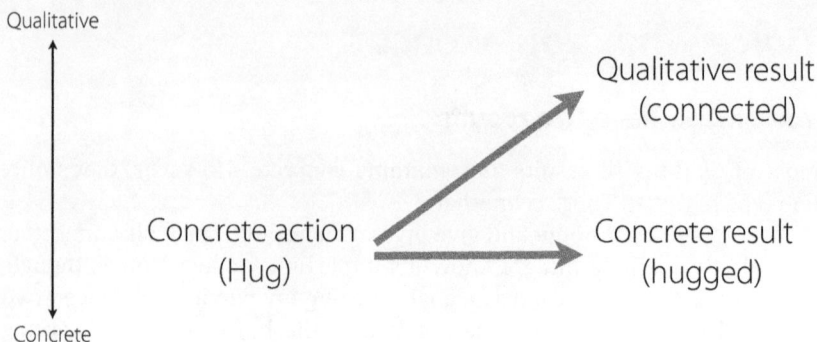

Qualitative

Qualitative result
(connected)

Concrete action
(Hug)

Concrete result
(hugged)

Concrete

Example of how an action has two results

For a given concrete result, there are many possible ways for achieving it. If I want a glass of water, I can get it myself, my partner can get it, or the dog can. If you are only interested in the concrete results, then any method or series of actions will do.

I could always demand that my partner fetch me a glass of water, though this will certainly evoke in her a certain qualitative result.

If you remember that every action also produces a qualitative result, and you value a particular qualitative result, then your method options narrow. I might prefer that I demonstrate self-responsibility and that my partner feel loved and appreciated. So I might ask myself, 'How can I do this in a way that demonstrates self-responsibility and elevates her experience of love and appreciation?' I'd eliminate the 'demand' option. I might choose to fetch a glass of water myself whenever I want one, offering her one too, and appreciate whenever she offers to give me one. In a sense, the qualitative result I want defines the constraints, boundaries or filters on the possibilities for concrete action. Only the actions that support creating the preferred qualitative result remain as options.

It's looking at your options through the lens of what matters.

One of the simplest starting points for action is to look at your own Value Stack. The front-line values that relate to concrete events, the values that are most concrete, directly relate to concrete circumstance and action. For example, Zaheed, whom you met earlier, puts 'acceptance' into practice. Look at the values in your Value Stack and ask which you can easily put into action. This is shown in the following diagram.

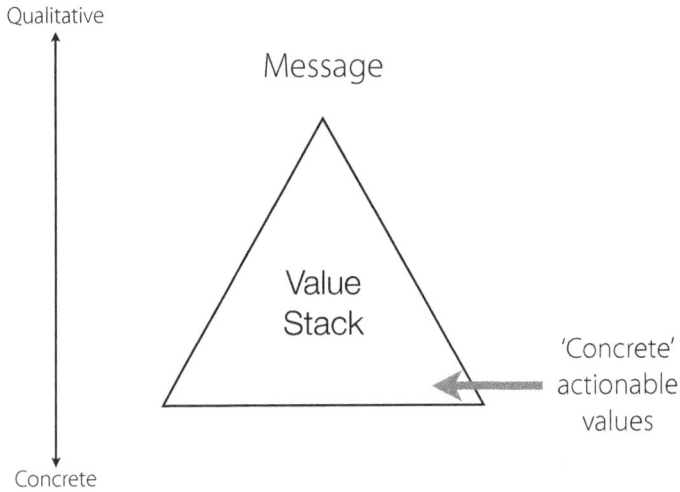

Qualitative

Message

Value
Stack

'Concrete'
actionable
values

Concrete

We can act on 'message' through our more 'concrete' or front-line values

The point of all of this is that:

1. Every action produces two results
   - Concrete
   - Qualitative
2. There are many possible ways or strategies to create a given concrete result
3. Every method and strategy also produces a qualitative result
4. If you have no interest in the qualitative result, then any action will do
5. If you do have an interest in the qualitative result, then 'any' action will no longer do
6. The qualitative result defines the extents, boundaries, constraints, limits or filters for the concrete action
7. Only the ones that produce the overall qualitative result remain viable and possible actions
8. Taking the qualities of the qualitative result you want, your method can be identified by answering, 'How can this be done in a way that is *quality*, *quality* and *quality*?

As an example of the last point above, let me tell you about some friends of mine in relationship. He is largely driven by 'freedom' that shows up as spontaneity, and she is driven by 'flow' that shows up as organisation. You could probably imagine the potential for domestic conflict when spontaneity and organisation collide, which is what they experienced. For example, they do not have a car, and he liked to come up with the last minute idea of going to a new cafe and would want to immediately head straight out the door and hope for the best getting there. She experienced this as chaotic. When they asked how they could interact and relate in a way that is both free and flows, they found answers that worked for them both. One way they found was when he comes up with the last minute idea of going to a new restaurant, she'll figure out how best to get there using public transport. For them, that's 'free flowing', jokingly called 'lava'.

Collectively we have two results

Though this example is an organisation of two people, it highlights where organisational culture change initiatives fail. Just as a person has an individual qualitative experience and a couple has a joint qualitative experience, organisational culture is a collective qualitative experience. Just as you cannot see qualitative experience even though it has a strong influence, you cannot see culture even though it has a huge influence on organisations.

Whenever culture change initiatives fail, the concrete actions are not congruent with the qualitative results—the new culture—desired. Most often, those actions are consistent with the current ways of working, and succeed only in propagating or further ingraining the current culture. Current behaviours experienced as the same message propagates the same culture. This is represented below.

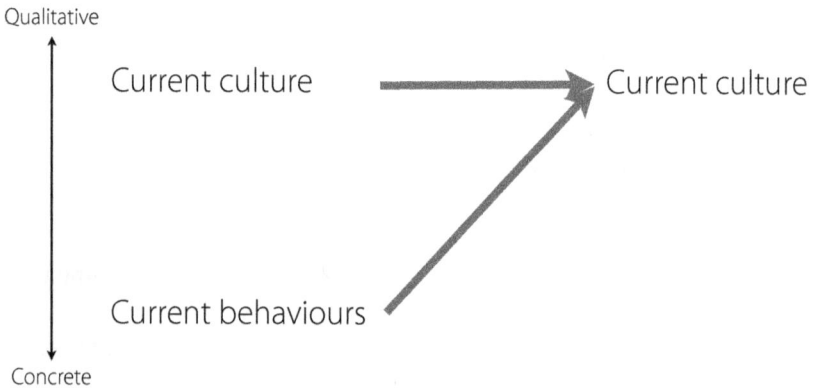

Qualitative

Current culture ⟶ Current culture

Current behaviours

Concrete

How culture continues

To create a new culture requires the creation of a new collective qualitative experience. New behaviours experienced as a different message supports and generates a different culture. The most immediate form of behaviour is language, which either supports the continuation or changing of culture. Donald Epstein succinctly describes this as, "language reflects and directs culture". This requires new behaviours, as shown below.

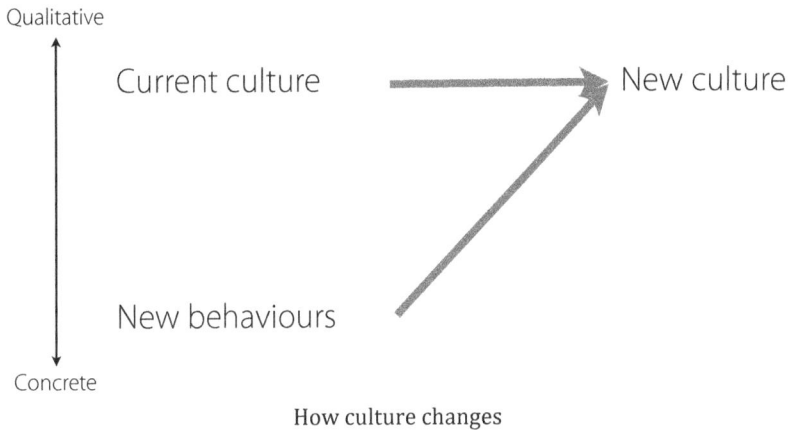

Qualitative

Current culture ⟶ New culture

New behaviours

Concrete

How culture changes

Simply complex

Different situation, different response

Have you ever gone to your car and seen that one of the tyres was flat? You could see immediately that you had a problem. This is a simple problem, as you could see straight away what the nature of the problem was. Many people can easily replace the flat tyre with their spare. That's why your car has a spare—the manufacturer knows that it is a common and simple problem to fix.

Unless you are a mechanic, when there's something else wrong with your car, you need to take it to one. You know there's a problem with your car, though you don't know yet what's causing it. Normally the mechanic will need to spend some time looking into and testing things out to determine what the cause of the problem is. Until the problem is identified, he cannot fix it. This is a complicated problem because there is time between the problem's showing up and the cause of the problem being known. Moreover, the cause required some form of investigation by an expert, in this case, a mechanic.

Have you ever gone to a mechanic and gone away with the feeling that you've been treated as though you were an idiot for not knowing about cars? Have you ever interacted with an I.T. or financial institution help desk and had the same experience? Somehow it's as if you're an idiot for not having their expertise. Though that expert is competent in their field and can solve complicated problems in that field, you experienced them in a different way, perhaps as disrespectful, condescending or arrogant. Have you ever had the experience of knowing a lot about a topic and have someone seeming to assume that you know nothing about it? You might have experienced that as disrespectful. Their ability to deal with complicated problems is not the issue. It is their ability to deal with the human at the other end that is. You'd probably prefer that they interacted with you in a different way. Humans are living, interactive and complex. We are not things that are simple or complicated. Yet how many times do we treat people as if they were?

If we treat every situation, including the people involved, as the same type of problem, then not only are we likely to get the situation wrong, we're almost certain to get it wrong with the people involved. Distinctions between things and people are not just useful—they're necessary.

During the late 1990s I came across the work of Dave Snowden, a researcher in knowledge management. He has developed a framework that helps people, such as managers in organisations, determine what is going on in a certain situation and identify the type of situation they are dealing with. His work helped me to clearly differentiate between things and people. Simple and complicated things do not have an inner experience, whereas complex people do. Situations and what's involved in situations have aspects of all three types. Snowden's research shows that different situations have different appropriate responses. Identifying the type of situation helps us to make more appropriate choices and decisions. In other words, the situation type informs the decisions to be made.

A simplified version of his original framework is shown in the following model. Things are either simple or complicated. They are simple when the problem and the cause are immediately known and the response is obvious. They are complicated when the cause of the problem is not immediately known and requires investigation. Some aspects of a complicated problem might well be simple.

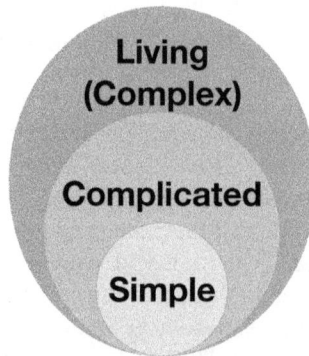

Types of systems

As a living complex human, you can have a simple problem, such as a broken bone. You can have a complicated problem such as a condition that requires many tests to diagnose. Then you can have problems that are complex, like relationship issues. No simple relationship advice is going to work for all people in all situations all the time. Snowden says that the only way to find out what works for a complex situation is to try different things out. When it works, do more of it. When it does not work, stop doing it. To try things out, in Snowden's words, is to probe the situation with 'safe fail' experiments—in a safe environment we knowingly experiment knowing it is likely to fail. These types of experiments serve to reveal what works and provide the feedback needed to learn. This is consistent with complex systems theory that says that we can only know about a system through interacting with it.

Because we humans are complex, any activity that we are exposed to will always have, as a minimum, a qualitative result. A bicycle or spreadsheet does not have a qualitative inner experience. Humans do. In a complex environment, which is the case whenever you have people involved, you need to interact and experiment to learn about the qualitative result that is being produced. Experimentation is all about learning what works and does not work. What works gets strengthened, and what does not work is discontinued.

Flow on purpose

Your message is your intent and motivation.
Your gift informs how to do it.
You choose your action.

What optimal experience?

Have you ever had the experience of being so involved in something that you lose track of time? Have you ever been so involved in what you're doing that you're just doing and there's no sense of self-consciousness? If you have, then you've experienced an optimal state of experience called 'flow'.

Flow can be experienced in any activity that affords the right balance of skill and challenge. It can be experienced in such things as walking, yoga, martial arts, knitting, cooking, writing, teaching, learning, digging, seeing aesthetics, listening to music, eating, reading a book, raising a family, conversation, solitude, and play. It can also be experienced in intellectual pursuits such as interpreting art, and playing with ideas in such fields as philosophy, science, poetry and maths.

To stay in the flow requires that you continually develop greater skill and apply it to greater challenges. Csíkszentmihályi describes this when he says: "One cannot enjoy doing the same thing at the same level (of performance) for long. We grow either bored or frustrated; and then the desire to enjoy ourselves again pushes us to stretch our skills, or to discover new opportunities for using them." Flow can be a driving force towards even greater levels of performance and creativity. This explains why flow activities lead to growth and discovery.

Csíkszentmihályi identifies the following factors as accompanying an experience of flow.

About you—the conditions for flow:

- **Clear objective.** You know the result you are after and have clear goals every step of the way.
- **Immediate feedback.** Progress towards your goal is self-evident while you are involved in the activity, enabling you to adjust your actions immediately.
- **Skill and challenge at the right balance.** You have confidence in your own abilities for the challenge at hand, and have belief that the objective will be reached.

About your activity:

- **Personal control.** You have a sense that the result is due entirely to your own actions. You have no worry about failure.
- **Intrinsic reward.** Just doing your activity is satisfying. It satisfies for its own sake. It is an end in and of itself.
- **Concentration.** You can give your attention to a narrow field of activity to such an extent that there's no self-consciousness about your activity or the results produced.

About your experience:

- **Time distortion.** A sense of time is altered.
- **Absorption.** Awareness only of the present. A lack of bodily need awareness, such as being hungry or fatigued and only realising this once the activity stops.
- **Merging.** A sense of doing where action and awareness merge such that there is action only.

You cannot force flow. It happens. It's the result of a number of factors, and may or may not occur even when those factors are present. You know you're in the sweet spot for your action choices when you have the conditions for flow and you're at the point of flow. Your target activity is one that's suitable for your current level of skill, that's sufficiently challenging not to be boring, and not so challenging that you're so anxious you've lost confidence in your ability to succeed. Your sweet spot is your flow-point.

Choose flow

Opportunities for acting on your calling abound. In essence, you're living true to what's important to you, from your message and including everything else that's important for you that supports your message. For example, your work and relationships provide a perfect opportunity for acting on your purpose. They are both situations that provide opportunity to actualise your calling and make a difference doing what is needed for others. You can always act in a way that is consistent with the values in your Value Stack.

Only you can choose to act on and create your calling, to carry out your 'concrete assignment' as Victor Frankl called it. Your calling is an abstract and qualitative experience. Your concrete assignment is whatever you choose it to be, whatever the form that appropriately satisfies the needs of others in a concrete way.

For anything to happen you need to commit to action and give yourself permission to act. This is said most succinctly in a section from the 1951 book, *'The Scottish Himalayan Expedition'*, written by William Hutchinson Murray (1913-1996), a Scottish mountaineer. It is a passage that is often attributed to Johann Wolfgang Von Goethe, and reads:

"Until one is committed, there is hesitancy, the chance to draw back, always ineffectiveness. Concerning all acts of initiative (and creation), there is one elementary truth the ignorance of which kills countless ideas and splendid plans: that the moment one definitely commits oneself, then providence moves too. A whole stream of events issues from the decision, raising in one's favour all manner of unforeseen incidents, meetings and material assistance, which no man could have dreamt would have come his way. I learned a deep respect for one of Goethe's couplets: Whatever you can do or dream you can, begin it. Boldness has genius, power and magic in it!"

The point is to get started. Try things.

The main point of Adrian Gilpin in the book, *'Unstoppable'*, is that you can start to do something before you know how to do it. You just need to start. You just have to know why you are doing it and know that that people succeed when they know what their individual purpose is. Ronald Heifetz, et al., in *'The Practice of Adaptive Leadership'*, says that to be adaptive we need to think experimentally to enable discovery of what does and does not work and to take corrective action. To be experimental, you need to start with an experiment.

John Izzo, author of *'Stepping Up'*, says that each of us has a sphere we can influence. To step up, you don't need to be on the world stage or have sublime skills. He says to do what matters to you, as your effort always matters. When everyone contributes and steps up into their role in change, no matter how large or small, it collectively creates large change. If you want things to change, start. What matters is that you take action and begin with one action that you can take.

You already have the power to make a difference. As you read the remainder of this section, think about your opportunities to serve and ask yourself whether you are willing to give it a go. Ask yourself: 'What matters? For whom does that problem exist? What can I do about it? Am I willing to do it? Do I give myself permission?'

Whatever you choose to do, ensure your activity is aligned with your gift, that it utilises your talents. While your gift informs and becomes how you deliver on whatever activities you choose, how do you choose those activities in the first place?

Criteria for actions that flow

Many years ago I considered what activities to undertake that would help me to grow in areas of my choosing. I knew that I had no motivation for activities that I considered to be boring. I also knew that I lost motivation if I ever doubted my ability to succeed. I didn't enjoy what I was doing if I was bored or anxious doing it. I used to have a sign above my desk that spelled out my criteria for a suitable activity or goal:

1. Challenging not easy
2. Interesting not boring
3. Achievable not doubting

I'd never found a satisfactory way of defining that more tightly until I came across Mihaly Csíkszentmihályi's work on 'flow'. According to Csíkszentmihályi, anything you can do is potentially enjoyable and therefore something through which you can experience flow, that being the word for 'optimal experience'. You know you've had optimal experience when you've experienced flow. Csíkszentmihályi makes clear that whenever flow happens, the activity is experienced as neither boring nor anxious. I remember excitedly reading about flow and then noticing the sign above my desk. You guessed it, I had another 'eureka moment'. I'd found my criteria! The factors for the flow experience are the same factors for choosing optimal activities and goals.

According to Csíkszentmihályi, there are three steps to transforming situations into an activity that can be controlled or contained, enjoyed and perhaps even experienced as flow:

1. **Self-assurance.** You have implicit belief and confidence in your own ability to navigate successfully and find a way through, that your destiny is in your own hands and your ability to respond to the circumstance. To do that you do not see yourself as needing to control your external situation, but

that your external situation is something that you are capable of responding to.

2. **Focus out.** Be involved with your environment. Your alert focus is both on your personal goal and on your surroundings insofar as you are open enough to notice opportunities to adapt to those external events. Remaining in touch with the situation allows you to notice possibilities for action as they emerge. In Mihaly's words, "People who know how to transform stress into enjoyable challenge spend very little time thinking about themselves."

3. **Be responsive.** Be open to your environment. When a situation is experienced as an obstacle and potentially stressful, there are two possible responses:

   - Focus on the perceived obstacle and move it out of the way

   - Focus on the entire situation, whether there are more appropriate goals, and develop different more adaptive solutions

Moreover, Csíkszentmihályi adds that the simplest act becomes enjoyable and can produce flow when:

1. You have a goal and as many sub-goals as feasible

2. You have ways of gauging progress towards the goals you have chosen

3. You concentrate on what you are doing as you are doing it, and keep making finer distinctions in the challenges involved in what you are doing

4. You have the skills needed to successfully interact with your situation

5. You keep raising your standard and level of challenge if the activity becomes boring

Csíkszentmihályi describes the characteristics of someone who converts situations into enjoyable challenges. Like all skills, these characteristics improve with discipline and persistence.

1. **Goals.** You have set your own goals. Moreover, you own your decisions and know that you are the one who has chosen your goal. The goal has not happened to you. As it's your goal, you can change it when it makes sense to do so.

2. **Feedback.** A challenge goal means that you'll eventually need to develop skills to keep it suitably challenging. To do that you'll need to monitor the feedback you get about your

progress. The more immediate the feedback, the better. Ideally you have feedback in action.

3. **Immersion.** You're deeply involved with and give your attention to what you are doing and the activities you chose for achieving your goal. This is a balance of the challenge in those actions with the skill you have while doing them. What you're doing is neither too anxious nor too boring for you.

4. **Attentiveness.** You pay attention to what's happening, and sustain your involvement. Your focus is out towards the situation, your activity and goal. You're not worried about how you are going and what others may be thinking.

5. **Enjoyment.** When you're setting suitable goals, acting on them, receiving feedback, adaptively developing skills, concentrating on what you're doing, and being involved, Csíkszentmihályi says that any situation can become enjoyable.

Choose both types of results

As was covered earlier, every concrete action that you take that affects others will always produce two results—concrete and qualitative. While you can see your concrete results, you can never see and know for sure the qualitative result that you have helped to create. Whenever you are interacting with other people, there is always a part of that situation that is complex. Qualitative results are always being produced. To find out what qualitative results you have produced, something needs to have happened for those qualitative results to have been produced. You need to have interacted in some way.

The advice for what to do to learn about complex situations is then your guide. To find out and learn about what is really going on for others, you have to interact, and then observe the results. Otherwise, you'll never know of the qualitative results that you have produced. Considering the results you generate, do more of what is helping to produce the results you want, and stop doing what is not.

Choose your support crew

One of the basic aspects of perturbation is the need for the pressures being experienced to be 'contained'. Containment is necessary for the pressures being experienced to become fuel for transforming in some way. Support from others as you are experiencing pressure increases the ability for that situation, and the pressures being experienced, to be successfully contained. It's almost like supportive others are bolstering the walls that help contain the situation for you. While support from others is no guarantee for the pressures to be contained, they certainly help to do so.

How to select your optimal choice

The factors for flow are the factors for your optimal activity choices. Add to this that, whenever you are interacting with others, there is always a part of that situation that is complex. Considering both of these, here are the criteria for assessing possible choices:

1. **Create goals**—establish your own suitably challenging goals towards creating your message
    *   They're neither so easy as to be boring, nor so challenging as to produce anxiety
    *   You have implicit belief and confidence in your own ability to succeed
    *   They're enjoyable to pursue
    *   Ensure you include the qualitative results that you want as part of your end goals
    *   If your overall goal produces anxiety, break it down so that your next goal is reduced to an achievable challenge that re-establishes your flow conditions

2. **Use your gift**—ensure your actions utilise your talents
    *   Your gift is the way you most effectively act on tasks and interact with people
    *   Use your gift to inform your activity choices for how you'll achieve your goals
    *   You have far greater potential skill and performance when you're working with your gift—so choose activities that utilise more of your talents than those which do not

3. **Know your qualitative results**—they are the qualities that are in your Value Stack and Message statement
    *   Your message defines what others ideally experience
    *   Use the qualitative results that you seek to define and refine your choice of actions
    *   Ensure your possible actions are qualitatively consistent with the qualitative result you want
    *   Allow only the actions that produce the overall qualitative result
    *   Ask yourself, 'How can I do this in a way that imbues the qualities of the qualitative result?'

4. **Interact**—you learn about the situation by interacting with it intentionally
    - Experiment and interact, try things out, experiment in a way that produces feedback so that you can adapt forwards towards your goal
    - Be attentive and pay attention to the feedback you get; notice how others respond
    - Stop doing what does not work, well, because it's not working
    - Enhance and keep doing what does work, because it's working

5. **Deliberately practise continually**—keep raising the standard of your performance
    - You can sustain your attention and involvement in your activity
    - You can concentrate and be deeply involved with what you are doing to achieve your goal
    - You can be attuned to and receive feedback both within yourself (are you becoming bored or anxious?) and about how your actions are progressing
    - Ensure you can keep raising the level of challenge if the activity becomes boring
    - As the challenge level increases, ensure you raise your skill and performance standard

6. **Find your support crew**—ensure that you have people who will
    - Be supportive of what you are seeking to achieve
    - Call you a success for trying
    - Celebrate your persistence
    - Encourage you when things inevitably don't quite go to plan
    - Help you see that 'obstacles' are simply necessary challenges

Choose 'transform' > 'actualise'

Now you have your criteria for whatever activities you choose. However, you may not automatically know some of the application options to choose from.

There are generally five different application areas that you can choose to work towards. These are shown in the following model. These are inclusive stages. Whatever stage you decide you want to work to, you need to include the essence of all the stages that lead to it. The stages of 'transform' and 'actualise' will be covered more thoroughly in the next two chapters.

Remember as you consider these application stages, that you always have two results, concrete and qualitative. The qualitative result is always your end goal. This is along with whatever your concrete goals are.

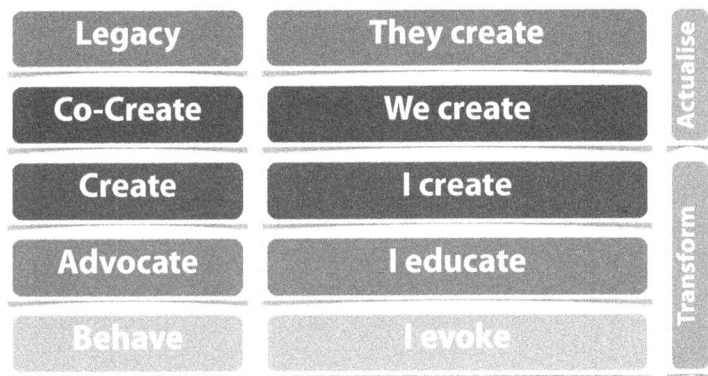

Legacy	They create	Actualise
Co-Create	We create	
Create	I create	Transform
Advocate	I educate	
Behave	I evoke	

Steps from transforming to actualising

To begin with, you always operate within an existing situation or context. You work in a cafe, firm, government agency, factory, a farm, or at home. This is the situation where you're achieving your concrete results. Within that context you seek to create the qualitative result you want—not at the expense of the concrete results, but along with them. You transform an existing situation to include the qualities that matter. For example, you're transforming your workplace to also be one of empowerment. You're transforming, which is detailed further in the next chapter, 'transforming'.

In the first stage, your behaviour directly evokes qualities in others. You need to know what qualitative result that you are after, what qualities you seek to evoke in others. When your behaviour is evoking the qualitative result that you are after, then you have achieved the essence of the behaviour stage and have created the foundations for all the other stages. For example, you behave in a way that helps others to be empowered.

Advocating is sending the message that certain qualities are important. Others are receiving that message. They're being educated about its importance. You're doing that implicitly through repeatedly evoking that quality in others; or explicitly through also giving voice to what's important and bringing it into your conversations. For example, you're advocating the importance of empowerment.

Next you initiate the creation of the qualitative result as an enduring feature and characteristic of the situation you're in. At home or at work, you create an enduring way of working that reflects and evokes the qualities that matter. The way you work or are in relationship evokes those qualities. You create a 'culture' that produces the qualitative result in an ongoing way. For example, you're creating an empowerment culture.

At a certain point, the qualitative result becomes explicit. It explicitly becomes what is to be created. Though qualitative, it has become an explicit and concrete goal in its own right. The qualitative result has become and is a concrete result to be achieved. For example, you are now helping others create empowerment for themselves. You're now actualising. This is detailed further in the final chapter.

At first you're creating that qualitative result together with others. You are co-creating. Regardless of the other concrete results that you work to achieve, your group works to achieve the qualitative results that matter. Together you are defining and creating ways of working and relating that produce the qualitative results. This is as true at home as it is at work. If you are in charge of groups and organisations you are in the perfect place for the creation and co-creation of the qualities that matter most for you. For example, you're working with others and helping them learn how to create empowerment for themselves and others.

At a certain point, you might decide to help people learn how to create and evoke those qualities for themselves as a deliberate and intentional act. In a real sense, you are leaving behind those qualities that matter. It's your legacy. At this stage, you might decide to act as an authority on your message. You might decide to become a coach and mentor. You might write and speak on the topic. You're helping others learn the fine art of creating that quality for themselves and for others that they interact with. Others are learning for themselves. It happens in your absence. Your message has become your legacy.

Choose to notice in giving we receive

Have you ever had the experience of being in a great mood and within a short time others around you are likewise in a great mood? In contrast, have you ever been in a great mood and interacted with someone in a bad mood, and soon enough, you too are in a bad mood? You can think of your ability to be in a particular mood as a tendency to resonate with a particular mood or vibration. In the first example, others resonate with your mood and synchronise with it, and in the second, you resonate with someone else's mood and synchronise with it.

If you take a tuning fork and strike it, it will make a particular sound as it vibrates at a particular tone. The tendency of the tuning fork to vibrate at one tone more than any others is an example of 'resonance'. If you have two similar tuning forks and strike one of them, the other will start to vibrate in unison. The other tuning fork has a harmonic likeness to the one that was struck, and vibrates in sympathetic resonance. As long as they are alike enough, the vibration of one will transfer energy to the other and they will tend to vibrate in unison. This ability to vibrate in unison can also result in synchronisation. In 1665, Dutch physicist Christiaan Huygens noticed that two grandfather clocks would synchronise their pendulum swings.

As you act towards creating the qualities of your message and your actions are congruent with the qualities you are seeking to create, you could say that you resonate with that quality. When you resonate with that quality, others will start to likewise resonate with that quality and synchronise with it. As you embody more of that quality, others are more likely to vibrate in unison with the qualities you imbue. To do that you must embody and be the quality you wish others to experience for themselves. As Ghandi said, "We must be the change we wish to see in the world."

When we're acting in alignment with and for the purposes of creating our message qualities, we're resonating with those qualities. It's not just that we're acting like a resonant tuning fork for our message though. One of the unforeseen aspects Scottish mountaineer, William Hutchinson Murray, describes that no-one 'could have dreamt' would happen, is that the intelligence of that quality can become known. When we act on creating our message, it's as though we become aware of the intelligence of that message. For some, it's like communing with grace.

Anthony's experience

Anthony grew up in Melbourne, the youngest of three brothers. He's spent a year travelling, and when he was sixteen he stood up to 20 friends who wanted to harass someone younger. He's now a married father of two very energetic young boys. Though he has a commerce degree, he works as manager of a successful agile software development team. For fun he likes to find ways to improve his exercise efficiency, play guitar, and sing. He enjoys learning about the history of any holiday location he goes to, especially when they're small towns.

His advice for anyone in search of meaning is that, "The meaning of life comes from purpose. Searching for purpose means we will never have it. Whereas if we just realise our own life and what is already purposeful in our lives, then we already have the meaning of our lives. Don't search for meaning. It comes as a result of living purposefully."

He's emphatic that the exterior of his life has not changed, though the awareness he brings to his life has. "Understanding your message does not mean that it changes your life. I had this expectation that understanding your message means that you have to go out and get a new job. That expectation was mistaken. As I have come to understand my message, I have realised that it hasn't actually changed my life. Yet, it has changed my life. The facts and circumstances of my life are as they were before. I am still who I am. How have I changed? I have become aware of something. I learnt one thing so profound it influences me forever now."

Anthony has realised that in giving, he receives. Like many others, he admits that at first "I didn't want my message to be that." However, his view changed after acting on his message. His message was 'Inclusion through self-awareness' and he reports, "In sharing self-awareness I have the experience of inclusion. Now I realise that it is as much a message to myself as it is to others. The quality that I put in was the quality that I got back."

What helped him to shift was the realisation that our purpose in life is our life. "In reality, it was there all along. It's your own life story. All I have done is give it some words. These words evoke a deeply felt response that identify my life's journey. Now I realise that there was nothing to attain. What I have attained is conscious knowing that it was already there. My purpose is not separate from my life as it already is."

His advice for others is to "Realise that purpose is not something external, something out there in the future. It is your life." He also suggests dropping the notion of trying to get it correct, advising, "Do not take your current realisation as absolute. It is going to change and things will come to you as you act."

Conduit

As Anthony shared, the other interesting thing that tends to happen when you are aligned with the qualities that are important for you, and you seek to create them in your environment, is that you tend to experience for yourself those qualities. Matt, the manager who seeks to achieve his concrete results and continually empower his staff at the same time, reports that he himself feels overwhelmingly empowered. His focus is not on trying to empower himself, but on ensuring others are empowered. He happens to be completely empowered as he works to ensure others are empowered. The more he works to ensure others feel energetic and are empowered, the more he feels energetic and is empowered.

He is so full of 'empowerment' that the question of whether he is empowered has become irrelevant for him. He finds that he is so full of the solution to the problem of his Great Wound, that the issue of his Great Wound has become irrelevant. In giving to others, he receives.

Through working to ensure others receive, you receive. It's not why you give to others. It happens to be what happens when you do.

Maree, whom we met earlier, shares an experience typical of those who put into action their message and act on what they are called to. For Maree, 'confidence' is part of 'worthiness'. "I simply sought to help others experience confidence, and my experiencing confidence and worthiness was a by-product. Seeking to help others have that confidence, I experience confidence. It doesn't even matter how they respond, so my experience is independent of how others respond. I drive my own worthiness. I am happier to be here."

For me personally, as long as I was seeking to answer my own fulfilment, as long as I was seeking for the answer from outside, as long as I was expecting others to give it to me, I felt miserable and the experience was perpetually painful. Moreover, I made life difficult for those around me. The moment I flipped that into helping others realise and act on their calling, I felt completely fulfilled. Any lack of a sense of purpose, meaning and calling, was simply no longer an issue. It was gone.

It's a question of how do we satisfy our craving and desire for those qualities we want to experience—success, confidence, fulfilment. We can:

- Seek for that to be supplied to us and satisfied from the outside. This will never satisfy.
- Generate that from inside in giving that to others. This is the only way it will ever be satisfied.

Many report that, as they immerse themselves in the goal of creating their message, that they just receive information about the message 'out of the blue'. Knowing seems to 'happen'. They see themselves as spontaneously receiving this information, like a scientist who suddenly understands the meaning of all of their observations. Albert Einstein said that, "The intuitive mind is a sacred gift and the rational mind is a faithful servant." Many who reported 'suddenly knowing things' investigated whether there was any research, evidence, or others that said the same things. They invariably found that, indeed, there was existing support for what they now knew. In many cases, that they 'suddenly just knew' was a refinement or extension of what others knew.

It's as though we've become a conduit for the intelligence of our message.

I know that this happened many times for myself. As I acted on helping people experience fulfilment through realising their calling, the intelligence of calling and fulfilment showed up. The most recent insight was when I was working to identify what were the best action choices to make and how to know which were the optimal choices for action. As quickly as I asked, I realised 'The optimal choices for action are the conditions for flow'. That sudden realisation led me to read more deeply Csíkszentmihályi's work,'*Flow*'. So be attentive to when insight reveals itself to you.

In acting on your calling you are like a resonant beacon for the energy and intelligence of that quality. The more you're a conduit for and share that energy and intelligence with others, the more you receive it.

Some will, some won't, so what

There's something to be aware of whenever we do something. When we move to act, including to create our message, many people tend to respond according to the four types described in the 'varieties of expertise model' described earlier. This happens particularly at the 'actualise' stage when we are explicitly creating our message. My suggestion is to be aware of the healthy and unhealthy ways people respond when you create:

1. **Applicator**
    - Some will apply what you create and appropriately attribute your creation to you, often finding and sharing refinements to your methods
    - Others will apply what you create without attribution to you, almost or literally as though they're claiming credit for it

2. **Scholar**
    - Some will apply and acknowledge your ideas as the basis for theirs, often extending your thinking and sharing that
    - Others will treat what you create as ideas to be thought about and discussed, often without application, and emphasise their ideas about your ideas, often invalidating them, without trying your ideas or acknowledging their usefulness

3. **Critic**
    - Some will think about, try out and evaluate what you create, often providing and sharing informed reviews, suggestions and enhancements
    - Others will look for, focus on, find fault with or denigrate you and what you create, including what you haven't done, regardless of your creation and its ability to help others

4. **Authority**
    - Some will use and extend what you create, and seek to attribute, where possible, what you create as the basis for the extensions they create and share (though it is not always easy to know the origins of what's been extended)
    - Others will use and extend what you create without recognition, attribution or acknowledgement of what they're extending or whose shoulders they're standing on, or even attempt to do so

Celebrate healthy responses. Don't be surprised or disturbed when people respond in the more problematic ways described above, though you might consider how you'll respond when they do.

Transforming

We've completed the 'learn' stage. We're now at the creation stages, the first of which is the 'transform' stage. The focus at this stage is on the methods we use for achieving results, and to do that we're ideally convinced about the qualities we seek to create.

Stage	Focus	Be
Being	Be	Grateful
Actualise	Result	Activated
Transform	**Method**	**Convinced**
Learn	Discover	Curious
Permit	Allow	Accepting
Identify	Explore	Honest
Denied	Accept	Open

Transform stage of the Stages of Actualisation

The end is nigh

If you work, then you have at least two situations or contexts in which you live your life—work and home. You might have many other situations in which you live, such as sport, recreation, and social groups. The 'transform' stage is essentially bringing your message qualities into those situations. You're innovating within your existing situation or context, where what you are introducing are ways to create or evoke the qualities that matter to you. You're putting time, energy and attention towards achieving your qualitative results.

For example, at work you're still achieving the tangible concrete goals, and achieving as much empowerment as practical and appropriate. At home, you're still raising a family, and going about it in a way that produces trust, respect and dignity for all involved.

A principle well known in the business world is that you cannot create a result separate from the method or strategy you use to create it. The results you get are a direct result of the strategy you used to achieve it. This is usually interpreted in concrete, tangible terms. What is not so well understood is that the same principle applies in qualitative terms.

Just as you have two types of results, concrete and qualitative, every method you use, every action you take, is both:

1. A concrete method (the action performed), and
2. A qualitative method (the qualities that the concrete methods embody and represent to others)

This means that you cannot create a qualitative result separate from the method or strategy you use to create them. It's the qualities that imbue your method that create the qualitative result you get. It's the qualities that imbue your method and strategy that define what your qualitative method and strategy are.

Therefore, the way you go about creating your qualitative results, the method you use, ideally embodies the qualitative results you're after. You are achieving your concrete goals, and creating an inner experience for those you're involved with while doing so. Your formula here is:

Message = qualitative method = qualitative result

In other words, the qualitative end result you're after defines the qualitative method you use. My mantra for this is:

The end is the method

For example, if you want empowerment, then your methods need to be empowering. If your methods reek of over-control, don't expect empowerment as the outcome. If you want love and trust at home, then your actions need to be loving and trusting as far as the other person is concerned. If you distrust and denigrate people around you, don't expect trust and love as the outcome.

Remember that your message is what others experience; your gift is your more effective way for how you do it. Your message is your qualitative result, and your gift your method. Your gift serves the creation of your message. Both your message and your gift inform and shape how.

When you act, you execute on a strategy. That strategy produces a concrete result as well as a qualitative one. This is represented in the following diagram.

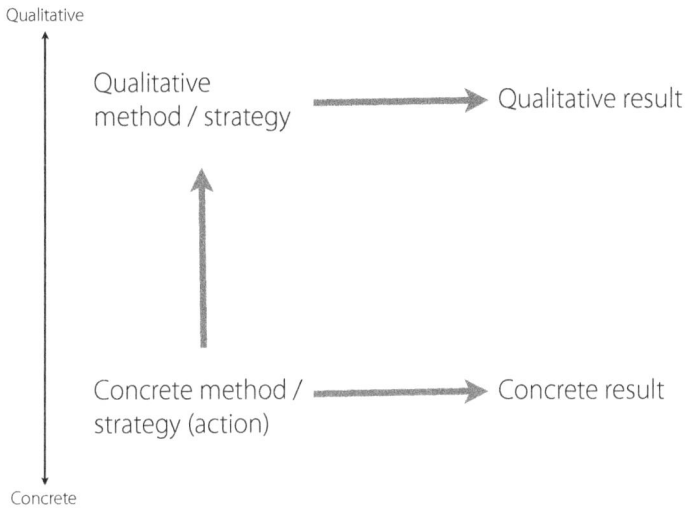

Why achieving both results needs a combined strategy

As most business people know, the concrete results you're after will inform the concrete strategy you use. You always start with the end in mind. Likewise, the desired qualitative results will inform your choice of qualitative strategy. Since the qualitative strategy is tied to and is a reflection of the concrete strategy, the required qualitative results will also need to inform the concrete strategy. The above diagram shows what happens once a strategy or method is acted on. Deciding on a strategy is a reverse engineering process, starting with both aspects of the end in mind. This is represented in the following diagram.

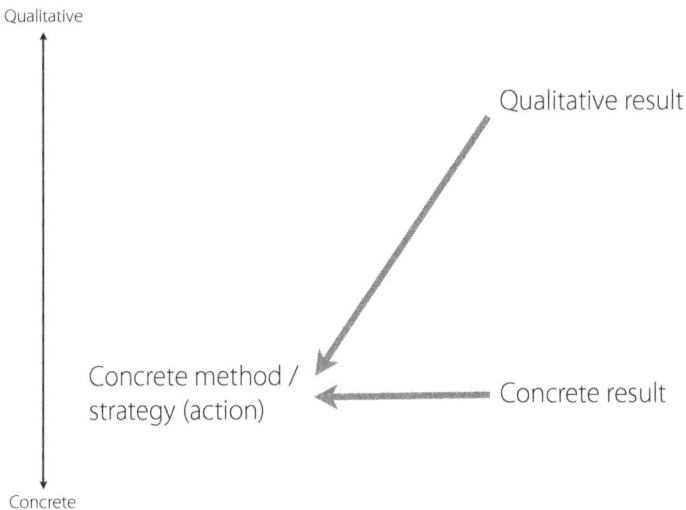

Strategy based on both types of results

Many years ago I worked with a rigidly bureaucratic organisation that seemed to expect people to do only as prescribed. This reveals more about me than the organisation, but their effect on people was such that I'd cynically called it the 'Dungeon of Human Suffering' (due to a perceived departure from freedom and dignity). They had an espoused corporate value of 'innovation', and spent much money on innovation programs. I had no doubt that they genuinely believed that innovation was important. They even included an innovation ideas box for people to submit ideas, which required a multipage 'Ideas Submission' form with some dozen or so questions. The form could not be completed in less than 45 minutes. If your idea got past the first checkpoint, there was even more paperwork and you were required to produce a complete and costed solution. What was promoted as a way to submit ideas was treated and reviewed as though it was a complete business proposal. People felt punished for their ideas. Any guesses about the levels of innovation that were produced? Few people submitted ideas. Generation of ideas dropped off all together. Nothing changed. I heard that a few years later the same organisation tried to kick-start an 'innovation culture' using virtually the same methods. By all accounts, staff were even more cynical than before.

When I was a teenager, I had the attention span of a gnat. Actually, that's unfair to gnats. I'd be easily distracted whenever I was in conversation with people, even though I was still listening. I'd still hear what was being said, though would come across as distracted. It was rare for others, let alone a girlfriend, to experience 'attention' as a result of my behaviour and actions. Whenever I was told that I 'was not listening', I'd recite back what had been said, giving the impression that I'd arrogantly proven them wrong. In my infinite wisdom, I'd compound a lack of attention with a lack of respect.

Both of these examples are perfectly understandable though. What I did not realise at the time of working with the controlling company was that the bureaucratic methods used by the organisation sent a clear message of control that served to stifle innovation. The way they went about trying to create an innovation culture was consistent with their existing control culture. Innovation would never take hold under those conditions. What I did not realise as a youth was that, while I was respectfully listening and heard whatever was being shared, the other person was experiencing me as its opposite, as not listening and disrespectful. The organisation's version of what they were intending to create was the opposite of what happened. My version of what I was doing was the opposite of those I interacted with. For a long time I could not understand how this could be so. Now I know that it could not have been otherwise.

Transforming transforms

The 'transform' stage is all about achieving qualitative goals along with whatever your concrete goals are. Your qualitative results define, shape and characterise the methods you use for achieving your concrete results. Your qualitative results are implicit while your concrete results are explicit. You achieve your qualitative results while achieving your concrete ones—by acting through your message.

Peter's experience

Peter is in his later 40s, is married with two teenage daughters, is himself one of two children, and has two cats. He grew up in country Australia, lived in the United Kingdom, has a Science Degree and a Masters in Accounting. Especially passionate about cycling, which he calls 'meditation on the move', he says that it satisfies his 'need for speed'.

Peter says that application of what's important for him has made a big difference in his life. "Being clear reveals what I need to put into practice. What matters is how I apply my values effectively. Application is really broad—work, family, and me individually."

Connecting with and applying his values means that Peter is "more at peace with myself. I am not trying to shut down my experience. I am listening and validating. That helps me work out what is and is not right in a situation, and how I need to address that. I know what the right effective thing is to do."

"I used to work on the assumption that, if I was feeling uncomfortable, this was my problem", says Peter. "Now it's, 'this is my problem and do something about that problem'. Don't bottle it up. Act effectively. I now have the questions to ask, which makes me more effective. There's not so much wondering about how I need to act. I just know how to act. This is because I understand and know what I stand for. I don't think I really knew what I stood for before."

Describing the shift in culture of his team, he explains, "I manage a new team with a large number of people. What I am finding now, which comes back to my message of self-trust and be courageous, I am much more focussed on supporting my team through things to show them that self-trust, rather than trying to protect them, which I did in the past." As a result of this, he says, "The culture comes through the broader team, as my people have teams themselves. The team is coming together really well, and have developed a deep trust very quickly."

Peter recognises the relationship between clarity and confidence. "Clarity and confidence go together," he explains. "In the past I might be unclear on what my position was because I wasn't listening to my own experience. Now I am a lot clearer and bring my own point of view to the table more, and trust that. I am just more confident about what I am doing, making decisions quicker, more willing to act sooner, more willing to trust myself and others."

Describing how the change in him ripples through his group, Peter says, "It wasn't a big change in behaviour for me. Those I support know they're supported. I am just more consistent in my behaviour—so others see it in evidence. The way my team manage their teams reflects the way I manage my team. There's more trust throughout the broader team and they're working across teams better."

Explaining how this has come about, Peter shares, "Doing something once has an effect, but when consistent it sticks. As an example, we're looking at outsourcing part of my team at the moment. Rather than hiding behind it, I've done what I can to be transparent and trust them with it. I've had the people involved actively engaged in the process. The open communication seems to have helped them understand the change, feel supported, and go with it, even though there's no decision yet. It's important for me that they're a participant in the process. It's not being done to them. They are a part of it. I trust them to know their stuff, and I trust them with the situation. The result is that there's more trust, increased engagement, and they're involved, even though we don't know yet what the outcome is. Even though the outcome may be they no longer have a role, they're contributing really positively to the whole process. That there is increased trust and participation, on its own, is already a great outcome. It's critical to the tangible outcome anyway."

Peter hasn't shared with his team his 'Be courageous through self-trust' message. His observation is that by being more courageous and showing greater trust in his team, his team showed greater courage and trust in positively dealing with a situation where their own roles were potentially at risk. Asked to reflect on this observation, he excitedly says, "That's part of why I'm in such a good place. It's just a buzz seeing the effects, seeing the interactions with the team move in a certain way, seeing a culture of trust grow. It's a form of love, of deep care. I am proud of them."

Like many others, Peter is clear that he is getting what he is giving. "You get a lot back from just doing it. What I am getting is trust. As I help foster trust I'm getting trust back from them and I trust myself more. As I seek to trust and elevate trust in others, I am more confident and trust myself. It doesn't mean you don't question what you are doing, but you have faith in what your intentions are and are happy to act and realise that you're improving the place and process as you go along."

Pausing for a moment, he adds, "It wouldn't even matter if I didn't get it (trust) back in kind, though it's great when it does. Even with those where it's not coming back, I am comfortable with that as I know that I have done what I can and what I am about. I've brought myself to the table properly."

Intangible achievement

The earlier 'learn' stage is essentially about trying things out and learning about what works and does not work, and why. What works ideally is strengthened, and what does not work is ideally discontinued.

At this stage you somewhat break with tradition and established methods and strategies. This is especially the case for the traditional concrete ways of achieving things for the situation and context that you are in. You break with established concrete methods—not necessarily all of them, but at least some of them—not to change the concrete results, as they are still important, but to include the qualitative results that are important. To do that, you need to be clear on both types of results you have and want as goals, and use them to define your combined strategy for action.

Message = qualitative method = qualitative result

Qualitative result + concrete result => combined strategy

There are three steps to the 'transform' stage:

1. Behave
2. Advocate
3. Create

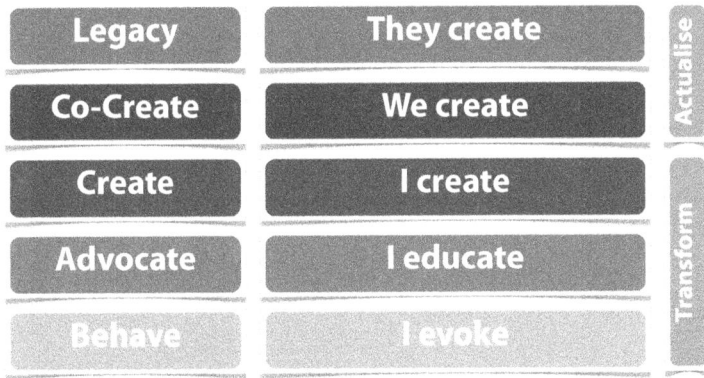

Steps from transforming to actualising

Behave

The first step is of behaviour. You act and behave in a way that evokes your qualitative result in others. You act in a way that evokes in others the qualities of your message.

For example, say that what matters for you is worthiness—so you point out when others have achieved a certain standard. They will perceive that in a certain way, and it could be in a variety of different ways such as worthiness, confidence and self-trust. As confidence and self-trust both occur in your Value Stack, you might decide that these qualitative results are all pointing to the same thing. In this case all of your qualitative results are consistent with your Value Stack. By giving compliments, you act in a way that others experience either directly or at least in part as 'being worthy'. Your compliments tend to evoke your qualitative result. You are acting in a way that that is congruent with what is important for you. You're being authentic.

Behaving is an interactive experience when it involves others. Your action creates an in-the-moment experience for others. Your action influences the qualitative result that's evoked. That qualitative result, for example the experience of confidence, is transitory. Your action is a transitory qualitative influence. It's an important influence. As you act, you influence others' experience. That influence is either towards or away from the qualities that are important for you.

As a guide towards how to behave, you have already identified behaviours that to you compromise the qualities that are important. As you created your Value Stack, you used behaviours that you experienced in your environment to identify what was important for you. If those behaviours compromise what is important for you, then the opposite of those behaviours create them.

From compromise behaviours, the opposite and creating actions can be readily identified. Examples of the creative opposite action are shown in the following table.

Compromise behaviour	Creative action
Student arrived into class after the second bell that indicated class commencement.	Arrive before second bell.
Mother talks about what she is missing in her life. Happens whenever we talk.	Talk about what you do have and appreciate about life.
He came into the meeting 10 minutes after it started. He told the group the story of how he became late. The attention of the group was on his story for 5 minutes.	Arrive on time. Stay relevant to agenda.
He went straight to study when he got home.	On arriving home, take a moment to hug and connect.

Examples of creative actions as opposite of compromise behaviour

A starting point to behave and act in a manner congruent with what's most important:

1. Know your gift, your most effective how
2. Know the qualities of what's important for you
3. Know the behaviours in others that compromise what's important
4. Identify the opposite of those behaviours
5. Act congruently with what's important

    - Behave and act to create what's important
    - Avoid the behaviours and actions that compromise what's important

Advocate

Behaving in a manner that is authentic for you is one thing—advocating and sharing with others the message of what's important for you, is another.

When your behaviour is consistent with what is important for you, you are being authentic. When you are behaving authentically and others receive the message about what's important for you, you are perceived by others as authentic. You are evoking the qualitative result as well as sending the message about it. To be perceived by others as authentic, they need to know what is important for you and experience it as true for themselves.

For example, 'respect' is important for me. If I act in a way that you perceive as respectful, you'll experience respect. If you experience respect each time we interact, you'd experience and associate with me a pattern of respect. You will tend to form an enduring impression of me as respectful. The frequency of the quality or respect that characterised our interaction sends a message. The message is implicit in the action and characterises the interaction. It's sending an implicit message.

It sends a message just as loudly as if I had given voice to it. If I then give voice to and share with you: 'You know, respect is really important for me' then that will confirm the pattern you've seen and the impression that you have already formed. More than likely you'll perceive me as being authentic, regarding the quality of 'respect' anyway. Giving voice to what's important sends an explicit message.

In another example, if whenever you interacted with someone who acted in a way that was true to their word, you'd probably get the message and assess them as having integrity.

Others receive in two ways the messages you send:

1. **Implicitly**—others experiencing patterns of your behaviour
2. **Explicitly**—others hearing from you about what's important

If you've not experienced respect as a result of our interactions and then I tell you that respect is important for me, you'll perceive me at best as inauthentic, maybe even a hypocrite. Making a message explicit before it is implicit is rarely perceived as being authentic. To be seen as authentic, the behaviours that follow an explicit message of what's important ought to be congruent with what was said to be important. For example, if you make claim that 'respect' is important for you and others have not yet experienced that characterising your patterns of behaviour, then a safe strategy is to ensure that they experience you as 'respectful' as quickly as practical. The safest ground towards authenticity is to advocate only when the behaviour is already showing up in you.

Proactive advocacy is one thing. Responsive advocacy is another.

In the above examples, you're proactive in demonstrating and acting in a way that is consistent with what is important for you. What about when others compromise what's important? How do you respond when that happens? The other side of advocacy is when others act in a way that compromises what's important for you.

Say for example, 'dignity' is important for you and someone acts in a manner that you experience as blatantly denigrating. In this situation you might choose to advocate the importance of dignity. You might choose to share with that person what is important for you and that what's important has been compromised. Notice I did not say to challenge them on 'being denigrating', as this is an arguable perception that is likely to lead to an argument. That dignity is important for you is unarguably true. Because 'dignity' is important, if this is the first time you two have talked about it, you might choose to have a one-to-one and private conversation with them, rather than bring it up in front of 20 people. As they may not know how to be clear themselves, it is useful to suggest options and possibilities for behaviour that would create what is important.

Robyn's experience

Robyn is the eldest of four children. She grew up on a dairy farm until 5 years old and then in a small town of 5,000 people. Someone who loves numbers and what numbers can represent, she studied maths and statistics at university. She plays tennis and golf, and is a regular participant of a book reading group. Her favourite television show is Australian Story, which is consistent with her love for connecting with people and hearing their stories. Working in the area of business improvement, she gets frustrated when things seem to be going too slowly, and she enjoys getting things done more effectively.

Robyn had a major shift around her understanding and application of her experience with anger. "A whole lot of stuff just went away when I realised that it was okay to feel anger. I used to think that anger was bad. So much energy was being used always pushing it down. Just being able to realise and identify what is important has been wonderful. I was never exploding in anger. I just feel calmer. No reason to explode, no reason to withhold. I feel like I am more me."

"I am clearer," she says of the importance of clarity. "In the workplace," she continues, "when I'm not connected with things and unclear, I just speak up. I am clear about why I am doing things and how they connect in to who I am and what I can deliver. Improving business services is creating clarity, and I feel so much more energised about that. I could do it all day."

Robyn is more connected with her work, feels more energised, and her relationships have improved. "When I wasn't clear, I'd make assumptions that people knew what I was thinking. I would be holding them accountable for things they had no idea about. Sharing what matters is also good for them. It's sharing the relationship properly."

"I am a lot less grumpy!" she laughs about the paradox of, "By giving myself permission to feel grumpy, I am a lot less grumpy." The effect of this is, "Happier relationships, less conflict."

Reflecting on the reciprocal nature of her own experience, Robyn shares, "By allowing myself to be, I'm allowing others to be. It's a lot less stressful." Her approach to her work has also changed. "I have more fun," she says, "there's not that sense of dread, that the project is about to go live, and will be a disaster. Anticipation was always dread, it was never hopeful anticipation. Now it's, well, we'll see what happens. No over-forecasting, just being present, as I still work to an overall project plan with key milestones, just not an over-engineered detailed one. Today is today and this is the best decision for today."

Robyn's message is about building trust. She says that, "All of a sudden, all of my life made sense. I was trying to build trust by avoiding anything that might lose trust. What I get now," she adds, "is that building trust is just right for my role. Business improvement requires everyone involved in that business to trust each other. So I share what I know, nothing is withheld, I do what I say, and everyone has a part to play."

The results are, "Better outcomes. People trust each other more. We have more of a piloting approach. We are all working together, all doing our bit, and we know in the end it's all going to be better than trying to control the whole thing. More is happening quicker, and people connect more positively with what they see happening. Things are less planned in detail, seemingly more chaotic, because I am dealing with what's there and that things are always changing."

Typical of the sentiment of many others, Robyn reflects that a day on purpose, while spent, is a day well spent. "Building trust," Robyn says, "feels right. It doesn't feel like hard work, even when it is."

Responsiveness responds

It's not just that something is important; to be congruent with what's important we act on what's important in a way that upholds it. Where and how you act is entirely up to you. Ideally, the way you respond is consistent with what is important for you. This is 'method integrity'. It's tough to have credibility advocating peace by being violent.

Responsive advocacy involves:

1. Something happening in your environment that you experience as a compromise of what's important
2. You are present to your own experience and can identify what is important for you personally
3. In a way that is consistent with what is important for you
   - Share what is important for you
   - Reveal that what is important has been compromised
   - Suggest options to experience what is important

What to do to advocate and influence for what's important:

1. Behave and act congruently with what's most important
2. Proactive advocacy
   - Be consistent with that behaviour to establish your actions as a pattern of behaviour, thereby sending an implicit message about what is important
   - Give voice to and nominate what's important for you, using your own behaviour as examples of what that looks like, thereby sending an explicit message about what's important
3. Responsive advocacy
   - Be present to when what is important for you is experienced to be compromised
   - Identify what is important for you that is unarguably true in a personal 1st person sense
   - Share what is important for you personally
   - Reveal that what's important has been compromised
   - Suggest options and possibilities for behaviour that create what's important

Create

Several years ago I had a role in the Leadership Development Unit of a large public company in Australia. The situation and context of my role was 'leadership development'. I had little interest in or motivation for management training, though I had much interest in and motivation for leadership development. Mind you, I had interest in a few aspects of leadership development and in only a few of the characteristics that led to greater leadership, not all of them. There are many approaches to the context of leadership development. There are many different characteristics that claim to be related to greater leadership effectiveness. Google 'leadership development' and you'll get 500 million results.

As you have been reading throughout this book, my personal message is around actualising your calling. Included with my message are 'purpose' and 'authenticity', as when you are living your message you are being most authentic and purposeful. Now as it happens, both 'purpose' and 'authenticity' are topics that already register highly in the context of leadership development. This means that there is already much evidence that shows that developing a sense of purpose and greater authenticity support more effective leadership. You can participate in specific programs that promise to develop your sense of purpose and authenticity. Moreover, there is research and evidence from The Leadership Circle, for example, that says that authenticity, including a sense of purpose, is the factor most highly correlated with leadership effectiveness. So far I have been describing to you the situation and context of 'leadership development', as that was the context in which I worked.

I was running my own practice at the time and had developed programs, methods and practices for supporting the development of authenticity and a sense of purpose. Utilising what I had created on my own, I offered a leadership development program for that organisation. The way that I presented that program was like this:

'Research shows that leadership effectiveness is fundamentally important for both individual and organisational performance. As leadership effectiveness increases, financial performance tends to rise. Though we know that developing greater leadership effectiveness is important, the problem is how to develop it effectively. The factor most highly related to leadership effectiveness is authenticity and a sense of purpose. Develop your authenticity and sense of purpose and you develop your leadership effectiveness. Doing so will tend to increase your overall performance. So this is a leadership development program that will focus on developing your single most important characteristic of leadership—your authenticity and purpose. Develop your authenticity and purpose, and you enhance your leadership effectiveness'.

I still completely agree with everything I said then. The point is that I had turned the existing context of 'leadership development' to be all about 'authenticity and purpose'. I had made 'authenticity and purpose' the solution and answer to the problem of and need for 'leadership development'. Authenticity and purpose are an expression of my message. Therefore I had changed the existing context to be my message. I had created a link from an existing context to my message. My message of 'authenticity and purpose' was now the solution, approach and method for the existing context of 'leadership development'. I was not trying to answer all aspects of leadership development, only the aspect that related to my message. I have done the same thing with authentic relating.

A friend of mine, Matt Church, makes leadership to be all about the clarity of spoken communication. Senior managers, John and a different Matt, both make leadership to be all about empowerment of staff. Peter makes leadership to be all about engagement and trust. Maree makes leadership to be all about the way you connect and engage with others. Adam makes leadership to be all about clarity and confidence. All of them demonstrate and are regarded by others as showing great leadership themselves. Moreover, all of them maintain high levels of engagement with their teams and achieve great performance.

What's more, look around and you'll find research and evidence that shows all of them to be true about leadership. There are books about each aspect of leadership they characterise. They each act through their gift, and the part of leadership they focus on is the aspect they care most about, which is what their lives are the solution to. You could say their signature leadership style is their message. Acting on that is their calling.

Your message is your leadership style

This happens in other contexts as well. Katrina makes engagement with students to be all about worthiness and certainty. Lucy makes her fine art to be all about freedom, inclusion and being held, helping people connect with their already connected and free nature. Pete makes accountability in coaching and mentoring to be all about integrity. Gerard makes social justice to be all about human dignity. Each of them is brilliant at what they do—gifted in how they work and passionate about what they are creating and leading.

The thing that all of these people have in common is that they made their message to be the factor necessary to achieve success in their situations. They made their message the primary method that others needed to experience for success to be achieved—it became their way of working with others. For all of them, their message was the factor that they regarded as most important for achieving what it meant to be a success when working with others in their field.

In other words, your message is likely to be the factor or quality necessary for success working with others towards achieving your concrete goals. It's your signature method or style for working with others. For example, though Katrina interacts with others through rapport, she does so for them to be worthy and feel certain.

Your message is your signature style

Wherever you interact with others you have the opportunity to create your message qualities. You're possibly already in the perfect place to act on and create your message through your gift.

In a given situation, you're ideally using your gift to produce your message. It's useful to define your ability to be effective in those situations that way. Use the following script to define and reframe your ability to be most effective. Use words from both your Gift Stack and Value Stack. Try this script and experience how it resonates for you: 'I'm most effective at ... *(context)* when I'm, by, or through ... *(gift)* ... *(message)*.'

For example, I'm most effective in leader development (context) when inspiring (gift) authenticity and purpose (message). I'm at my best fostering relationship communication and connection by illuminating what's mutually important.

To create your message in an existing situation, and to use it to change the way you approach that existing context:

1. Know your existing situation—professional or personal. For example, school teacher, business leader, entrepreneur, artist, or relationship.

2. Decide whether it works and makes sense for you (not necessarily for others) to make the qualities of your gift and message essential for success in that situation. For example, is it true for you to say that rapport and engagement (your gift) in the classroom is key to success as a teacher, and that to achieve success in the classroom the students must feel worthy and certain (your message)? As another example, is it true for you to say that to achieve success in business others must feel motivated and empowered?

3. Redefine your existing situation according to your message. For Katrina it is, 'I'm at my best as a teacher (context) when I'm engaging (gift) and my students know they are worthy and feel certain (message)'. For Lucy it could be something like, 'I do my best fine art (gift) when my commission (context) represents freedom and inclusion (message)'.

4. Do it. See what happens.

Actualising

We've completed the 'transform' stage. We're now at the 'actualise' stage. The focus at this stage is on the direct creation of our message—making it explicit. To do that we're explicit about our message being the result to be achieved, and activated about achieving it.

Stage	Focus	Be
Being	Be	Grateful
Actualise	Result	Activated
Transform	Method	Convinced
Learn	Discover	Curious
Permit	Allow	Accepting
Identify	Explore	Honest
Denied	Accept	Open

Actualise stage of the Stages of Actualisation

Explicitly explicit

Jeri's experience

Jeri was born in India and grew up in the Middle East, moving to Australia when he was 12 years old. At high school he held the 100m sprint record and captained the soccer team. He trains in Krav Maga, an Israeli martial art, loves the character Superman, and is his friends call him a playful prankster. He's married and has a 3 year-old son.

"I have been much more relaxed. It's like a re-injection of confidence," Jeri shares of his experience, "and this comes from understanding what's important for me, of what I need in an experience of something or else it doesn't work for me."

His group mirrors his personal experience. "In sharing my experience my direct team had a better understanding of where I was coming from. They just got it. As I relaxed, the people around me relaxed. As I was confident, others around me were confident."

"What caused this," Jeri explains, "was uncovering what's important, my core values. As long as I am acting according to that, I am happy. In the past, a lot of my frustration came from not acting on that, but I did not know that at the time. I used to think, 'I don't like that, what do I do?' Now it's more like, 'I don't think that's right because of the following'. These changes have come from knowing that trust and respect are important for me."

The positive influence on others has been significant for Jeri. "I have gone from being uncomfortable with something to being able to say why. It had never entered my mind before just where I could take a conversation and what kind of effect it could have by taking it there."

Jeri has found his immediate team and broader group have responded positively. "I find that people listen more and are actually waiting to hear it," he explains. "The concrete result is achieved in a way that achieves what's important, that uplifts and upholds what's important. Being able to have that discussion that involves both aspects, when before I didn't because it never entered my mind, enables me to have a more effective conversation."

Reflecting an attitude of having a role and interacting with others as humans, Jeri shares, "I have one of those roles where it's very easy for people to feel intimidated. I've realised how easy it is to have a high level of formal authority that comes from my role, and still be an approachable human being that treats people according to what's important. It's amazing how powerful it is to share what's important, be consistent in my behaviour, to keep my word, and to do what I say."

Describing his approach to building a highly functioning team, Jeri explains, "Respect is important. I just do it. I don't have to engineer a situation; the situation is already there. This does not mean you're not delivering an unpopular decision, though you can do it with openness and respect that lets people know what's needed to make the goal the reality. I can share that something isn't working any more and that we have to do it in a new way, and my teams tell me there's much more buy-in than ever before. I realise that my job is to help them understand what the core principle is and what we need to be as a team. They are involved in figuring out how to make that shift."

Describing the usefulness of having both a concrete and qualitative objective, Jeri continues, "Where you want to get to needs to make sense. If people see that it makes sense to them, it makes things a lot easier, and it makes finding a way a lot simpler. You might have a generic thing like 'improved profitability'. Business planning is usually defined by that outcome or a particular number. Now, it's more around, 'well, what do we need to do to get that as well as what's important, and then work back from it'. How do we need to act, and still get those results?

Challenging my team with that has helped them be a lot more creative, lateral, and come up with new approaches, many of which we can take forward, and will be the basis of a new look for the organisation. I haven't heard someone say outright 'no!' Or someone not agree."

When asked about what advice he might give to others, Jeri gets animated. "There's an old saying that a team is a reflection of their leader. I've always kind of believed it, but I haven't understood it as much as I understand it now. It's not the showboat stuff that makes a difference; it has to be the stuff that happens everyday that will give you that credit from your staff. Showboating can easily backfire when it's not consistent with what happens everyday. Without a doubt, you must be consistent. The message you send just has to be consistent."

For Jeri, right action not only produces the right concrete result but also produces the right experience for those involved. "You need to get the right result through right action. If not, you need to change how you are doing it, and do that upfront next time. The right effort is the one that produces the right results."

Message method, message result

Transforming is where your message is implicit. Actualising is where your message is explicit. Your message transforms an existing context; at the actualise stage it is the context.

Transforming is all about adding your qualitative results to whatever your concrete results are, or redefining the concrete results according to the qualitative ones. Your qualitative goals define and characterise the methods you use for achieving your concrete goals. Your qualitative results were implicit while your concrete results were explicit. The 'create' step was essentially innovating within an existing context (your concrete goals) and reshaping how you achieve that context to be in accordance to your message (your qualitative goals). Your concrete objectives are still achieved, though the method for achieving those results is reframed in accordance with your message. The method for achieving results in that situation was characterised by your message. In other words, in the transform stage:

Method = Message

Transforming a situation can be entirely satisfying and fulfilling. Your existing work context might well be the perfect place for the fulfilment of your purpose. The actualising stage goes one step further, for those who wish to go there.

Actualising is all about making your qualitative results explicit. You make your qualitative goal a concrete goal in its own right. It does not replace other concrete goals, but becomes one itself.

The actualise stage is all about effectively creating a new goal, a new context. This is where your context and goal is your message. Here the objective or result you seek to achieve is explicitly the quality of your message. In other words, in the actualise stage:

Result = Message

Co-create

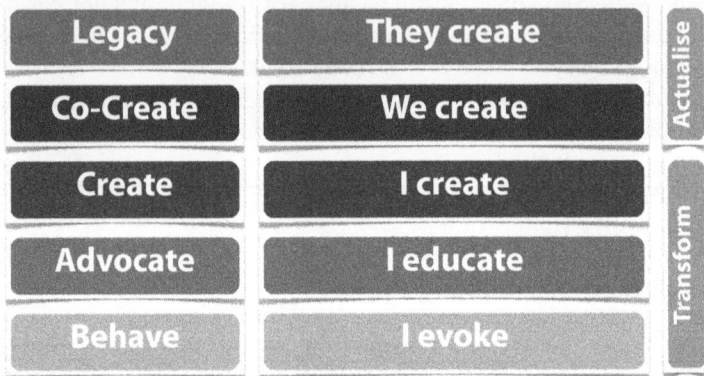

From transforming to actualising

The essential difference between the 'create' and 'co-create' steps is:

- Create is where I make my message explicit ***in*** a context
- Co-create is where we make it explicit ***as*** the context

Behaving in a manner that is authentic for you is one thing. Advocating and sharing with others the message of what's important for you, is another. Actively creating what's important as an enduring characteristic of your situation is yet another. Different again to do so with others.

The step beyond sending the message of what's important is to not just evoke that quality as a transitory experience or enduring impression, but together to explicitly create it in your environment. Here you lead and co-create a qualitative influence that endures—a new context called your message. Co-creation usually happens organically as people choose to explicitly participate with its creation.

Every action creates two types of results, concrete and qualitative. If you consistently behave in a manner that is experienced by others as respectful and has integrity, they experience your authenticity. They receive the message of respect and integrity, though it is implicit in your behaviour. If you then give voice to and advocate respect and integrity as important, you send an explicit message. When your implicit and explicit messages are the same, you are congruent and others perceive you are authentic. If others likewise become convinced that respect and integrity are important, and their actions likewise reflect those qualities, then you have created a culture—a culture of respect and integrity.

When people normalise to a particular qualitative result as a characteristic of how they work, they have a culture that reflects that quality. You have a culture of respect and integrity only when the way you work is interpreted and experienced by people as reflecting respect and integrity. When a group of people choose to consistently act in a way they know creates a certain qualitative result, say respect, then you have a co-created culture of respect. At home with your intimate partner, if the two of you explicitly act in a way that you both consistently experience as respect, you have co-created a respectful relationship.

Have you ever worked for an organisation that had 'innovation' as one of its corporate values, and whenever someone shared an idea they were ridiculed? You probably have a culture of disrespect. You do not have an innovation culture. As long as attempts to innovate receive ridicule, a culture of innovation cannot exist. By the way, if you try to enforce a new culture through tightly defined behaviours and punitive measures, then you're creating a culture of control and compliance, regardless of what you imagine you might be creating.

Each time you act, you send a single message. Others hear a single message. A single action is not yet a pattern of behaviour, and you have not yet sent a consistent message. For example, you might once send the message of 'trust', though if your existing pattern is a message of 'distrust', then others are likely to be sceptical of the single message of trust. A consistent message requires a consistent pattern of behaviour sending the same message. When you have a pattern of the same behaviour, you have a pattern of sending the same message. When others repeatedly receive the same message, they 'get' the message, and may follow your lead. If you consistently act in a way that sends the message of 'trust', others will eventually get that as a message about you. When they likewise implicitly choose to participate, you're creating trust. When others explicitly choose to create trust and do so together, you're co-creating trust.

The create step of the transform stage is where you're the driving influence that transforms an existing context. It's something that others might pick up on and emulate. The co-create step is where the group you're part of decides to do so deliberately as an objective or goal in its own right.

You co-create culture anywhere there's other people—in your personal or professional life, at home, at work, or with friends. Your collective focus is the qualitative aspect of how people act and the qualitative experience it results in.

The create step is through individual leadership; the co-create step through joint leadership. One often organically leads to the other.

Matt's experience

Matt's the eldest of three boys. His mother worked as a lawyer and his father in sports administration. Passionate about football, his early ambition was to play in the Australian Football League. He has a degree in Behavioural Science after initially wanting to become a psychologist. Professionally he has gravitated towards operational leadership roles because of the large number of people involved, and the ability for creating greater effectiveness. A volunteer with the Big Brother organisation, he regularly mentors a ten-year-old Sudanese boy.

Like many others, Matt relates to the aspiration to be like someone else. "My attempts to find message in the past, were scatter-gun," Matt shares, "typically identifying people who were delivering a message that was appealing to me at the time. That changed regularly, and it was always someone else's message. I'd never taken the time to identify my own personal message. I'd deliver on someone else's message, and then move on to what I thought was better. I wanted to be like my dad, a footballer, a musician, or some clever person who wrote a book, because at that time, their message appealed to me. I'd seek to emulate them and their message."

Understanding his message helped Matt to appreciate aspects of his own drives. Matt explains, "I had a strong desire to start a family. I realise now that this was one form of wanting to help people fulfil their potential. I now realise there are other ways to do that. Now that I know my message, I can see the obviousness of my desire to have a family. It was a playing out of my desire to help others develop, and instil energy in them about their ability to develop their capability. This is what the role of 'parent' was to me. My whole 'start a family' thing was actually 'I need to nurture'."

He has a renewed understanding of how he was contributing to workplace conflicts. "I've had clashes at the senior leadership level, particularly around people matters," Matt shares, "and now the pressure is off. My drive to develop people, to empower people, is not everyone's message. My attempts to make empowerment the primary consideration were causing these clashes with people for whom it may be a secondary consideration. It was a relief, as it seemed like I was getting everything wrong. I was driven for a course of action and didn't understand why I was butting heads with others. The manner in which I was going about it was causing the butting of heads and the frustration I felt. That for me was some serious progress. I needed to sit down and understand exactly what they thought."

"In essence," he says, "I went from not knowing what was driving me and not knowing why I was butting heads with people, to knowing what was driving me and curious about what was driving others."

Like many others, Matt reports greater confidence. "There's a number of situations (at work) where I thought I'd failed. The outcomes weren't a success according to what others considered them to be. What I realise now is that I had actually acted according to what's important, and had been acting to achieve my purpose and message. I've gone from being concerned about those past events to being satisfied that I have acted according to what's important. Even when the tangible result wasn't what I wanted, I'm satisfied that I had acted with integrity to the best of my ability at the time. I no longer think of those events as possible failures, and I'm proud of myself even, to know that, without knowing it, I had tried to achieve what's important. I'm relieved of all that doubt. Even now, I'm satisfied with what I've done because I know I'm doing what matters. I don't second-guess my decisions any more."

Matt found that his message explained a lot. "I never knew why I would get so frustrated. I understand now that I was always in pursuit of my message or purpose without realising it, and I realise that others were also in pursuit of what was important for them. I see now that neither of us understood this and butting heads was inevitable."

The answer for Matt was to make his purpose explicit. "Now I share with others what my purpose is and that I will always pursue it, and have a conversation with others about their purpose. Each of us will have a different purpose, and they will all be complementary when we figure out how to bring them together. But we can only do that when we all know what each person's purpose is." Matt and his leadership team made 'empowerment' an explicit objective.

The change in his experience of his work couldn't be more different. His is a clear example of message being intrinsically motivating. "I have endless energy and excitement for my work now too. Here we are, 4:30pm on Friday and I am still raring to go. I started at 8:30 this morning and have been back-to-back the whole day, and I feel like I've just started. Others don't believe me—or think I'm a workaholic—to be so energised and enthusiastic about my work. It's just that I feel so great at work, and then go home with a full tank and I'm energised through the evening. I've gone from not being so enthusiastic about work; from I could take it or leave it, to being excited to be at work. Even when it's tiring and I need to travel, it's still in a good way, a satisfying way. I've just spent the past two days interstate, I started at 8:30 this morning, and I'm still energetic. Because I know why I'm doing it, I know that I am doing it, and realise that my work is the perfect place to live my purpose, to have people come together, to create situations where they solve their own problems and choose for themselves to take the initiative."

Not only has Matt gone from ambivalent to excited about his work almost overnight, he realises that, "My purpose means that being a leader and manager is perfect for me. I love it. I focus on helping others to be at their best, and the results happen. I don't even have to worry about whether we'll achieve them."

As we approached 5:00pm, he asked to close the conversation, sharing that he'd asked people from two geographically separated teams to solve a mutual business problem. Completely confident that they'd solve the issue, he excitedly shared, "I can't wait to get back and find out what answers the working group has come up with."

It's no surprise that Matt's message is 'Energetic through empowerment'.

Recently, Matt and his leadership team realised that their central defining value is 'trust', of which Matt's 'empowerment' is a part. They're intrinsically motivated to create more trust through the way they work as a team. As a minimum they've decided to do what they can to eliminate mistrust and enhance trust through their conversation and behaviour.

Co-creative relationships

Remember the earlier example of an argument about the bedroom window that goes back and forth. One wanted fresh air and the other warmth, yet the conversation came out like this:

> "I want the window open."
> "I want the window closed."

Eventually it could result in mutual frustration and their judging the other according to something like this:

> "You're being disrespectful!"
> "You're being inconsiderate!"

What's really going on? There are two conversations. One conversation is about the result that's wanted. The other conversation is about the method of conversation. Each of them has two parts:

1. Result—conversation about the desired result
    *   Window open or closed (concrete topic)
    *   Fresh air and warmth (qualitative topic)

2. Method—conversation about how the conversation was done
    *   Inconsiderate and disrespectful (the qualitative result of the conversation)
    *   Respect and consideration (the method of conversation that mattered)

At the window open or closed level of discussion, it's a win-lose situation. Assuming the couple want increasing levels of connection and intimacy, then it's a win-lose problem. This is because there will be one who gets their way, and the other who does not. It is the wrong problem because, by its nature, it will push people away—not bring them together. It will compromise what they both want. The problem of 'open or closed' is defined in terms that are too concrete. 'Either-or' conflict exists only over concrete means for solving a problem or achieving what's important. You cannot have 'window open and closed' at the same time. There is conflict only due to the lack of clarity about what the topic is really about and what to do about it.

Conflict is the lack of clarity about how to achieve what's mutually important

A better problem is the one that defines the problem in its qualitative terms. The 'win-win' problem of 'air and warmth' is a better one, as it is more likely to contribute towards connection and intimacy. If the couple could redefine their problem and realise that they were really discussing fresh air and warmth, then they could work together on how to best solve that better problem. Their problem would be 'How do we create both fresh air and warmth?' They'd discover that there are many different options that are now available. The previous 'open or closed' version is no longer an option as it does not provide for both 'air *and* warmth'. As we discussed earlier, one option might be to open a window in an adjacent room, and the person who wants fresh air sleeps closest to the door. They have created this solution together; they have co-created a concrete result that they both want.

Furthermore, during the conversation they both experienced that something was compromised. Respect and consideration were both compromised. If neither realises that their argument was really about respect and consideration, they might continue to act in ways where the other continues to perceive that what is important is being compromised. The way they are having conversations isn't working as well as it could. Their method for conversing has room for improvement. Just as there was a better problem that led to a better solution, there's a better way for them to be in conversation.

What was compromised is now the 'conversation method' problem that needs to be factored into the way they have their conversations. Realising what the problem was with their conversation, they could then work together and ask: "How can we converse in a way that is both respectful and considerate?" They could then start to work together on how to do things differently in a way where both experience what is important—not the compromise of what is important. They'd discover that there are many different options that are now available that would produce the qualitative results of respect and consideration. They then have co-created a method that produces that qualitative result they want. When they both act and behave consistent with their agreement, they are co-creating a culture of respect and consideration.

This is represented in the following model. A conversation that was about the window open or closed, showed that air and warmth are wanted. A conversation that was experienced as disrespectful and inconsiderate, reveals that respect and consideration are wanted. Argue about the window in a way that's inconsiderate and disrespectful; or create air and warmth in a way that's respectful and considerate.

Conversations have an intent and they are done in a certain way. We can be unclear on both fronts—about what we want the result to be, and how we want to experience it. This framework can help clarify what a conversation is truly about. Useful for deepening connection. Especially useful when there's conflict.

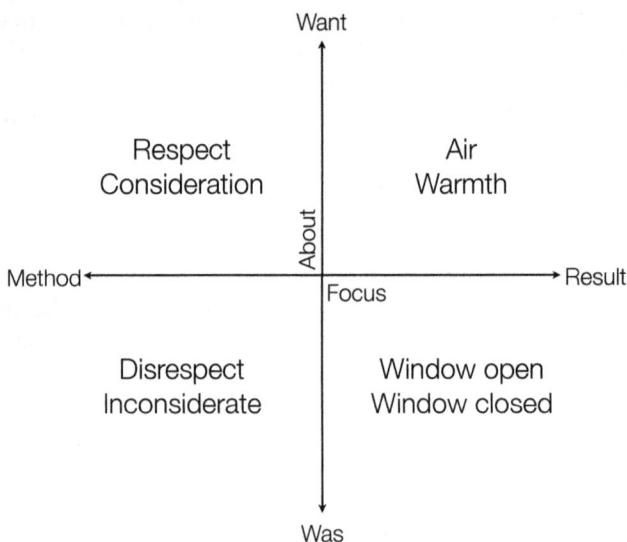

Dimensions of conversation model

The next time a potential conflict arises, they could put into place their co-created conversation method to arrive at a concrete solution that both of them are happy with. They are happy about both aspects—happy with their result, and with their method for achieving it. They have simultaneously achieved a concrete and qualitative result that they both wanted. However, they can only do that when they are both aware of both the concrete and qualitative results that they want. They know that from knowing what previous conflict was really about. Without that earlier conflict, they'd not now know what is mutually important and could not use it to shape their development of a superior method.

Conflict is simply feedback that the qualitative method is not working as well as it could be, or the qualitative result is not as it should be. Conflict is simply feedback about a lack of clarity. Used effectively, conflict clarifies what's important.

I've found the conversation about the conversation to be the most important conversation.

Conflict is a lack of clarity

Conflict is feedback

Conflict clarifies

When you mutually create, you co-create. Co-creation is about working to methods that simultaneously achieve the desired concrete and qualitative results. Co-creation is knowingly creating with others the concrete result and culture you're after. It's your combined creation.

Cultures at work

Just as there was method and behaviour in the personal relationship example, the same is true with larger groups of people, such as in organisations. A relationship is an organisation of two people. In the usual sense of an organisation, the actions to be done and method followed is generally called 'the work'. The work is the strategy for achieving certain results. However, the actions to be done and method followed, is not the whole picture. As the work is being done, people are behaving in certain ways. As such, there are two aspects to doing work:

1. Work design—the design of the work that needs to be done, the actions and methods needed
2. Behaviour—the behaviour of the people as they are doing the work

All aspects of the work, the work design and the behaviour of the people performing the work, have qualitative counterparts. Just as people's behaviour sends certain messages, the work design itself sends certain messages. Just as behaviour creates qualitative outcomes, so does the design of the work itself. You could have the most trusting manager in the world, but if you are working to a process that constantly checks and rechecks your work as if it's assumed you're constantly making mistakes, you're not likely to regard the workplace as a trusting one. 'I'm not trusted by the organisation', would be a common complaint. Working to a process that has no room for interpretation and innovation is likely to be experienced as a highly controlled one—not an empowering one.

When you have qualitative results in mind, it's important to have as many as possible of the concrete aspects of the methods reflect the qualitative goals. For example, you might have a qualitative goal of empowerment, which means the culture you want is characterised this way. Therefore, the work design needs to be experienced as empowering, and the way people behave needs to be experienced likewise. If the work design is highly restrictive, and the people doing the work operate in a way that is widely regarded as lacking honesty, then you have a problem. The more the work design and people's behaviour produce a qualitative result that opposes empowerment, such as restriction and dishonesty, the less empowered and more restrictive and dishonest the work environment culture will be.

To find out the qualities that are represented by and experienced as a result of the current work design and behaviours, review the qualitative results currently being achieved and review the current culture.

To create the work according to the desired qualitative results, consider what the work would look like when it imbues what's important. This is represented in the following diagram.

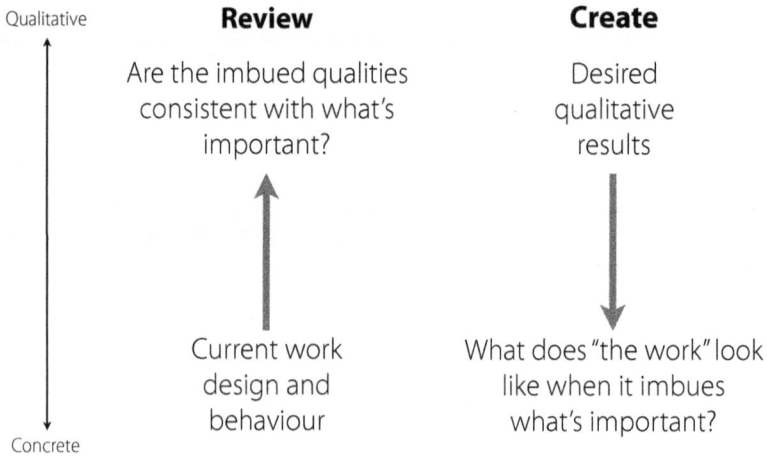

Qualitative work design

This describes how both a method and results focus is important, as are both the concrete and qualitative aspects of both. The following model represents this. It shows the four domains that interact and need to be considered together when both concrete and qualitative results are important to be achieved. This model applies for both defined and revealed cultures—anywhere you have people.

A given strategy is both the work design and behaviour of those performing the work. That strategy will be interpreted and experienced by people in a particular way. That strategy and experience will create a qualitative, cultural outcome, and a concrete outcome. To determine the appropriate strategy requires an appreciation of its experiential effects as well as back-casting. The qualitative outcome (culture) and concrete outcome inform and are constraints for the strategy that is needed to produce those outcomes.

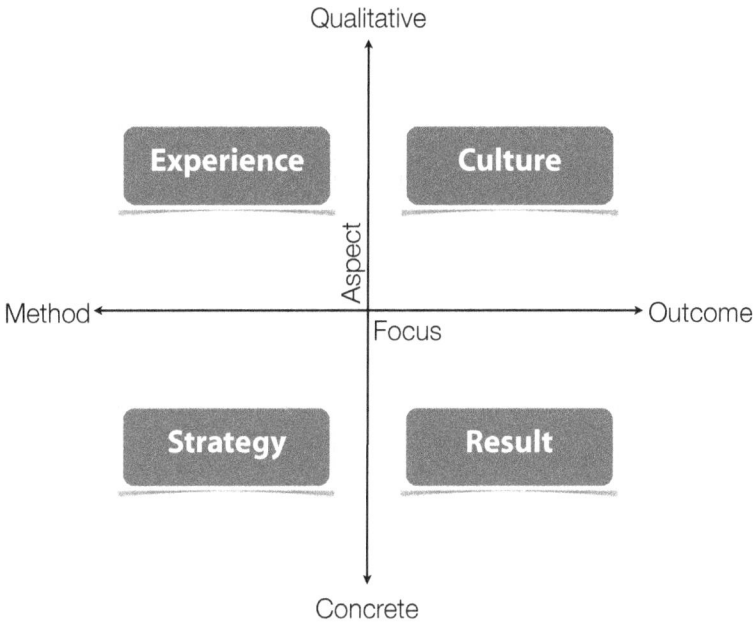

The four interrelated domains of the group work model

The problem with defined cultures

A common approach to culture and culture change is to define what you want it to be, review the current culture for compliance, and then to initiate a culture change program to align with the defined culture. This typical approach that many take to creating a predefined culture is usually a process of:

1. **Define.** Define what the culture or group values should be.
2. **Review.** Analyse the gap between the defined and actual culture. Produce recommendations to close the gap.
3. **Act.** Act to close that gap, usually through culture change initiatives, strategies or programs.

The problem is that the vast majority of people experience this approach as being 'done to'. Many people groan when culture initiatives are announced. Rarely is the culture change done in a way that reflects the intended qualitative result. Indeed, it is usually done in a way that compromises the innate values of the employees.

Just as there is a risk to advocating something as important that is not experienced by others as being so, there is risk in advocating a defined culture without the team, organisation and community experiencing it as such. Cynicism is one natural result when the 'defined and announced values' oppose what is experienced by people as already true. The above approach makes sense if you think of culture in concrete terms, as a concrete 'thing' that can be created in a linear and concrete way, and does not have a qualitative counterpart.

We cannot pursue culture the same way we pursue other concrete objectives—for the simple reason that culture is experienced, not concrete.

Put simply, the usual approach to creating culture is a process of define, review and act—define what you want it to be, review for compliance, and act to align. This approach suggests that the current culture, the current set of collective qualitative results is somehow wrong or broken. What if it's not broken? What if what's collectively important for people is being expressed in an unhelpful way, which people then label as a 'dysfunctional culture'? Just as an individual can express what's important for her or him in an unhelpful way, so too can a group of people.

An unhealthy expression of a value does not make the value wrong. Similarly, the unhealthy or dysfunctional expressions of a collective value does not make it wrong. It's merely unhealthy.

Remember how empowerment, trust, and engagement, all served the individual's ability to achieve? What if the innate values of people in any relationship, group or organisation, will always serve the concrete objectives of those involved?

My primary values define how I naturally experience my humanity. I react to the absence or compromise of what's important. I'm always seeking the experience of what matters—even when I'm not consciously aware of what that is.

It's the same for a group of people. The group values as they already are defines how the people involved naturally experience their humanity. They will react to the absence or compromise of what's important for them. If it continues to be compromised, they'll disengage. They're always a community seeking the experience of what matters—even if they're not consciously aware of what that is.

What if it's not that the current culture is wrong—it's that the innate group value is being expressed and sought in an unhealthy way? What if what is called 'dysfunction' is really the unrecognised and unhealthy attempt to realign with what's important? What if this is as true for an individual as it is for a group?

Revealed cultures

The alternative is to remember that there are always two results— concrete and qualitative. This means to think of culture as a collective dynamic between concrete factors and qualitative experience. The alternative to deciding on and announcing what the culture is supposed to be—what the collective qualitative results and culture are to be—is to realise and align with what the culture is already trying to become in a functional way. Align with the values already there.

The dysfunctional or unhealthy aspects of a culture does not mean the values seeking to be experienced are wrong. It's the unhealthy expression of the desire to experience what matters.

A community of people already unconsciously knows what's important—they react to its absence. The better way is to allow the values that are already wanting to be present to show up in a healthy way.

The alternative to making people fit to have alignment, is to reveal the fit that is already there and then align with that in a way that is functional. This is not about creating alignment that's not yet there. It is about realising and choosing to focus on creating the collective alignment that already is and will always seek to be—and doing so in a healthy way.

This means to align according to what's important for people already, the culture that is already being revealed, albeit possibly disruptively, as the one that people are wanting.

We have already covered these two ways, though on a personal level. In the chapter on 'What's important', approaches to the topic of 'values' were described in two general categories—those that were externally identified and defined, and those that were internally revealed.

This book has been dedicated to revealing what is already there for you on a personal level. You went through a process to:

1. Reveal what is already important for you
2. Align with what's already important for you
3. Create what's already important for you

The same approach and methodology can be used by a group of people. A group of people, such as the people in an intimate relationship, a team, or an organisation, can do the same though on a collective level.

As the brief example with Matt's management team showed, groups can go through the same process to:

1. Reveal what is already important for us
2. Align with what's already important for us
3. Create what's already important for us

Just as our calling is a product of our 'gift', what's 'important' and the 'need', culture is a product of 'behaviour', what's 'important' and the 'work design'. The crossing point of behaviour with what's important is collective interpretation. The meeting of what's important with the work design is its qualitative characteristics. Where behaviour meets the work is the contribution. This is shown in the following model.

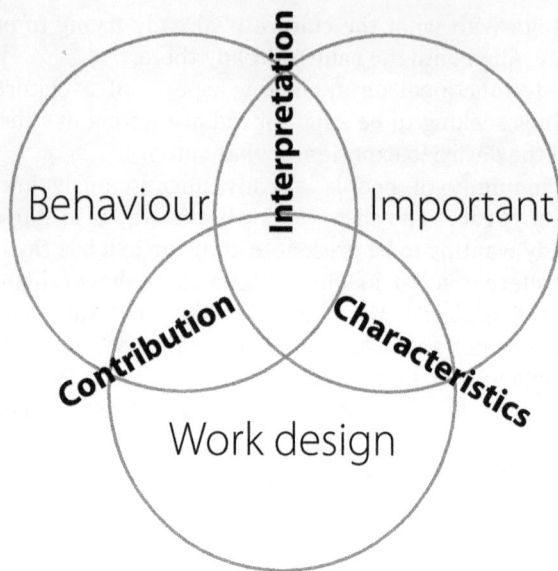

Culture model

I'd much rather see culture change be about creating healthy expressions of what already matters for the community of people involved.

Collective calling

A specific form of a collective, qualitative result or culture is the culture defined by its collective calling. This occurs when those involved have unified their individual calling into one that encompasses and defines them all. Each person's calling is then an integral part of the collective one.

For you personally, the highest aspect of 'important' is what's most important, your message. Just as you can identify your message and gift, a group of people can likewise identify their collective message and collective gift. It's the same process you followed as an individual, with the additional step of adding the messages together and the gifts together. You add those qualities together and collectively ask, 'What's that about?'

Realising and releasing a group's collective calling is the ultimate in co-creation, and potentially, of legacy. From a single person to the largest organisation, the only thing that changes is the number of people involved in defining what we're called to. Each individual, relationship, team, group, organisation, nation, and so on to all of humanity, is called to something.

Wouldn't you want to know what the communities you're part of are called to? Wouldn't you want to know how what you're called to contributes?

Legacy

In my earlier transform stage example of delivering 'leadership development' through 'authenticity and purpose', the explicit topic and concrete result to be achieved was 'leadership development'. Though 'authenticity and purpose' was explicitly stated as the method for achieving it, the overall topic was implicitly about 'authenticity and purpose'.

In the actualise stage it becomes all about achieving authenticity and purpose. 'Actualising your calling' is now the explicit topic and the result we're after. The topic becomes what it is really about qualitatively. In the previous transforming stage, I would say that the most direct path to leadership effectiveness is authenticity and its highest form, purpose. If you're authentic and on purpose, then more likely your leadership will be effective, inspirational, and create trust. This is still true.

At this actualising stage, I drop the leadership context. It's no longer about how you achieve leadership effectiveness. It is now 'I want to help you realise and create your life on purpose and experience the fulfilment that comes with that'. This also happens to still be the factor that will drive leadership effectiveness.

This is what 'legacy' is all about. It's when you're helping others know how to create that experience, result and quality for themselves. You're teaching, interacting, giving instruction on, or otherwise passing on the knowledge, practice and methods for others to be able to have and to do so for themselves. You do what you can to share how others can experience more of your message for themselves. Others then put what you share into practice. Others putting into practice what you have created becomes a self-propagating creation of your message by others.

What you have created develops a momentum that is carried on through time—its remains after you've left, and continues on in your absence like ripples in a pond. It becomes your legacy.

Your message is your legacy

For example, this book is an artefact. You're reading it in my absence. It's intended to support you to realise and create your message and calling for yourself—it's part of my legacy.

Let's look at Katrina's message of 'be worthy and feel secure' as an example. Her message in its simplest form is, 'Worthy through certainty'. Her calling is, 'Through rapport others know they're worthy and feel secure'. She observes that high engagement is a result of rapport.

In the transform stage, whether she communicates her message with others is up to her, as it's regarding an existing situation or context. Her message in the transform stage form can be elaborated to include her context, such as, "I'm at my best as a teacher (context) when I'm engaging (gift) and my students know they are worthy and feel certain (message)."

To give you an idea of how that helps to derive the transform stage versions of the same message, here are some transform stage examples:

- 'Successful teaching is all about how you engage with your students in a way that they know they are worthy and feel certain'.

- 'Effective relationships are all about engaging with others so that they know they are worthy and feel certain'.

- 'Sales is all about engagement and how quickly customers feel certain and good about what they are buying'.

Her message is one that can apply to many other types of situations and contexts. She can elaborate her message and tailor it with different emphasis. The transform stage is all about doing so, and it is absolutely appropriate when applying ourselves within an existing context—whatever that applicable context may be.

At the actualise stage, we make our message an objective on its own. Since it's a generic objective, it is context independent. We make our message the explicit result to be achieved and experienced. Our message is what others seek for themselves.

Returning to Katrina, at the actualise stage, she can express her message in many different ways such as:

- 'Creating worthiness through certainty'

- 'Creating engagement through worthiness and certainty'

- 'How changing your ability to be certain enhances your experience of worthiness'

Steve's experience

Steve was born and raised in the United States of America, has a Bachelor of Science Degree and a Doctorate in Chiropractic. He immigrated to Australia some 19 years ago, is passionate about living a happy life with his wife, watching his two boys grow, and seeing others shine. Steve runs a Wellness Centre, is constantly on the move, and when excited is spontaneous with his language. He's the healthiest, and most animated and supportive person I know. From Steve I've learned much about acceptance.

Through awareness, Steve helps people be who they truly are and feel alive. That's also what he tells people he does. It's what people come to him for and to learn. His message is 'Be who you truly are and feel alive'. Steve's example is one whose message is made explicit and is something that others explicitly want.

Describing how he's integrated his message into his work, Steve explains, "When I'm talking to people and getting to the real source of what I do, I say my message. It's fantastic. People really are excited. That's what they want. It's looking at what they want, that's what they're looking for and why they come to my practice. That's satisfying to me to know I'm on the right track. I'm grateful to have an opportunity to share my gifts. People understand where I'm coming from. It just feels great. It feels great to have that clarity. I feel a lot more powerful with that. I have greater clarity in my view that that's what I'm here for, what I can accomplish with an individual, a common thread between what they are looking for and what I am there to give. It's just empowering for both. It's empowering for me to know that I have got the person with an understanding of what I can help them experience, and they are excited about the prospects of that experience. It's what I offer, and it's what they want."

Steve's clarity is helping him be more intentional, more deliberate about aligning what he offers and what others are seeking. "That's what makes this empowering," he says, "it has enhanced my ability to communicate and share what I am doing. Always getting back to helping people to discover and become who they really are is a great way to communicate what I do. It makes it easier to have that simple explanation. It gives a greater definition to what I do and how I can help people. It's the focus of where I can go with my work, the communication is clear, the understanding of what I do is clearer, and the person can get a better understanding of what I can do. We have a common direction of where we want to go, so the focus is more about their becoming more of who they are and being more enlivened with where that individual is."

Steve animatedly shares, "It's just really exciting when there's a match between what I offer and what someone wants. To have an aligned purpose with the individual that I am working with just feels good. It's fulfilling. It's me being who I am and I feel alive."

He remembers being very excited when he established his message. In part this was due to the way he'd looked at or appreciated his own experience of his life which was previously very complicated. "My message was a culmination of many different things I've had in the past. Taking apart what has been a very complex thing for me, and all of a sudden having the clarity, the direction, and creating the opportunity for me to really shine with it, was fantastic. It's just a lot easier to do the things I do, more aligned with what I am really working to accomplish with people."

Steve's final words reflect the typical experience when people create their legacy. He concludes, "I now have a simple, not simplistic, clarity and direction for what I do, and it is the very thing those I work with want."

View from the top

Throughout this book I've mentioned the importance of remaining alert to what happens, to notice the effect, and to tune in to other people's experience, especially when it is unexpected. One such situation, as I was helping people realise their calling, opened my eyes to something delightful, something I'd hoped would happen and show up. I was working in a coaching and mentoring capacity with Anthony, whom we met earlier, a manager in a large organisation. He had just articulated his message, which at the time was, 'Feel included through self-acceptance'— a great message for someone in a leadership role and directly affecting many people's lives. As he was exploring how this was helping him make sense of his life, he stopped and looked at me. Holding my gaze, he shared with me: "You know, throughout working with you, I've felt totally included and completely accepted. I've experienced with you what matters most for me." Deeply touched by what Anthony shared, I felt joyous. We sat in silence for a while.

His experience makes perfect sense. I asked others to find out whether that experience was consistent, and sure enough, it was. When I've worked with people who chose to work with me around realising their message, they happened to experience their message through the process of doing so. A woman whose message is 'connection' was deeply connected; a man whose message is trust, trusted himself. A senior manager whose message is 'empowerment' experienced being empowered. One whose message is about respect, experienced respect. Another whose message involves freedom, felt free.

Creating one message can simultaneously create another. Katrina has a message around worthiness. In her view, my work in helping people actualise (realise and act on) their calling helps them to know themselves to be worthy. I trust her view on that, as her life of sensitivity is around worthiness, and she'll know what resonates with worthiness and what does not. As such she enthusiastically supports what I do. Though my work is not explicitly about being worthy, she experiences it as such.

Similarly, Justine, whom you met earlier, has a message around inclusion. My Value Stack does not include 'inclusion'—so much so that it's difficult for me to know whether something I create imbues inclusion or not and I stumble when I try to design for it. Because I know that 'inclusion' is important for many people, I'll ask her to assess whether my program outline adequately reflects that quality. I seek her perspective as I trust her sensitivity to 'inclusion' and she is brilliant at it. Within a heartbeat she knows whether something demonstrates inclusion, or not. She's incredulous when I say that 'inclusion' is missing from my Value Stack, as in her view, those programs strongly imbue it.

It makes sense that what I experience as 'dignity', 'freedom', and 'fulfilment', others will experience as 'acceptance', 'inclusion', and 'worthiness'. They're all different aspects of one love—personal love together universal.

I trust people's message and gift. When I want access to a quality, I'll seek out someone who has that as their message. When I want access to an ability, I'll seek out someone who has that as their gift. This is the best way I know of to help people actualise their calling—I ask them to share it. I call for it.

Imagine if we all call for, share and receive each others calling?

Earlier I said that our message is a particular form of love. When others are intentionally interacting with us in the capacity of receiving our message, they interact with us in our form of love. Others interact with us and receive the solution to the problem we know about, which is love in our particular form. As Anthony pointed out, others may experience that interaction with us according to love in their particular form.

We love our way such that others experience love their way.

Conclusion

Congratulations—you've finished this book and the Life Calling Method™. My overall method for helping you realise your purpose is illumination. 'Insight' and 'power' occur in my Gift Stack as well. So according to my Gift Stack, to help you illuminate your own life, I'm at my best when I help you realise your own insights in a way that is empowering for you.

What will not work for me is if I try to 'tell' you what your purpose is. Those who have asked me to do just that, know this. That would not be your insight. Nor will I tell you what the interpretation of your experience is, for I trust that you come to your own conclusion. I may suggest alternative interpretations, but you are the one who decides.

This is also consistent with my Value Stack that puts dignity, freedom and empowerment as highly important for me. To tell you would be inconsistent with what matters to me, with what my version of love is. It's important for me that I help you celebrate and manifest the magnificence of your own life as well as that of others.

I am not the expert on your life—you are. I develop methods through which you can derive insight into your own life in a way that illuminates, liberates and empowers. I do this to help you realise what your life is the answer to, the gift you have that will best help you to make that happen, and to directly or indirectly share your message with others.

It was with you in mind that I wrote this book. As you participate with life, I have three wishes for you:

Realise: That you decipher your own life and discover what's important for you, uncover your message, and discern what your natural talents are. It's not about trying to get it right or perfect, just clear enough in a way that resonates for you.

Act: That you put into action what you realise and discover. Share your message. Remember that it is not for you alone. Besides, you won't really know how true your message is until you put your calling to action.

Adapt: That you pay attention to what happens for you and others when you act. This is your feedback that informs your ability to improve what you do and how you go about it. Live your message and remain flexible about how you create it.

My hope is that together we can bring even more love into our own and others lives, weave together our message threads, and give and receive the gifts of each others magnificence.

I'd love to hear how you go, what your message and gift are, what your experience was like, and what this has meant for you. Send me a message via or visit www.philipoudevrielink.com or www.life-calling.com for additional resources, to stay in touch, and to be notified of programs.

References

1. Boyle, Patricia, Lisa Barnes, Aron Buchman, and David Bennett. "Purpose in life is associated with mortality among community-dwelling older persons." Psychosomatic Medicine 71.5 (2009): 574-579. Online.

2. Chida, Yoichi, and Andrew Steptoe. "Positive psychological well-being and mortality: a quantitative review of prospective observational studies." Psychosomatic Medicine 70.7 (2008): 741-756. Online.

3. Church, Matt, Scott Stein, and Michael Henderson. Thought leaders: how to capture, package and deliver your ideas for greater commercial success. Auckland, N.Z.: HarperCollins, 2011. Print.

4. Csikszentmihalyi, Mihaly. Flow: the psychology of optimal experience. New York: Harper & Row, 1990. Print.

5. Csikszentmihalyi, Mihaly. Finding flow: the psychology of engagement with everyday life. New York: BasicBooks, 1997. Print.

6. Eiseley, Loren C. The unexpected universe. New York: Harcourt, Brace & World, 1969. Print.

7. Epstein, Donald M., and Nathaniel Altman. The 12 stages of healing: a network approach to wholeness. San Rafael, Calif.: Amber-Allen Pub., 1994. Print.

8. Epstein, Donald M.. Healing myths, healing magic: breaking the spell of old illusions : reclaiming our power to heal. San Rafael, Calif.: Amber-Allen Pub., 2000. Print.

9. Ericsson, Anders, Michael Prietula, and Edward Cokely. "The making of an expert." Harvard Business Review 85.7-8 (2007): na. Print.

10. Frankl, Viktor E. Man's search for meaning: an introduction to logotherapy. 4th ed. Boston: Beacon Press, 1992. Print.

11. Gallwey, W. Timothy. The inner game of work. New York: Random House, 2000. Print.

12. Geisel, Theodor Seuss (Dr. Seuss). GoodReads. N.p., n.d. Web. 9 Jan. 2013. <http://www.goodreads.com/quotes/497473-be-who-you-are-and-say-what-you-feel-because>. Online.

13. George, Bill, and Peter Sims. True north: discover your authentic leadership. San Francisco, Calif.: Jossey-Bass/John Wiley & Sons, 2007. Print.

14. Gibran, Khalil. BrainyQuote. N.p., n.d. Web. 9 Jan. 2013. <http://www.brainyquote.com/quotes/quotes/k/khalilgibr119996.html>. Online.

15. Gilpin, Adrian. Unstoppable the pathway to living an inspired life. Chichester: Capstone, 2004. Print.

16. Heifetz, Ronald A., Alexander Grashow, and Martin Linsky. The practice of adaptive leadership: tools and tactics for changing your organization and the world. Boston, Mass.: Harvard Business Press, 2009. Print.

17. Izzo, John. Stepping up: how taking responsibility changes everything. San Francisco, CA: Berrett-Koehler Publ., 2012. Print.

18. Jordan, Michael. BrainyQuote. N.p., n.d. Web. 9 Jan. 2013. <http://www.brainyquote.com/quotes/quotes/m/michaeljor385092.html>. Online.

19. Kegan, Robert, and Lisa Laskow Lahey. Immunity to change: how to overcome it and unlock potential in yourself and your organization. Boston, Mass.: Harvard Business Press, 2009. Print.

20. Layard, Richard. Happiness: lessons from a new science. New York: Penguin Press, 2005. Print.

21. Lyubomirsky, Sonja. The how of happiness: a new approach to getting the life you want. New York: Penguin Books, 2008. Print.

22. Merzel, Dennis Genpo. Big mind, big heart: finding your way. Salt Lake City, UT: Big Mind Pub., 2007. Print.

23. MetLife Mature Market Institute. "Discovering What Matters: Balancing Money, Medicine, and Meaning." Web. 5 July 2012. <https://www.metlife.com/assets/cao/mmi/publications/studies/mmi-discovering-what-matters-study.pdf>. Online.

24. Niblick, Jay. What's Your Genius. USA: St. James Books, 2009. Print.

25. Prigogine, I., and Isabelle Stengers. Order out of chaos: man's new dialogue with nature. Toronto: Bantam Books, 1984. Print.

26. Quindlen, Anna. GoodReads. N.p., n.d. Web. 10 Jan. 2013. <http://www.goodreads.com/quotes/113654-the-life-you-have-led-doesn-t-need-to-be-the>. Online.

27. Rath, Tom. Strengths finder 2.0. New York: Gallup Press, 2007. Print.

28. Seligman, Martin E. P. Authentic happiness. North Sydney, N.S.W.: Random House Australia, 2011. Print.

29. Schweitzer, Albert. BrainyQuote. N.p., n.d. Web. 9 Jan. 2013. <http://www.brainyquote.com/quotes/quotes/a/albertschw133001.html>. Online.

30. Sone, Toshimasa, Naoki Nakaya, Kaori Ohmori, Taichi Shimazu, Mizuka Higashiguchi, Masako Kakizaki, Nobutaka Kikuchi, Shinichi Kuriyama, and Ichiro Tsuji. "Sense of Life Worth Living (Ikigai) and Mortality in Japan: Ohsaki Study." Psychosomatic Medicine, Journal of Biobehavioural Medicine 70.July/August (2008): 709-715. Online.

31. Steptoe, Andrew, Panayotes Demakakos, Cesar de Oliveira, and Jane Wardle. "Distinctive biological correlates of positive psychological well-being in older men and women." Psychosomatic Medicine 74.5 (2012): 501-508. Online.

32. The Leadership Circle. N.p., n.d. Web. 9 Jan. 2013. <http://www.theleadershipcircle.com>. Online.

33. Thich Nhat Hanh. The heart of the Buddha's teaching: transforming suffering into peace, joy & liberation : the four noble truths, the noble eightfold path, and other basic Buddhist teachings. New York: Broadway Books, 1999. Print.

34. Tolle, Eckhart. A new earth: awakening to your life's purpose. New York: Plume, 2006. Print.

35. Wilber, Ken. The collected works of Ken Wilber. Boston: Shambhala :, 1999. Print.

36. Wilde, Oscar. GoodReads. N.p., n.d. Web. 9 Jan. 2013. <http://www.goodreads.com/quotes/19884-be-yourself-everyone-else-is-already-taken>. Online.

37. Williamson, Marianne. A return to love: reflections on the principles of a Course in miracles. New York, NY: HarperCollins, 1992. Print.